McFarlin Library
WITHDRAWN

SHAW 2

continuing

The Shaw Review

Stanley Weintraub, *General Editor*

| John R. Pfeiffer | Rodelle Weintraub | Louise Goldschmidt |
| Bibliographer | Assistant Editor | Editorial Assistant |

Editorial Board: Elsie B. Adams, California State University, San Diego; Sidney P. Albert, California State University, Los Angeles (Emeritus); Charles A. Berst, University of California at Los Angeles; Bernard F. Dukore, University of Hawaii; Robert Chapman, Harvard University; Louis Crompton, University of Nebraska; Frederick P. W. McDowell, University of Iowa; Michael J. Mendelsohn, University of Tampa; Ann Saddlemyer, Graduate Center for Study of Drama, University of Toronto; Warren S. Smith, Pennsylvania State University (Emeritus); Barbara Bellow Watson, City University of New York; Jonathan L. Wisenthal, University of British Columbia.

SHAW

The Annual of Bernard Shaw Studies
Volume Two

Edited by
Stanley Weintraub

The Pennsylvania State University Press
University Park and London

Quotations from published Bernard Shaw writings are utilized in this volume with the permission of the Estate of Bernard Shaw. Shaw's additions and corrections to Cecil Lewis's "Pen Study" © 1982 The Trustees of the British Museum, The Governors and Guardians of the National Library of Ireland, and the Royal Academy of Dramatic Art.

ISBN 0-271-00305-7

Copyright © 1982 The Pennsylvania State University
All rights reserved
Printed in the United States of America

CONTENTS

GBS AND THE LOIN OF PORK *Ray Bradbury*	1
MRS WARREN'S PROFESSION: IN THE GARDEN OF RESPECTABILITY *Tony Jason Stafford*	3
CANDIDA AS A "MYSTERY" *Thomas P. Adler*	13
CLIMATE AND CHARACTER IN *JOHN BULL'S OTHER ISLAND* *Joseph M. Hassett*	17
SIEGFRIED ELEMENTS IN THE PLAYS OF BERNARD SHAW *Robert Coskren*	27
EPICURUS AND ARISTOTLE—AND SATAN AND JUAN *Robert Wexelblatt*	47
BERNARD SHAW: THE EMERGENCE OF A REPUBLICAN ROYALIST *Thomas F. Hale*	57
"THE LADY AUTOMATON" BY E. E. KELLETT: A *PYGMALION* SOURCE? *Philip Klass*	75
THE SHAW/DICKENS FILE: 1914 TO 1950. AN ANNOTATED CHECKLIST (CONCLUDED). *Edgar Rosenberg*	101
GEORGE BERNARD SHAW. A PEN STUDY *Cecil Lewis*	147

MR SHAW'S *ST. JOAN* 155
Christopher Hollis

RATTIGAN VERSUS SHAW: THE "DRAMA OF IDEAS"
DEBATE 171
Susan Rusinko

THE STATE AND FUTURE OF SHAW RESEARCH:
THE MLA CONFERENCE TRANSCRIPT 179
Margot Peters, Charles Berst, Daniel Leary

REVIEWS

    BERNARD SHAW, FILM-MAKER 195
    Stanley Weintraub

    NOT BY SHAW 200
    Alexander Seabrook

    TAILORING *HEARTBREAK HOUSE* FOR THE
    STAGE 201
    Robert Chapman

A CONTINUING CHECKLIST OF SHAVIANA 207
John R. Pfeiffer

CONTRIBUTORS 218

Ray Bradbury

GBS AND THE LOIN OF PORK

> Mrs. Campbell to George Bernard Shaw:
> "Sir, if you should ever eat a porkchop,
> from that day on, God protect all women!"

There he sits in the restaurant,
The porkchop on his plate.
We wait to see if he will cut the beast . . .
Shaw thrusts his beard southwest, nor-east;
The fates of half a billion women wait on this.
Will G.B. hover, savor, kiss
The darling flesh,
And, kissing, stop, deplore,
Leap up, and want no more?
Or try again and find that pork embellishes
And perks one's curiosity and need for relishes
Put up in ladies shapes and girlish bloomers?
The rumors
Have it Shaw may well this night
Fall to and bite and chew, then brood
On how his vegetarian-prone life has fixed his mood.
The loin of pork, undressed, no sauce, a simple food,
With neither eye of salmon, mouth of cod,
Or breathless gill,
Thrills to know Shaw the God
Stares down at it, his tongue and tone like knives.
The wives and daughters of the world suspend
Their chat, they live in little breaths,
Is this the end?
A thousand deaths occur while watching G.B. hover,
Will now the atheist of meat turn carnal lover?

Copyright 1981 by Ray Bradbury.

The wine lies waiting, too.
But, no popping the cork!
His mind is all pork!
His fiery beard-tines quiver,
A thousand women's sweetmeats shiver, stop, wait.
Shaw trembles his fork,
The pork shudders on plate.
Shaw slams his eyes shut, his summation complete,
Leaping up, G.B. cries,
"You may *kill,* I'll not *eat!*"
He stands, waiting proudly
Applause rushing loudly roves wild fields of hands,
Hurling table aside,
G.B. Shaw/Dr. Jekyll leaves loinpork ghost Hyde,
He strides out the door.
Applause dies on the shore.
The good wine still lies there, untouched, uncorked,
The women unwomened and the pork unporked.
Ten million Moms tonight write poems,
Shaw's fled back to rice and beets,
Safe our daughters, safe our streets;
God rest our happy homes!

Tony Jason Stafford

MRS WARREN'S PROFESSION: IN THE GARDEN OF RESPECTABILITY

When Shaw tried to get *Mrs Warren's Profession* licensed for production in 1893, he encountered the first of a long succession of indignant rebuffs to his "prostitution" play. In fact, it was not until 1902 that the London Stage Society agreed to give it a showing, and even they, in looking for a place to put it on, were turned down by twelve theatres, two music halls, three hotel ballrooms, and several picture galleries before giving it two private performances at The New Lyric Club on January 5 and 6. The critics of course denounced the play for its decadence and immorality. In New York, it opened at the Garrick Theatre on the night of October 30, 1905—and closed the same night. The cast was arrested for disorderly conduct.[1]

Shaw was predictably bemused by this self-righteous outcry. Wrote he, "a really good performance would keep its audience out of the hands of women of the street for a fortnight at least."[2] Subsequently, scholars have come to the playwright's defense to show that the play really is a serious treatment of a variety of things, including capitalism,[3] "the wrongs of . . . [a] society which in effect left [Kitty Warren] with no alternative course of action,"[4] "parent-child relationships" and "conventional" thinking habits,[5] and even good and evil in the "morality play" sense.[6]

But Shaw's flippant, off-hand jest may provide a clue for looking at the play in another way. While his quip sounds as though the play has the moral intent of keeping men "out of the hands of prostitutes," another implication of his double-edged remark is that the members of the play's first audiences who were raising indignant voices against his play were the very ones who were active customers of prostitutes. Thus his comment is aimed not only at defending the morality of his play but also at suggesting the widespread hypocrisy in society.

This interpretation of the playwright's comment takes us to the play again where, given this new clue, we can see that Shaw is indeed systematically and thoroughly examining society's habit of pretending one thing in order to hide something else. We can also find that, in order to support and develop this theme, Shaw draws upon a location, that of the English garden where society's hypocritical practices are often in evidence, and uses it in his setting, structure, action, and names of characters often enough to make the garden a metaphor for middle-class conduct. Parenthetically, it might be noted that Shaw generally is highly cognizant of settings and their relationship to the behavior of the particular society which inhabits them. One need think only of his use of the country house in *Misalliance* and *Heartbreak House* as a metaphor for upper-class and upper-middle-class manners to see that his practice here is consistent with his treatment of setting elsewhere.

Shaw, knowing that an audience's first impression is gained through the on-stage setting, makes his play, or three-quarters of it anyway, a garden play. The opening line of the first stage description establishes the scene: "Summer afternoon in a cottage garden on the eastern slope of a hill."[7] He goes on to say that a "paling completely shuts in the garden, except for a gate on the right" and that "the common rises uphill beyond the paling to the skyline" (p. 25). This image, an enclosed garden with a background of open field beyond a fence that is repeated in a later act and reinforced with other images, figures into the action and even suggests an underlying meaning to the play. Moreover, throughout Act I, the commons beyond the fence is emphasized by the fact that several entering characters appear on the commons first, and all five arrivals come on stage by means of the gate (instead of through the cottage). Only Vivie is already in the garden at the beginning; only she seeks escape from it later.

In Act II, nightfall forces the characters indoors, but Shaw does not let the audience forget about the garden. He shifts the point of view 180° so that the audience is facing the window and door which it had seen from the garden in Act I, thus stressing the interaction between inside and outside and keeping the garden present. At the beginning of the act, each character makes an entrance from the garden; by mid-act characters start exiting into it again; and at the end, Vivie opens the door, comments on the beauty of the night, and "draws aside the curtains of the window" to reveal the scene "bathed in the radiance of the harvest moon rising over Blackdown" (p. 60). The curtain comes down with the audience looking at the garden and the open land beyond the fence once again.

In Act III, Shaw transfers the action to another garden, that of Rev. Samuel Gardner. The stage description begins, "In the Rectory garden next morning, with the sun shining from a cloudless sky" (p. 62). The garden wall and gate are again present: "the garden wall has a five-barred wooden gate, wide enough to admit a carriage, in the middle" (p. 62). And again, Shaw makes the audience aware of the scene on the other side. "Beyond the gate is seen the dusty high road, parallel with the wall, bounded on the farther side by a strip of turf and an unfenced pine wood" (p. 62). Although the act begins with Frank and his father in the garden, action from beyond the wall intrudes. Shortly after Praed has come in through the hedge, the Reverend announces in great dismay that "Mrs Warren and her daughter are coming across the heath with Crofts" (p. 65)—toward the garden, of course, where the remainder of the action is centered, with garden, wall, gate, and the terrain beyond clearly in view. Once inside, no one uses the main gate again, except Vivie at the end of the act, as though Shaw were saving the gate for the right moment and the right meaning.

But there appears to be nothing inherent in the action or dramaturgy which necessitates a garden setting. All that is clear is that the audience has a visual image of pleasant gardens, claustrophobic fences, and a view of open fields, and perhaps freedom, beyond.

The garden idea also functions in the play's structure and movement. The first three acts highlight the garden setting, but the fourth does not. The movement of the play takes the action elsewhere, and it is precisely at the climax that the movement away from the garden begins. What brings the action to the turning point is that Vivie, from the beginning and up until the end of Act II, resents her mother as long as she excludes Vivie from the secrets of her private life. But when Mrs. Warren explains the impoverishment of her girlhood which forced her into prostitution, Vivie not only sympathizes with her mother but rejoices in her fortitude: "My dear mother: . . . you are stronger than all England" (p. 59). They are thus reconciled and stay that way until Crofts blunders out that Kitty Warren is still in the business, now as a bawd. Vivie is sickened by the knowledge, the tenuous bond between mother and daughter is thereupon severed, and the play moves toward its conclusion. This climactic moment between Sir George and Vivie not only provides information which alters the course of the play, but also contains a link between the garden motif and society's system of pretense which enables Sir George and Kitty Warren to function in acceptable society. Shaw creates a vivid, tableau-like effect in order to draw attention to Vivie's change as well as to initiate the final movement of the play. Incensed with Crofts and what she learns from him about society, Vivie seeks flight from the garden: "she raises the latch of the gate to open it and go out. He follows her and puts his hand heavily on the top bar to prevent its opening" (p.

75). They wrangle briefly in this position. Then Frank arrives, Crofts leaves, and Frank tries to entice Vivie, with his game of "babes in the wood," into remaining in the garden. But nothing can stop her exit. "Goodbye," she says to Frank, and when he asks, "Where shall we find you," she announces, standing in the gate, "At Honoria Fraser's chambers, 67 Chancery Lane, for the rest of my life" (p. 76). Vivie's exit through the gate, the effect heightened by Shaw's reserving it until this moment and utilizing it as part of the physical conflict of the scene, marks the basic progress of the play and calls attention to the metaphorical possibilities of the garden motif.

Act IV is located in the law office of Honoria Fraser at the top of New Stone Buildings, London, with "the chimneys of Lincoln's Inn and the western sky" (p. 77) clearly in view. Through exact geography, Shaw makes it clear that the achievement of the last act is a complete reversal of the first three. The audience now faces westward (or southwestward), looking toward those gardens in Surrey from which Vivie has escaped. The progress of the play then, and by implication of Vivie, is from those tightly enclosed and carefully controlled little plots of land to the city, the new challenge, where country gardens do not exist but freedom does.

Shaw also underscores the garden theme by giving all his characters, except for Vivie, names associated with land, especially land which is fenced in and intended for some type of cultivation. Although Shaw, to avoid libel allegations, apparently used London street names as a source for some of his characters—Praed Street and Warren Street for example—he still chose, out of all the streets he could have used, names harmonious with his garden motif. In the case of the title character, it is true that a "warren" seems an appropriate name for a prostitute and a brothel-keeper, but it is also consistent with the encircled-land image in that the word is formally defined as "a piece of land enclosed for the breeding of game."[8] Moreover, when Rev. Gardner knew Kitty years before, she was Miss Vavasour, and a vavasour, a term from the Middle Ages, is one who holds lands from a superior lord and has landholders under him.

Sir George Crofts bears a family name that is defined as a "small enclosed field." The Reverend Samuel Gardner and his son Frank are associated with the common word "garden" and require no formal definition. The name Praed, while a proper name familiar to the residents of London, exists in our language in the root of the adjective "praedial," which means "of or relating to land" or "landed." Whether Shaw knew this word or not, it would not have been against his nature for him to have researched into the word's Latin origins (*praedium:*

farm, estate) and perceived its relationship to the garden image and to the other names in the play.

Of course none of the details of their lives or their characters connects them with the land. None are outdoor, country types, nor are any of them dependent on farming. In fact, they dislike the country and feel more at home in the city. Kitty Warren says, "I dont know which is the worst of the country, the walking or the sitting at home with nothing to do" (p. 40) and adds later, "I'd a good deal rather be in Vienna" (p. 40). Crofts, although of the landed class, prefers to invest his money in brothels in Brussels, Ostend, and Vienna, where he spends most of his time, while Praed, an architect, is more comfortable among the museums, concert halls, and buildings of the cities of Europe. Only Sam Gardner lives in the country, and that is not by choice but by necessity. The reason behind Shaw's choice of such names, then, must originate more from their metaphorical usefulness than from what they denote.

Through the use of related names, Shaw has linked together all the characters in the play except Vivie. Moreover, all the members of this group share some common traits and receive similar treatment. Each is guilty of some type of pretension, and all are exposed for their hypocrisy, mostly by Vivie in her quest for honesty. Ironically, while most of them pride themselves on their rejection of cant, they are prone to falsehoods in spite of themselves. In addition, each of the major characters has at least one scene that utilizes the garden setting in a meaningful way.

Praed, an artistic, free-thinking type, admits to the pretenses imposed on him by society in his youth, labeling his own behavior as "affected as it could be" and governed by the rule of "always saying no when you meant yes" (p. 26). But he does believe in beauty. Vivie, however, thinks of cultural pursuits as phony and gives Praed several examples of why she thinks so. Praed is astonished at her attitude, but when in Act III Praed extolls the beauty of Brussels and Ostend, she is vindicated: these European cities are the very ones where Vivie's mother operates brothels. Beauty among such degradation, she feels, can only be hypocritical, and Praed's belief in art is exposed as such by her biting cynicism.

The candor implied in Frank Gardner's first name is belied by the garden overtone of the second. Although he tries to be unpretentious and brutally frank, especially with his father, his insistence on "love's young dream" is scorned by Vivie as an illusion, and his desire to play the garden game of "babes in the wood" and to be "covered up with leaves" is jeered by Vivie with "Ah, not that, not that. You make all my flesh creep" (p. 76). Moreover, while he may like Vivie for the person that she is, he also likes her mother's financial condition. His duplicity is best seen when he realizes that Vivie will not touch her mother's tainted money. Says he to Praed, "I cant marry her now." When Praed asks him, "Was that what you were going to marry on," Frank confesses, "What else? I havent any money, nor the smallest turn for making it" (p. 86).

Frank's father, Reverend Sam, is so blatantly a sham that his pathetic efforts at honesty are merely comical. He pretends to write his own sermons but buys them instead; he does not want Kitty Warren, a whore, to come to his house but is implicated in a past affair with her; he upbraids his son for being a wastrel but cannot remember what he did in his drunkenness the night before; and he works to maintain respectability but cannot even gain the respect of his son. The essence of Sam Gardner is dramatized by means of the garden image in Act I as he arrives at the garden gate to speak to his son. When Frank tells him to come inside, the Reverend replies, "No sir; not until I know whose garden I am entering" (p. 37). Reverend Gardener knows the value of gardens in establishing one's respectability.

Sir George Crofts is also one who insists on no pretenses. Although he is a man with a title, he does not pretend to enjoy the pleasures of his class. Even Vivie admires him "for being strongminded enough to enjoy himself in his own way... instead of living the usual shooting, hunting, dining-out, tailoring, loafing life of his set" (p. 91). He thinks of himself as devoid of the lies of society: "When I say a thing I mean it; when I feel a sentiment I feel it in earnest; and what I value I pay hard money for" (p. 70). But what he says later belies this kind of openness and, in fact, because he has inside knowledge of how it works, he becomes the chief expositor for the system. At the climactic scene, when he and Vivie have their confrontation, the audience as well as Vivie learns through Sir George the truth about respectable society. First, in spite of his self-professed honesty, when the subject of Kitty Warren's profession comes up, Crofts pretends that he and Kitty Warren are in the hotel business, and when Vivie warns him that she already knows the truth, he reveals his intention to lie about it: "I'd never have told you" (p. 73). After Vivie calls him a scoundrel, he defends himself by revealing that the Duke of Belgravia's rents are "earned in queer ways" and that the Archbishop of Canterbury has "a few publicans and sinners among his tenants" (p. 73). When Vivie expresses guilt over spending her mother's money, Crofts tries to reassure her by explaining how society operates: "As long as you dont fly openly in the face of society, society doesnt ask any inconvenient questions" (p. 74). He then articulates the cardinal principle: "There are no secrets better kept than the secrets everybody knows" (p. 74). This is the epiphany in the play for Vivie. When she learns that the code of the garden is never to speak the truth about what people want to hide, she flees through the garden gate.

Kitty Warren is also critical of the pretensions of society. She says, "The hypocrisy of the world makes me sick!" (p. 58) and "I cant stand saying one thing when everyone knows I mean another. Whats the use in such hypocrisy?" (p. 60). But she is not free from hypocrisy herself. In her first private talk with her daughter, she reveals that "respectability" is the most important thing in her scale of values, using the word over and over. By conversation's end, it is clear that for Kitty Warren, respectability is not based on what one does but on how well one deceives society, on what one might call "keeping face." And it is all carried off through polite pretenses. The garden motif helps to dramatize in one brief scene how it all works when Frank, who has just called Mrs. Warren a "wicked old devil" (p. 66), sees her approaching, turns to her as she enters the garden, and, as Shaw describes it, in "an ecstacy of dissimulation," says "Ever so delighted to see you Mrs Warren. This quiet old rectory garden becomes you perfectly" (p. 66). Whether he means it or not is irrelevant; it is what she wants to hear: "Well, I never! Did you hear that, George? He says I look well in a quiet old rectory garden" (p. 66). Of course the audience knows that in Kitty's mind, because of her constant references to her sister, a former prostitute who now lives next to the cathedral in Winchester, a rectory garden is the epitome of respectability. Vivie sees Frank's game in a different light and scolds him: "You were making fun of my mother just now when you said that about the rectory garden. That is barred in future. Please treat my mother with as much respect as you treat your own" (p. 67). Vivie wants respect for her mother, but Frank gives her respectability. The scene dramatizes in miniature how the hypocrisy of society functions, as well as the difference between Vivie and her mother.

This difference is brought out even more clearly in their final confrontation. After each argues her own point of view and it becomes clear that Vivie intends never to see her mother again, Kitty begins to lament that she tried to make her daughter into a "good woman," and swears from this point on she will "do wrong and nothing but wrong" to her "last hour" (p. 94). Vivie praises that declaration of honesty. "Yes: it's better to choose your line and go through with it" (p. 94). She also makes it clear that she is not judging her mother on moral grounds, even admitting that she might well have done the same thing as her mother had she been in her mother's position. Then she gives the real reason why she is rejecting her mother: "but I would not have lived one life and believed in another." It is the practice of this convention that causes her to say, "That is why I am bidding you goodbye now" (p. 94).

Vivie is set apart from the other characters in the play, in name as well as in nature. Shaw very carefully spares her any real association with the garden-related names of the others. On the one hand, no one, not even Kitty herself, knows for sure who Vivie's father is. All that Kitty can tell her daughter is that it is none that "you have ever met. I'm sure of that, at least" (p. 53). On the other hand, since Warren is a name assumed by her mother, it cannot be Vivie's real name either. All that is certain is that her name is Vivie, a name which suggests "life." Indeed, Vivie does seem to embody traits of someone in touch with her "life force," especially as she is able to defy society's dictates and live according to her own personhood. Vivie wants honesty in all things, with no pretenses, no illusions, and no dreams, and seems to live as honestly as she can, even if it means admitting that she studied only for the money she would get, that her education has made her an "ignorant barbarian," that art and culture are boring, or that Praed, Frank, Crofts, and her own mother are all hypocrites.

Because Vivie is dissociated from the garden motif, because she is determined to be painfully truthful and realistic in all matters, and because she is contrasted with the garden-related characters, the audience gets a better understanding of the significance of the garden image. The garden functions in the play as a superficially pleasant place for social intercourse, which really means maintaining a respectable surface on everything, and even though it is surrounded by an entrapping fence, it allows a view of freedom beyond. Vivie, repulsed by garden conduct, is the only one who can grasp for this freedom. She flees from her garden to the city where, she hopes, honesty, hard work, and ability have a better chance to succeed.

Notes

1. Alan S. Downer, "Introduction to *Mrs Warren's Profession*," *The Theatre of Bernard Shaw* (New York: Dodd, Mead, 1969), I, 21.
2. Ibid.
3. Charles A. Carpenter, *Bernard Shaw and the Art of Destroying Ideals* (Madison, WI: University of Wisconsin Press, 1969), p. 52.
4. Alfred Turco, *Shaw's Moral Vision: The Self and Salvation* (Ithaca, NY: Cornell University Press, 1976), pp. 75, 70.

5. Bernard F. Dukore, *Bernard Shaw, Playwright: Aspects of Shavian Drama* (Columbia, MO: University of Missouri Press, 1973), pp. 77, 70.

6. Charles A. Berst, "Propaganda and Art in *Mrs Warren's Profession*," *English Literary History*, 33 (September, 1966), 390–404.

7. Downer, p. 23. All citations are from this edition.

8. David B. Guralnik, ed., *Webster's New World Dictionary* (World Publishing Company, 1978). All definitions are from this source.

Thomas P. Adler

CANDIDA AS A "MYSTERY"

Critics have advanced a number of reasons to explain why G. B. Shaw subtitled *Candida* a "Mystery"; Louis Crompton, emphasizing the relationship between Candida and the Reverend Morell, proposes, for example, that "The Mystery celebrated in the play is, of course, the sacrament of marriage. But what makes marriage sacred in Shaw's eyes is not the legal tie or sexual purity but the nature of the life the couple lead together."[1] Maurice Valency approaches more closely my position when he writes: "Possibly he [Shaw] saw in the Candida situation an analogy to a play about Mary, Joseph, and their unruly son."[2] Yet Valency does not cite specifically the probable biblical analogy, and even retreats from the notion of "mystery" with this qualification: "In that case, he might have done better to have called it a morality, for its symbols, if symbols they are, come closer to the personificaton of the medieval moral plays than to the Bible stories enacted in the mystery cycles." But the reference here to "medieval moral plays" is not precisely correct in its suggestion of such dramas as *The Castle of Perseverance* and *Everyman* as an illuminating frame of reference for *Candida*. Valency instead might more accurately have written "medieval miracle plays," for among Shaw's chief symbols, the one most visible throughout what the author himself termed his "Virgin Mother play"[3] is, of course, the "large autotype of the chief figure in Titian's Assumption of the Virgin"[4] hanging above the mantelpiece. The Assumption, as a non-biblical episode from the life of Mary, would have been, in medieval times, appropriate material for a miracle (or saint's) play. What has gone unnoticed on this point, however, is that Eugene Marchbanks' description of Candida in terms of the Virgin—"her shawl, her wings, the wreath of stars on her head, the lilies in her hand, the crescent moon beneath her feet" (p. 62)—does have a close biblical counterpart in the visionary description in Revelation 12:1: "And there appeared a great wonder in heaven; a woman clothed with the sun, and the moon under her feet, and upon her head a crown of twelve stars." Marchbanks' description, in fact, seems to correspond even more closely to Murillo's famous painting of the Immaculate Conception than to the Titian in the stage set.

A second visual image in Act III, that of Candida holding the fireplace "poker, a light brass one . . . upright in her hand" (p. 56), followed by Marchbanks' comment to Morell that "Then she became an angel; and there was a flaming sword that turned every way, so that I couldn't go in; for I saw that that gate was really the gate of Hell" (p. 60), alludes specifically to Genesis 3:24: "So he [God] drove out the man: and he placed at the east of the garden of Eden cherubim, and a flaming sword which turned every way, to keep the way of the tree of life." If the phallic nature of the poker, which Candida gazes at "intently" and in rapt "absorption," escapes Marchbanks—who likens the poker to a "drawn sword" in medieval heroic literature placed between a couple to keep them chaste—clearly Candida understands that there could never be a physical relationship between herself and the young poet, that, indeed, that kind of paradise was not for him but would only deflect him from his true vocation as poet.

The presence of these two definite verbal echoes of Revelation and Genesis, heightened and underscored by the visual symbology or iconography, suggests that Shaw may have had in mind a specific biblical occasion involving "Mary, Joseph, and their unruly son" that would justify his terming *Candida* a "Mystery" and thus link it with the medieval mystery cycles which dramatized sacred history. And this biblical episode—the finding of the child Jesus in the Temple—dovetails nicely with Shaw's mystical philosophy. At play's end, when Marchbanks, for whom this has been an interlude of education at the hands of Candida and Morell, leaves their household forever, the audience might well think of the Jesus/Mary/Joseph configuration, especially of the incident in which Jesus astonishes the doctors with a level of wisdom and understanding far beyond his years. When Mary and Joseph find him on the third day and ask why he made them endure this anguish, Jesus responds, "How is it that ye sought me? wist ye not that I must be about my Father's business?" (Luke 2:49)—which might be an enlightening gloss for Marchbanks' somewhat ambiguous curtain line: "But I have a better secret than that [the disparity between his and Candida's ages] in my heart. Let me go now. The night outside grows impatient" (p. 75). From the very first, Morell has known about and been instructing Marchbanks in his role as an incipient poet in the evolution of the Life Force, in nudging towards perfection the Kingdom of God on earth: "You will be one of the makers of the Kingdom of Heaven on earth . . . for dont think, my boy, that I cannot see in you . . . promise of higher powers than I can ever pretend to. I well know that it is in the poet that the holy spirit of man—the god within him—is most godlike. It should make you tremble to think of that—to think that the heavy burthen and great gift of a poet may be laid upon you" (p. 29). Marchbanks, indeed, "must be about [his] Father's business."

Notes

1. *Shaw the Dramatist* (Lincoln: University of Nebraska Press, 1969), pp. 43–44.
2. *The Cart and the Trumpet: The Plays of George Bernard Shaw* (New York: Oxford University Press, 1973), p. 132.
3. *Bernard Shaw: Collected Letters 1874–1897*, ed. Dan H. Laurence (New York: Dodd, Mead, and Co., 1965), pp. 623, 632.
4. *Candida* (New York: Penguin Books, 1977), p. 7. Further references appear within parentheses in the text.

Joseph M. Hassett

CLIMATE AND CHARACTER IN *JOHN BULL'S OTHER ISLAND*

In the preface to *John Bull's Other Island* Shaw makes the arresting assertion that there is no such thing as the Irish race but that "[t]here *is* an Irish climate, which will stamp an immigrant more deeply and durably in two years, apparently, than the English climate will in two hundred."[1] Shaw thus takes implicit issue with Matthew Arnold's view that there is a racially derived Celtic element in literature,[2] and sets the scene for the play's rich examination of the relationship among race, climate, and culture.

John Bull's Other Island was written for the Abbey Theatre at the request of William Butler Yeats, who nonetheless rejected it.[3] Yeats had reacted with "admiration and hate" to Shaw's *Arms and the Man* when it shared the bill with his own *The Land of Heart's Desire* at London's Avenue Theatre in 1894, thinking this early Shaw play portrayed "inorganic logical straightness and not the crooked road of life." Its author appeared to Yeats in a dream as a perpetually smiling sewing machine.[4]

A more organic Shaw animates *John Bull's Other Island*. In this play, Larry Doyle and Peter Keegan, speaking with a conviction that bespeaks the playwright's authoritative voice, sound a mystical note that transcends "inorganic logical straightness."

Could it be that the tantalizing possibilities inherent in the question of the effect of climate on culture permitted Doyle and Keegan to lead Shaw down "the crooked road of life"? Yeats had thought this unlikely, although by *Man and Superman* (1901–03) Shaw had shown, in the *Don Juan in Hell* interlude, that he was reaching well beyond rationalism. In *A Vision,* Yeats consigned Shaw to the twenty-first phase of the moon, a realm in which intellect dominates passion, and the creative writer fashions characters who "must go his road and not theirs and perpetually demonstrate his thesis."[5] However, Larry Doyle and Peter Keegan entice Shaw to join them on a path that rejects the narrow road of pure logic and embraces a note of mysticism that becomes increasingly prevalent in Shaw.[6]

Early in the play Larry Doyle elaborates on Shaw's prefatory assertion that the Irish climate creates a distinctive temperament. His oft-quoted speech posits the relationship between the misty climate and the dreamy temperament:

> Your wits cant thicken in that soft moist air, on those white springy roads, in those misty rushes and brown bogs, on those hillsides of granite rocks and the magenta heather. Youve [in England] no such colors in the sky, no such lure in the distances, no such sadness in the evenings. Oh, the dreaming! the dreaming! the torturing, heartscalding, never satisfying dreaming, dreaming, dreaming, dreaming.[7]

Doyle continues with a passionate lament that, as a result of the climate-induced dreaming, "The Irishman's imagination never lets him alone, never convinces him, never satisfies him, but makes him so that he cant face reality, nor deal with it nor conquer it."[8]

In short, Doyle, elaborating Shaw's theme, asserts (1) that there is an identifiable Irish state of mind or temperament; (2) that its chief characteristic is an insatiable imagination; and (3) that it is the result not of racial trait, but of a moist climate, misty rushes, and alluring, dream-inducing distances. Doyle's views echo those of Spenser's Eudoxus who, marvelling at the power of Ireland to make the English in Ireland more Irish than the Irish, exclaimed: "Lord, how quickly doth that country alter men's natures."[9] Shaw himself had advanced similar views in "Notes to Caesar and Cleopatra," where he rejected the claim "that it is not scientific to treat character as a product of climate" as merely illustrative of "the wide range between common knowledge and the intellectual game called science."[10]

More pointedly, Doyle's views evoke Matthew Arnold's essay on the study of Celtic literature. An analysis of the areas of agreement and disagreement between Shaw and Arnold as to the relationship among climate, culture and temperament, spiced with some observations by Yeats and Wilde, provides useful background to an examination of the stance ultimately taken by the characters in *John Bull's Other Island*.

The Shaw-Doyle viewpoint is completely in accord with Arnold as to the existence and nature of a Celtic temperament. (Their disagreement would have been over its source.) Arnold calls the Celtic temperament "sentimental," but gives the term a unique definition, equating it with being "always ready to react against the despotism of fact."[11] It is this "vehement reaction against the despotism of fact,"[12] this profound dissatisfaction with the smallness and misery of life, that gives Celtic literature its "passionate, penetrating melancholy"[13] tinged with "piercing regret."[14] Arnold highlights the nature of the Celtic element by noting that it finds its anti-self in Southey's self-satisfied lines:

> Praise be to God who made me what
> I am, Other I would not be.[15]

Other the Celt *would* be. In tones that make clear that he and Larry Doyle are speaking the same language, Arnold concludes that the Celtic "sentiment cannot satisfy itself, cannot even find a resting place in color and form; it presses on to the impalpable, the ideal."[16]

It is the tension between the sweet ideal and the bitter reality in which it is perceived that gives rise to what Arnold's predecessor Ernest Renan called the "delicious sadness" of the Celt's national melodies and those "poetic memories which simultaneously intercross all the sensations of life, so vague, so deep, so penetrative, that one might die from them without being able to say whether it was from bitterness or sweetness."[17] Do we not sense this element still breathing, for example, in Dylan Thomas's "Fern Hill":

> Oh as I was young and easy in the Mercy of his means,
> Time held me green and dying
> Though I sang in my chains like the sea.[18]

By definition, the bitter-sweet is not all sweet. Doyle's bitter catalogue of the negative outgrowths of the Irish imagination finds congruent, if more politely phrased, expression in Arnold. The defects of the Celtic imagination are "ineffectualness and self will."[19]

Thus far we find agreement between Doyle and Arnold both as to the existence of a Celtic element and its content. What, then, of its source? Does Arnold subscribe to the Doyle theory of moist climate, misty rushes, and alluring distances? At first, he feints in that direction, linking the Celtic sensibility with "the secret of natural beauty and natural magic."[20] Perhaps Arnold is here swept along by the influence of Renan, who proclaimed that the contrast between the climates of Normandy and Brittany reflected "the same contrast . . . in the people," and added that "[a] like change is apparent, I am told," in passing from England to Western Ireland.[21]

Ultimately, however, Arnold will not stray too far into the Celtic mist. Climate, he concludes, may influence the development of an aptitude, but not alone determine it:

> Modes of life, institutions, Government, climate and so forth,—let me say it once and for all,—will further or hinder the development of an aptitude, but they will not by themselves create the aptitude or explain it. On the other hand, a people's habit and complexion of nature go far

to determine its modes of life, institutions, and Government, and even to prescribe the limits within which the influences of climate shall tell upon it.[22]

Yeats, of course, would not heed Arnold's plea that he be allowed to "say it once and for all." In his 1897 essay "The Celtic Element In Literature" Yeats sets out to "re-state a little Renan's and Arnold's argument."[23] Arnold's "Celtic element" is not uniquely Celtic at all, says Yeats. It "is but the ancient religion of the world, the ancient worship of Nature and that troubled ecstacy before her, that certainty of all beautiful places being haunted, which it brought into men's minds."[24] In this ancient religion,

> Life was so weighted down by the emptiness of the great forests and by the mystery of all things, and by the greatness of its own desires, and, as I think, by the loneliness of much beauty; and seemed so little and so fragile and so brief, that nothing could be more sweet in the memory than a tale that ended in death and than a wild and beautiful lamentation.... Men did not mourn merely because their beloved was married to another, or because learning was bitter in the mouth, for such mourning believes that life might be happy were it different, and is therefore the less mourning, but because they had been born and must die with their great thirst unslaked.[25]

In robbing Arnold of the last word, Yeats says every word, and obscures somewhat the relationship between the "loneliness of much beauty" and the mournfulness of the onlooker. Renan clarifies the point in his description, echoed in Yeats, of "the sorrowful feeling that man knows when, face to face with [nature], he believes that he hears her commune with him concerning his origin and his destiny."[26]

What, then, did the Celt hear when nature communed with him about his destiny? He heard, through his priest, the druid, that this life was but a way-station on the way to a greater life beyond the grave, that death was the gateway to reincarnation and a more enduring life. These Celtic beliefs are memorialized as early as 50 years after the death of Christ in Lucan's apostrophe to the Druids:

> To you only is given knowledge or ignorance (whichever it be) of the Gods and the powers of Heaven; your dwelling is in the lone heart of the forest. From you we learn that the bourne of man's ghost is not the senseless grave, not the pale realm of the monarch below; in another world his spirit survives still; Death, if your lore be true, is but the passage to enduring life.[27]

This is a fundamental belief about the way things are that is bound to be reflected in literature. One who believes that there is a more complete life beyond the grave may be excused if he or she dreams of the other world, and grows melancholy at the incompleteness of the here and now. All of mankind is linked with the believer's past and future in a way that minimizes the importance of his own life as "a personal adventure, undertaken by each man on his own account," and he sees it instead as "a link in a long chain, a gift received and handed on, a debt paid and a duty done."[28] The believer in a life beyond the grave feels something of an exile in this world—like Yeats, his soul sick with desire and fastened to a dying animal[29]—and, since he believes that the real life lies in another world, he cannot avoid believing that those who treat this life as the real one are a little mad.

If these be characteristics of the Celtic temperament, whence do they derive? To return to our original question, is temperament the result, as Larry Doyle asserts, of "soft moist air" and "misty rushes"? Or, as Oscar Wilde would have it, is climate the result of temperament? Wilde sees temperament as causing the softness of the air and the mistiness of the rushes:

> Where, if not from the Impressionists, do we get those wonderful brown fogs that come creeping down our streets? . . . To whom if not to them and their master do we owe the lovely silver mists that brood over our river, and turn to faint forms and fading grace curved bridge and swaying barge? The extraordinary change that has taken place in the climate of London over the last ten years is entirely due to this particular school of Art.[30]

Somewhere between Shaw and Wilde climate has been transformed from the cause of sensibility to its effect. Wilde explains the paradox by saying that to look at something is not to see it: "One does not see anything until one sees its beauty" and "what we see, and how we see it, depends on the Arts that have influenced us." People see fogs, not merely because there are fogs, "but because poets and painters have taught them the mysterious loveliness of such effects. There may have been fogs for centuries in London. . . . But no one saw them. . . ."[31] In Wilde's view Larry Doyle sees misty rushes because poets and painters—and why exclude Druids?—have taught him to.

If Wilde's reputation as a *poseur* cautions against a too ready assent to his views, it is worth remembering that Wilde's claim that the Impressionists created London's fogs is only a colorful version of one of the principal tenets of the Romantic movement. According to Coleridge, it was Wordsworth's objective in *Lyrical Ballads*

> to give the charm of novelty to things of every day, and to excite a feeling analogous to the supernatural, by awakening the mind's attention from the lethargy of custom, and directing it to the loveliness and the wonders of the world before us; an inexhaustible treasure, but for

which, in consequence of the film of familiarity and selfish solicitude we have eyes, yet we see not, and hearts that neither feel nor understand.[32]

As Coleridge summarizes, Wordsworth sought, through "freshness of sensation,"[33] to "invest the world with the modifying colors of imagination."[34] In short, both Wilde and Wordsworth evidence that when we look into the mist, we see what our culture has taught us to see.

When the Romantic gazed into the mist, he too, like the aboriginal Celt, felt a longing for a life greater and more enduring than our earthly strut. But while the Celt believed he could find such a life in the next world—and so dreamed of it in this one—the Romantic could not bring himself to believe in the world for which he longed.[35] The Romantic thus sought to heal man's longing in the here and now through the transforming power of imagination "to excite a feeling analogous to the supernatural."[36] As Abrams nicely puts it, "the very discrepancy between [man's] infinite reach and his finite grasp"[37] became the fuel of the Romantic imagination.

Shaw senses the prick of the same discrepancy. It is the force in the misty rushes that sets Doyle dreaming. Peter Keegan, the defrocked priest who shares the views of a Hindu believer in reincarnation, makes this explicit. He suggests to the sad grasshopper that what "wring[s] your heart and mine" is the "sight of Heaven" in the sunset and the heart-punishing knowledge that "you can only look at Heaven from here: you cant reach it."[38]

Keegan's lament places him firmly in the Celtic tradition as defined by Arnold. Indeed, he is a very Druid. Brooding at the round tower like Lucan's Druid in "the lone heart of the forest," Keegan experienced the "intense melancholy" (p. 97) of the Celt communing with nature. This life is no gratifying personal adventure, but a travail "to expiate crimes committed ... in a former existence" (p. 155). This world, whether it be hell as twice suggested, or only purgatory, is "very clearly a place of torment and penance" (p. 155) and Keegan is not at home in it. Alienated from his world, he is thought to be mad, to be living the dream of a madman.

If Keegan exhibits the traits of the Celtic temperament, what is the cause therefor? It may be remembered that there are "great breadths of silken green in the Irish sky" (p. 97) as Keegan discerns the sight of heaven in the sunset and laments the disparity between his reach and grasp. Is then Keegan's temperament the product of the Irish climate? Well, yes and no. Yes, to the extent he sees his vision in the Irish sky. This is Larry Doyle's mist. No, to the extent that what he sees is the product of his mind. Keegan concedes that his vision is one of those wonders that "had been there all the time" but not seen because "my eyes had never been opened to them" (p. 103). This is Wilde's Impressionist fog. In short, Keegan's vision is the product of a fertile marriage between nature and imagination. To this extent, it may be said to reflect the Romantic sensibility.

However, in the moving finish of the play, Keegan, speaking with all the intensity and finality Shaw could give him, transcends both the Romantic and the Celtic imaginations. Whereas the Celt longed for the other world, and the Romantic despaired of ever obtaining it, Keegan boldly drags the other world into this one. Keegan dreams of

> a country where the State is the Church and the Church the people: three in one and one in three. It is a commonwealth in which work is play and play is life: three in one and one in three. It is a temple in which the priest is the worshipper and the worshipper the worshipped: three in one and one in three. It is a godhead in which all life is human and all humanity divine: three in one and one in three. It is, in short, the dream of a madman. (P. 179)

Keegan envisions an Ireland in which the "heart [is] purified of hatred" (p. 179) through the infusion of elements of the other world, a vision analogous to Yeats's hard-won realization that "all hatred driven hence/ the soul recovers radical innocence."[39]

Keegan's dream is "the dream of a madman," but, as Sean O'Casey puts it, "the dream of an Irishman too."[40] Shaw permits Keegan's vision to predominate over Tom Broadbent's doctrine that "[e]fficiency is the thing" (p. 177). Broadbent promises to make Keegan's town a Garden city, complete with higher wages, "a library, a Polytechnic (undenominational, of course), a gymnasium, a cricket club, perhaps an art school" (p. 176). Even the round tower will be repaired and restored. Although Broadbent may be right that "[t]he world belongs to the efficient" (p. 177), the play ends with the other-worldly Keegan passionately dreaming his vision at the round tower.

Larry Doyle laments that Keegan is still the victim of mere "dreaming, dreaming, dreaming, dreaming" (p. 181). Shaw-like, he will return to London. Shaw himself once reminisced that:

> If I had gone to the hills nearby to look upon Dublin and to ponder upon myself, I too might have become a poet like Yeats, Synge and the rest of them. But I prided myself on thinking clearly, and therefore could not stay.[41]

Clear-thinking Shaw left dreamy Ireland, but, by letting Peter Keegan ponder on the hillside, powerfully realized a poet's dream in *John Bull's Other Island*.

Notes

1. G. B. Shaw, "Preface for Politicians," in *The Works of Bernard Shaw* (London: Constable, 1930), XI, 18.
2. Matthew Arnold, *The Study of Celtic Literature* (1867; rpt. Port Washington, N.Y.: Kennikat, 1970).
3. Shaw, "Preface for Politicians," XI, 13.
4. W. B. Yeats, *The Autobiography of William Butler Yeats* (1935; rpt. New York: Collier, 1965), p. 188.
5. W. B. Yeats, *A Vision* (1937; rpt. New York: Collier, 1966), p. 157.
6. See, e.g., John Stewart Collis, "Religion and Philosophy," in *The Genius of Shaw*, ed. Michael Holroyd (London: Hodder & Stoughton, 1979).
7. G. B. Shaw, *John Bull's Other Island*, in *The Works of Bernard Shaw* (London: Constable, 1930), XI, 86–87.
8. Ibid.
9. Edmund Spenser, *A View of the Present State of Ireland* (London: Oxford University Press, 1970), p. 151.
10. Shaw, "Notes to Caesar and Cleopatra," in *The Works of Bernard Shaw*, IX, 208.
11. Arnold, pp. 84–85.
12. Ibid., p. 127.
13. Ibid., p. 84.
14. Ibid., p. 127.
15. Ibid., p. 132.
16. Ibid., pp. 101–102.
17. Ernest Renan, *The Poetry of the Celtic Races* (1859; rpt. Port Washington, N.Y.: Kennikat, 1970), pp. 7–8.
18. Dylan Thomas, "Fern Hill," in *The Norton Anthology of Poetry*, ed. Alexander Allison et al., rev. ed. (New York: Norton, 1970), p. 1166.
19. Arnold, p. 97.
20. Ibid., p. 91.
21. Renan, pp. 1–2.
22. Arnold, p. 100.
23. W. B. Yeats, "The Celtic Element in Literature," in *Essays and Introductions* (1961; rpt. New York: Collier, 1968), p. 174.
24. Ibid., p. 176.
25. Ibid., p. 182.
26. Renan, p. 22.
27. Arnold quotes this passage from Lucan at p. 42 but does not emphasize it.
28. Renan, p. 6.
29. W. B. Yeats, "Sailing to Byzantium," in *The Collected Poems of W. B. Yeats*, 2nd ed. (1950; rpt. London: Macmillan, 1963), p. 217.
30. Oscar Wilde, "The Decay of Lying," in *The Artist as Critic*, ed. Richard Ellmann (London: Allen, 1970), p. 312.
31. Ibid.
32. Samuel Taylor Coleridge, *Biographia Literaria* (1817; rpt. Oxford: Clarendon Press, 1907), II, 6.
33. Ibid., I, 60.
34. Ibid., II, 3.
35. Meyer H. Abrams, *Natural Supernaturalism* (New York: Norton, 1973), p. 216.
36. Coleridge, II, 6.

37. Abrams, p. 216.

38. *John Bull's Other Island*, p. 98. Page references to this work hereinafter will be given in parentheses in the text.

39. W. B. Yeats, "A Prayer For My Daughter," *Collected Poems*, p. 211.

40. Sean O'Casey, "Drums Under the Windows," in *The Autobiographies of Sean O'Casey* (New York: Macmillan, 1958), I, 259.

41. Quoted in *The Genius of the Irish Theatre*, ed. Sylvan Barnet, Morton Berman and William Burto (New York: Mentor, 1960), p. 13.

November 25, 1889 suggest his immersion. On that muddy, rainy Sunday in London he played *Siegfried* for himself all afternoon and into the evening. The next day he did nothing—he confessed—but play *Siegfried* until William Archer interrupted at five. But by eight Archer had gone, and Shaw was on his way to visit Fabian friends, Alfred Dryhurst and his wife, carrying with him Wagner's scores. It was after midnight when he left them. *Siegfried* took some time.[4]

A feature of Shaw's response to *Siegfried* directly related to the prominence of motifs in the plays is the peculiarly rich intellectual structure which he attributed to it, particularly in relation to *Das Rheingold* and *Die Walküre*. Out of his allegorical reading of *The Ring* expounded in *The Perfect Wagnerite*, *Das Rheingold* emerges one-dimensionally, an exposé of the evils of capitalism. Also one-dimensional is *Die Walküre*, an exemplum for Shaw of the moral travail involved in government. *Siegfried,* on the other hand, Shaw conceives more complexly: he sees in the picaresque adventures of the hero an action which includes and furthers the allegorical issues of both the *Rheingold* and *Walküre* dramas; also, one which introduces the theme of romantic love—what Shaw calls the "Love Panacea"—through which he relates it to the later drama, *Götterdämmerung*.

Shaw's conception of *Siegfried* as embodying these three related but distinct concepts—the "Rheingold" element (evoked through the greedy interaction of Alberich, Fafner, Mime), the "Walküre" element (centered, for Shaw, in the Wanderer and in the incidents which culminate in his loss of power at the hands of the Hero), and the "Love Panacea" (evoked through the romantic ecstasies of Brunnhild and Siegfried)—underlies his use of this drama in the plays. Whether employed as direct allusions, or as subject to Shaw's own formidable powers of parody and ironic transformation, motifs from *Siegfried* which emerge in the plays take as their point of reference one or more of these concepts.

One further point: the sort of use to which Shaw puts *Siegfried* motifs—and Wagnerian motifs generally—alters radically after the turn of the century, a change in method no doubt attributable to the systematic formulations of *The Perfect Wagnerite*. Motifs in such early plays as *Widowers' Houses* and *Candida* represent little more than isolated allusions, included to achieve effects essentially parodic. In the later, more important plays—in *Major Barbara, Back to Methusaleh,* and *Saint Joan*—*Siegfried* elements (while often treated parodically) function in the context of Shaw's allegorical understanding of *The Ring* and contribute to a revision—distinct in each play—of the allegory according to the program outlined in his *Wagnerite* treatise.

The earliest Shaw play to include a *Siegfried* element is in fact his earliest play, *Widowers' Houses* (1884–92). That this should be so might at first glance be surprising, since the overall tenor of the play is hardly "heroic." There is here, obviously, no character conceived within the *Siegfried* mold. On the contrary, the cast consists for the most part of types drawn from the nineteenth-century drawing room comedy—a tradition virtually antithetical to Wagner's. Also, the play reveals no ostensible parallels with *Siegfried;* in fact, dramatic affinities in this respect are to be found with another *Ring* drama, Shaw's admitted model for the play as a whole, *Das Rheingold*.[5] Nonetheless, for all the apparent discrepancies of tone and temper, it is demonstrable that Shaw has fashioned one scene, at least, of *Widowers' Houses* after *Siegfried:* the Act III confrontaiton between Sartorius and Lickcheese taking as its prototype the Act II confrontation between Alberich and Mime. Underlying both incidents is the common motif of greed conniving over a lucrative corpse: in Wagner, of the legendary dragon newly slain; in Shaw, its modern and unpleasant equivalent—the urban slum.

That suggestions of *Siegfried* emerge in what is essentially his *Rheingold* play is consistent with the apparent hold which *Siegfried* had upon his imagination. The confrontation of Alberich and Mime in Act II of *Siegfried,* in any case, represents an extension of the *Rheingold* theme of greed, an overlapping of resonances. In *Siegfried* the brother-dwarfs meet at the entrance to Fafner's cave. Expecting at any moment to become inheritors of the slain dragon's booty, they enter into a squabble over division of the spoils. The point of contention is (among other treasures) Tarnhelm, the magic helmet fashioned by Mime, which empowers its possessor to appear in any shape or to disappear altogether. About this helmet Shaw himself had some very specific ideas. It was for him a symbol of the power of wealth to make corruption invisible, and to transform the corrupt rich into the very model of respectability. "This helmet," he remarks in *The Perfect Wagnerite,* "is a very common article in our streets, where it generally takes the form of a tall hat. It makes a man invisible as a shareholder, and changes him into various shapes, such as a pious Christian, a subscriber to hospitals, a benefactor to the poor, a model husband and father, a shrewd, practical, independent Englishman, and whatnot, when he is really a pitiful parasite on the commonwealth, consuming a great deal, and producing nothing, feeling nothing, knowing nothing, believing nothing. . . ."

The relevance of these lines to the Act III encounter of Sartorius and Lickcheese should be immediately apparent: for it is to acquire precisely such power as Shaw describes that they meet; only what is to be transformed is Sartorius' slums, and to be concealed, are their greedy motives. As the scene begins, who should be in possession of

Tarnhelm but Lickcheese himself. Arriving at Sartorius' drawing room sporting a *"silk hat of the glossiest black,"* he is manifestly transformed: in place of the poor scoundrel of the first act, he stands, peacock proud, the "independent" gentleman of means.[6] Moreover, as, in *Siegfried,* Mime is willing to barter away the power of Tarnhelm in exchange for cold cash (a share in the slain dragon's gold), so Lickcheese proposes a deal whereby, for a share in the profits, he will relinquish to Sartorius the modern equivalent of Tarnhelm, that is, the principle of "compensation." The possessor of this magic power finds that at almost no cost to himself he is able to transform ill-paying slum dwellings into sham respectability and thereby reap enormous profits. The Mime in Lickcheese proffers Tarnhelm through his advice to the Alberich in Sartorius that he "Spend a little money on the block at the Cribbs Market end: enough to make it look like a model dwelling.... youll be compensated to the tune of double the present valuation with the cost of improvements thrown in." In return, the former overseer seeks only a piece of the pie: "let the other blocks to me on fair terms for a depot of the North Thames Iced Mutton Company."

In representing this union of cunning and greed, Shaw has, in one respect at least, gone beyond his Wagnerian model in depicting the success of the enterprise. In Wagner's drama, the dwarfs, for all their conniving, attain neither gold nor Tarnhelm, being too stupid and—ultimately—too powerless to attain their desires. Shaw's modern dwarfs promise to fare quite differently since they have acquired both the knowledge and the capital to make good their scheming. All this is, in fact, in keeping with Shaw's conception of the modern, enlightened Alberich, a type who, as he remarked in *The Perfect Wagnerite,* "is not to be dismissed as lightly as Alberic in the *Ring,*" for "the pursebearer," he remains "under Destiny, the real master of the situation."

In *Widowers' Houses* Shaw has reached forward, so to speak, to *Siegfried,* extracting from it the *"Rheingold* element" in order to complete the re-evaluation of *Das Rheingold* which underlies the play as a whole. The next of Shaw's plays to draw upon *Siegfried* is *Candida;* here the Wagnerian element is used more narrowly, as one of a series of "heroic" motifs, manipulated for essentially parodic effects. Among the heroic trappings of *Candida* is a Siegfried in the person of the poet Eugene Marchbanks, young, ardent, and impossibly romantic. The role assigned him—nothing less than a mountaintop wooing of the Brunnhild in Candida Morell—results, alas, in something less than ideally heroic.

As the third act of *Candida* opens, Marchbanks and his beloved are, Shaw tells us, *"seated at the fire."* That this is no ordinary fire is immediately evident to souls of a really romantic cast: like the young poet, they transport themselves to a Wagnerian landscape where Brunnhild slumbers. Candida is therefore found to be *"profoundly unconscious . . . with her feet towards the blaze and her heels resting on the fender."* But what good a sleeping Brunnhild—fire included—without a mountaintop? Thus, completing the effect, Marchbanks queries with sly allusiveness, "Where would you have me spend my moments if not on the summits?" Moreover, the impetuous ardor with which the true hero embraces his maiden (Wagner's speaks of "glowing blood . . . enkindled, as our burning glances are meeting, as I clasp you, blazing with ardor") is a trick not beyond the imaginative grasp of our hero who places himself *"hands clasped and his arms on her lap . . . his blood beginning to stir."*

As it happens, Marchbanks makes a rather poor showing as Siegfried. The role itself of course he embraces eagerly enough, remarking of his moment at the fire, "how heroic it was." But all this is naught beside Shaw's own formidable powers of parody. Perhaps what is funniest in this mock-heroic is that whereas Wagner's hero successfully wakens his maiden from slumber, Shaw's has the misfortune to place his Brunnhild into it, his poetry having, to his dismay, an unanticipated narcotic effect. Perhaps more embarrassing yet, Shaw's Siegfried never even manages to approach the desired goal. The fire, after all, through which Wagner's intrepid hero successfully maneuvered, serves only, it seems, to intimidate his more sensitive hide. "There was," he admits— *"musically"*—"a flaming sword that turned every way, so that I couldn't go in. . . ." Other ironic jabs at this self-styled Siegfried are too numerous to mention. What is abundantly clear is that in this opening scene of Act III Shaw has fashioned from the Wagnerian "hero" motif a very effective mock-heroic device.

Ten years were to pass before *Siegfried* found its way into another Shaw play. This play, one of his greatest, was *Major Barbara*. During that period came the writing of *The Perfect Wagnerite* and a complete formulation of the allegorical scheme of *The Ring* as Shaw conceived it. Clearly reflecting that experience, *Major Barbara* is the most thoroughly Wagnerian of all the plays. More than one critic, for example, has uncovered in Act II prototypes for a host of *Ring* characters drawn from both *Das Rheingold* and *Die Walküre*.[7] And indeed, in the second act Shaw attempts to lay the foundations for a new *Ring* revised along the lines suggested in the *Wagnerite*. This dramatic overhauling carries over unmistakably into Act III where Shaw turns to the climactic drama of the allegory, to *Siegfried*. At the same time, the *Siegfried* which emerges in *Major Barbara* is not to be mistaken for the original. Rather, it is full of dramatic inversions bespeaking a thoroughly altered conception of both the nature of the hero and the terms of his realization. For an explanation of these we must now turn to *The Perfect Wagnerite*. Here Shaw reveals himself basically disenchanted with Wagner's heroic type; at the same time he lays down a sort of game plan for his later use of Wagner's drama in *Major Barbara*.

It is a fact, never too often pointed out, that for all his admiration of *The Ring* as a work of the imagination, Shaw thought it a philosophical failure. Specifically, the type of new humanity envisioned in Wagner's Siegfried never, in his view, materialized, history having arranged matters rather differently. "The Siegfrieds of 1848 were," Shaw maintained, "hopeless political failures, whereas the Wotans and Alberics were conspicuous political successes."

Among the historical inaccuracies of *The Ring* none was for Shaw more glaring than Wagner's failure to envision the importance which the Alberich type was to assume in the capitalist scheme, and particularly, the necessary evolution of the type within that scheme. In effect, Shaw faults Wagner for failing to recognize that, within an evolving capitalism, Alberich the dwarf becomes Alberich the industrialist, who becomes Alberich the statesman and philanthropist:

> He discovers that to be a dull, greedy, narrow-minded money-grubber is not the way to make money on a large scale; for though greed may suffice to turn tens into hundreds and even hundreds into thousands, to turn thousands into hundreds of thousands requires economic magnanimity and a will to power as well as to pelf. And to turn hundreds of thousands into millions, Alberic must make himself an earthly Providence for masses of workmen, creating towns, and governing markets.... Consequently, although Alberic in 1850 may have been merely the vulgar Manchester factory-owner portrayed in Friedrich Engels' *The Condition of the Working Class in England in 1844,* in 1876 he was well on his way towards becoming exoterically a model philanthropic employer and esoterically a financier.... Wotan is hardly less dependent on him than Fafnir: the War-Lord visits his works, acclaims them in stirring speeches.... And he owns and controls a new god, called The Press, which manufactures public opinion on his side, and organizes the persecution and suppression of Siegfried.

This having been the course which history did indeed take, Shaw conceives for the modern Siegfried a role radically different than that assigned by Wagner: he must grow up and accept the responsibilities of power in a capitalistic civilization. "Alberic's work, like Wotan's work and Loki's work, is necessary work, and ... therefore Alberic can never be superceded by a warrior, but only by a capable man of business who is prepared to continue his work without a day's intermission." The modern Siegfried must, in short, "learn Alberic's trade and shoulder Alberic's burden."

Alfred Turco has remarked that "*Major Barbara* is Shaw's attempt to rewrite *Siegfried* in terms valid for the twentieth century."[8] And it is fascinating within this context to observe how in Act III Shaw manages consistently to mold the action according to *Siegfried* patterns even as he quite as consistently transforms the tenor of the action according to his own conceptions. For example, the third act opens upon a world in one respect very like that of Wagner's drama: it is a world explicitly in need of a redeemer. Shaw underscores the parallel by providing his armsmaker a brooding speech strongly reminiscent of a lament uttered by Wagner's god. Wotan had recognized the need for a man who "can manage what I don't dare, a hero, never helped by my power; who, strange to the gods, is free of their grace. . . . This one can do what I fear to try, and never urged him to do."[9] Similarly, as act three opens Undershaft announces his search for a "man with no relations and no schooling; that is, a man who would be out of the running altogether if he were not a strong man."

It is, by the way, important to keep in mind this aspect of Undershaft's need and its apparent Wagnerian derivation; otherwise one is liable to misjudge the quality of his strength and, consequently, the nature of his contribution to the dialectic of power within Act III. Three current views of Undershaft illustrate the danger. Robert Jordan has spoken of the "strange limitations" of Shaw's armsmaker, remarking as odd that "Undershaft's intellectual and spiritual power does not drive him beyond this to pursue the higher forms."[10] J. L. Wisenthal, on the other hand, while acknowledging the limitations of Undershaft, thinks this not strange but necessary, writing that "Although he has a stronger grasp of the actual world than Barbara or Cusins, he is less highly evolved than either of them."[11] Recently this debate has taken an about-face, Arthur Ganz arguing against Wisenthal that, yes indeed, Undershaft is to be taken as *the* figure of power in the play:

> But the problem with Wisenthal's view is that it contravenes not only the Undershaft of the Preface but the Undershaft of the play as well. When he answers Cusins' question about what drives Perivale with the reply, "A will of which I am a part," Undershaft means not the will of society (as Wisenthal, astonishingly, says) but the Life Force and thus offers Barbara a glimpse of a religion nobler than her previous one. And it is Undershaft who offers to Cusins the vision of Perivale as a center of revolutionary force. "Poverty and slavery," he tells Cusins, "have stood up for centuries to your sermons and leading articles: they will not stand up to my machine guns. Dont preach at them: dont reason with them. Kill them."

Ganz concludes that "though we may have reservations about Wisenthal's view of Undershaft as a characterization, we need not doubt that he is correct in equating the master of Perivale and the lord of Walhall."[12]

But surely Wisenthal's view of Undershaft is the correct one, and for precisely the reason which Ganz acknowledges: Undershaft's role is that of the crippled son of Valhalla. That he is driven by what Ganz calls the Life Force does not mitigate his essential impotence any more than it does Wotan's in *The Ring*. The point is that Wagner's god has tied his spiritual aspirations (promptings of the Life Force) to material binds—Wotan admits, "I who by treaties was lord, by these treaties now am a slave." So, too, Shaw's armsmaker. Realization of this fact underlies Cusins' jibe that "You have no power.... This place is driven by the most rascally part of society, the money hunters, the pleasure hunters, the military promotion hunters; and he is their slave."

That Shaw himself considered Undershaft impotent in precisely the manner of Wotan is more than evident in the parallels between the great laments provided the respective god figures. In one of the great set pieces of *Die Walküre,* and in a bitter utterance which is at the center of the *Ring* allegory, Wotan had narrated as an inexorable chain of past evils his stymied present: "When young love vanished, with its delights, my spirit aspired to power, and spurred by former wishes, I went and won myself the world. I thought no falsehood, yet I did falsely, carried out contracts where harm lay hid." This dark confession returns in Undershaft's own moving admission of an unsavory past; his "*tone dropping into one of bitter and brooding remembrance,*" he recalls: "I was an east ender. I moralized and starved until one day I swore that I would be a full fed man at all costs; that nothing should stop me except a bullet, neither reason nor morals nor the lives of other men. I said 'Thou shalt starve ere I starve'; and with that word I became free and great." Like Wotan, Undershaft has linked vital aspiration to past evils, and is to an extent still bound by them. Both are to be seen as "slaves" awaiting the arrival of the free man.

But such is the only real similarity between the two figures. For the rest, Shaw proceeds to demonstrate that even if Undershaft's power is qualified in the manner of Wotan, yet its extent is far greater than that of Wagner's god and infinitely more assured; this a development in keeping with the evolution of Wotan as depicted in *The Perfect Wagnerite*. In short, Undershaft/Wotan has achieved a coalition with Alberich: the capitalist has become ruler, the ruler capitalist. This alteration is symbolized in Perivale St Andrews, whose features are drawn to suggest simultaneously the Niebelheim of the dwarf and the shining home of the gods.

The Valhalla pedigree of Undershaft's foundry town is evident enough. As Wotan's domain assumes the form of "a castle with glittering pinnacles, which stands on a cliff in the background," so Perivale St Andrews is shaped according to a similar ideal: situated *"between hills,"* it is *"an almost smokeless town of white walls, roofs of narrow green slates and red tiles, tall trees, domes. . . . beautifully situated and beautiful in itself. . . ."*

It is, however, as a structural alteration unimagined by Wagner that the home of Shaw's twentieth-century god should acquire the lineaments of a renovated Niebelheim as well. Its renovation at the hands of the modern Alberich in Undershaft (Shaw had remarked in *The Perfect Wagnerite* that Alberich "had found that Niebelheim was a very gloomy place") is hinted at in an exchange between Barbara and her father. Barbara, still in the nineteenth century, believes melodramatically that the workplace of the capitalist-industrialist must inevitably assume the sleazy character of the home of Wagner's dwarf. "I have always thought," she admits, "of it as a sort of pit where lost creatures with blackened faces stirred up smoking fires and were driven and tormented by my father." To this, *"scandalized,"* the enlightened Alberich in Undershaft can only reply, "My dear! it is a spotlessly clean and beautiful hillside town."

It is noteworthy, then, that if Wotan and Undershaft share a fundamental impotence, Undershaft retains a strength which is all his own. His is the potency born of political realism and of the command of an economic punch to which Wagner's doomed god has no access. And for this reason the hero which Shaw's Wotan seeks represents a type worlds away from that of the young rabble rouser of Wagnerian fame: not an anarchist who will destroy Valhalla, but a capable ruler who will sustain it. As *Major Barbara* concludes, the role of the new Siegfried falls to Cusins. In the meantime he is put through a strict apprenticeship under the Wotan in Undershaft and the Brunnhild in Barbara. His lesson?—that which for Shaw is utterly requisite for the enlightened Siegfried: he is "to learn Alberic's trade and shoulder Alberic's burden."

"Cusins," writes J. L. Wisenthal, "at the end of *Major Barbara* . . . is the Siegfried . . . in a *Ring* which has been brought up to date. Shaw has undertaken the revisions which he says Wagner did not attempt."[13] Extending this insight, Arthur Ganz points out what seems to be a distinctly Wagnerian allusion fashioned into Shaw's young foundling: "Although Wisenthal refers once to 'Cusins/Siegfried,' he makes no attempt to relate these figures; and yet they have similarities, especially in regard to their progenitors. Both, after all, are orphans. Siegfried is a child of incest. . . . The comic equivalent in *Major Barbara* is Cusins' claim that he is a foundling because his mother is his 'father's deceased wife's sister' and her marrriage is thus illegal in England."[14]

The apprenticeship of Shaw's burgeoning young hero consists of his assuming the role of his prototype in two key scenes from *Siegfried*. The first occurs by way of the extended, heated—and thematically crucial—discourse between Cusins and Undershaft, which is fashioned to suggest the climactic—and for Shaw allegorically crucial—encounter between Siegfried and the Wanderer. The meeting in each respective drama assumes the character of a contest in which impetuous youth taunts experience and age. In *Siegfried*, the Wanderer (the disguised Wotan) is made to feel his waning strength:

> WANDERER. Why then I must hinder your way! For still do I hold the mighty haft. The sword that you swing once broke upon this shaft: yet once again let it splinter upon this spear!
> SIEGFRIED. So my father's foe faces me here? Sweet is the vengeance that comes my way! Swing with your sword and let it split on my sword!

In Shaw's drama Cusins' taunts assume a similar tenor:

> UNDERSHAFT. Don't come here lusting for power, young man.
> CUSINS. If power were my aim I should not come here for it. You have no power.
> UNDERSHAFT. None of my own, certainly.
> CUSINS. I have more power than you....

It must be borne in mind that the hero and god which Shaw draws together here have a significance quite unlike that which they had for Wagner. Shaw's Wotan, unlike his prototype, has the experience of a successful capitalism behind him as well as the economic power of Alberich; he is, in short, an enlightened god infinitely more vital and formidable than his prototype. Conversely, Shaw believed the Siegfried underlying Cusins to be a failed type very much in need of renovation. Consequently, fashioned into this otherwise Wagnerian encounter are some distinctly un-Wagnerian *coups de théâtre*.

In the first place, Shaw's Wotan understands what the modern Siegfried must learn: that his rebellion is to be creative, not destructive, and practical as well as idealistic. For this reason, interpolated within the verbal clash is a little lecture on the realities of power not to be found in Wagner's libretto. The modern Wotan—so the modern Siegfried must understand—is sufficiently strong not to have to yield to brute force and intends to relinquish the reins only to a mature hero: "Ought! Ought! Ought! ... Turn your oughts into shalls, man. Come and make explosives with me. Whatever can blow up men can blow up society. The history of the world is the history of those who have had courage enough to embrace this truth." Moreover, as if to underscore this new conception of a Wotan strong in his commitment to the fact of power, Shaw reverses the outcome of this Wagnerian clash of heroes, and withholds from his Siegfried the ultimate victory granted his prototype.

In *Siegfried* the heroic youth overcomes the god effortlessly, his sword smashing through Wotan's spear with the force of necessity itself. The *Major Barbara* equivalent finds the Wotan in Undershaft quite the equal—and more—of his challenger. His is the upper hand: "You are fencing, Euripides. You are weakening: your grip is slipping. Come! try your last weapon. Pity and love have broken in your hand: forgiveness is still left." The function, then, of this parody is ultimately to deflate the notion that "strength" is to be equated with the untoward gyrations of a "blonde beast." As Shaw accepts the term, "strength" is rather the courage to accept the truth and to act according to the dictates of reality and of necessity. It is this truth which the Siegfried in Cusins learns as the first of his lessons in the ways of the world.

The second stage of Cusins' growth is marked by an incident of Wagnerian mood as well; this in the Act II union of the young professor of Greek with Barbara, which retains echoes of the love duet between Siegfried and Brunnhild. In Wagner's drama the love duet follows immediately upon the hero's overthrow of the gods and represents a union now utterly free and tremendously vital. In its fierce and exulting passion, it represents the emergence of the heroic age out of the ashes of Wotan's defeat. Similarly, the "love duet" which concludes *Major Barbara* follows closely upon Cusins' re-enactment of the Siegfried/Wotan clash. It initiates the transfer of power from the Wotan in Undershaft to the Siegfried and Brunnhild in Cusins and Barbara. Ultimately, Shaw's finale marks the dawn of a new, spiritually vital age out of the darkness of Undershaft's rule.

There are parallels between the finales of Wagner and Shaw. The fiery mountaintop, for example, upon which Wagner's lovers unite, is suggested in the smoking chimneys and hillside setting of Perivale St Andrews. Even the incendiary element is not lacking, Shaw having provided in Bilton a Loki who "*opens the box and deliberately drops the matches into the fire-bucket.*" Moreover, as Shaw had, in *The Perfect Wagnerite*, interpreted Siegfried's penetration through the fire as a victory of truth over illusion—"And never a hair of his head is singed. These frightful flames which have scared mankind for centuries have not heat enough in them to make a child shut its eyes"—so Cusins approaches Barbara with a like commitment to truth: "What I am selling it [his soul] for is neither money nor position nor comfort, but for reality and for power."

The "libretto" of Shaw's finale has something in it of Wagner as well. Siegfried unites with Brunnhild in "*ecstasy*"; he "*fastens his lips on hers,*" while she, for her part, "*throws herself in Siegfried's arms.*" In a manner similar although somewhat less impetuous—Shaw's, after all, are Anglo-Saxon lovers—Barbara, "*seizing* [Cusins] *with both hands, kisses him.*" Moreover, the curious chanting quality of Shaw's dialogue is not unlike Wagner's: the ecstatic Brunnhild swoons, "Hail, O sun-lord! Hail, O light," while Barbara, similarly transported, exclaims, "Glory Halleluja!" Also, the gloriously illuminated world achieved in the union of Siegfried and Brunnhild—Siegfried's "Hail, O light, that have burst from the night" is typical—returns in Barbara's biblical vision of "the raising of hell to heaven and of man to God, through the unveiling of an eternal light in the Valley of the Shadow." Finally, if in Brunnhild's frenzy she imagines herself as having passed right out of this world—"I see, still shining, Siegfried's star!"—so Cusins remarks of Barbara that "she has gone right up into the skies."

For all these parallels, however, it can hardly escape notice that in one respect at least Shaw's version of the "love duet" is not only unlike, but positively antithetical to Wagner's—this in its utter disregard for the sentiment of romantic love. Indeed, while the world in which Wagner's lovers unite contracts (even, paradoxically, as it expands) to the scope of their private ecstasy, the world in which Barbara and Cusins meet is that most unromantic world of humanity at large, the world of money and power, the world of poverty and need. "There are larger loves and diviner dreams than the fireside ones," Barbara remarks in what may be an ironic reference to the fireside romance of their prototypes.

This de-romanticizing of the "love duet" represents a revision of *Siegfried* according to the criticism which Shaw had levelled against it in *The Perfect Wagnerite*. In the finale, claimed Shaw, Wagner had abandoned "the perfectly clear allegorical design" of *The Ring* in favor of what he went on to call "THE LOVE PANACEA," that is, the "prescription of a romantic nostrum for all human ills." This of course Shaw's own lovers reject. Emblematic in fact of the change in the emotional climate are the quite different terms upon which each Brunnhild chooses to unite with her Siegfried. Wagner's warrior maid, in a very delirium of erotic bliss, rejects "Valhall's radiant world! Let fall your glittering towers to dust!" Shaw's, on the other hand, more levelheaded (even hard-headed), accepts the love of Cusins only on the condition that he assume the rule of Undershaft's Valhalla/Niebelheim/Perivale St Andrews: "Do you know what would have happened if you had refused papa's offer? . . . I should have given you up and married the man who accepted it."

And it is in this, Barbara's insistence upon concrete reality, that she weans the incipient Siegfried in Cusins away from the romance of love precisely as Undershaft had, earlier, been weaned from the romance of power. As a result, in this scene is revealed the new, legitimate Siegfried. Having rejected what Colin Wilson calls Cusins's "Celtic twilight of dreams," having embraced in its place reality and power, having united with an enlightened Brunnhild to assume the burdens of Alberich and Wotan, Cusins has achieved the only strength compatible, for Shaw, with the truly heroic: this is the strength born of, and sustained by, the encounter with truth. Shaw's Siegfried has thus arrived, and with his arrival the completion of the *Ring* element in *Major Barbara*.

Shaw has referred to *Back to Methuselah* both as a "metabiological pentateuch" and as his "Ring drama."[15] And two more incongruous elements (myth and biology) it would be hard to imagine as coherently co-existing in one play. What Shaw has done, however, is to adapt the biological program of the play—i.e., the idea of a vastly extended span of human life—to a sort of *Ring* treatment, long life emerging as the principle upon which he undertakes the second major overhauling of *The Ring* in his career. Prominent among the *Ring* elements in the play are those drawn from *Siegfried;* and these too have been subjected to a biological overhauling, such that the heroic type which in Wagner had been conceived as a spontaneous occurrence, Shaw fashions as developing in time, the dramatic result of a long process of biological evolution. In form, *Back to Methusaleh* may be compared to *Major Barbara;* the first two of its cycle of five plays represent, like the first two acts of *Major Barbara,* a world awaiting the arrival of the hero. In *The Thing Happens* that hero, and the new humanity which he symbolizes, arrives at long, at very long, last on the scene.

J. L. Wisenthal has remarked of *In the Beginning* that it "is the prelude to *Back to Methusaleh* as *The Rheingold* is the prelude to Wagner's *Ring*."[16] This may be true in a strictly analogical sense, but the *Ring* drama to which the play is especially indebted is *Siegfried*. Closer to the mark in this respect is Louis Crompton, who has called the part of Cain that of a "brilliant heldentenor."[17] Indeed, the Edenic world of this first of the *Methusaleh* plays is steeped in the heroic element and has for its self-proclaimed "hero" an incipient Siegfried in Cain. Shaw relates his warrior to Wagner's at a number of points. Certainly the motif of parental rebellion is distinctly Wagnerian, the series of skirmishes in which Cain engages his father occurring in a spirit very like that which binds Siegfried antagonistically to Mime. As, for example, Siegfried ridicules the dwarf's craft ("blustering bungler" he calls him), so Cain taunts Adam as a "stupid old digger." Moreover, as Wagner's intrepid youth voices a preference even for the company of four-footed Bruin to that of his guardian ("Then a bear broke through the woods ... and I liked him better than you"), so Cain insists to Adam, "I had rather be a bear than a man.... If you are content, like the bear, I am not."

Finally, the fear motif which so clearly distinguishes Wagner's pair (Mime being a creature of fear; Siegfried utterly intrepid) returns to distinguish Shaw's father and son: Adam acknowledges that "fear will drive me to anything," while his blustering son can announce, "Danger and fear follow my footsteps everywhere."

In *The Perfect Wagnerite* Shaw had characterized as an ideal type the Siegfried who emerged from the early scenes of Wagner's drama. Compared to the cringing dwarf, he wrote, the young hero "is, in short, a totally unmoral person, a born anarchist, the ideal of Bakoonin, an anticipation of the 'overman' of Nietzsche.... Altogether an inspiring young forester, a son of the morning, in whom the heroic race has come out into the sunshine from the clouds of his grandfather's majestic entanglement with law...." Similarly, in the antagonistic relation between his Adam and Cain, Shaw demonstrates that, compared to the timid, plodding, conventional Mime in Adam, the brash and vital Cain represents an evolutionary leap towards the Siegfried type. Indeed, significant in this respect is Cain's own recognition—only in part ironic—that "There is something higher than man. There is hero and superman." Shaw goes on to underscore this ideally heroic aspect of Cain by attributing to him Siegfried's power of understanding the voice of birds. In Wagner's drama this talent is associated with the hero's being in touch with truths perceptible only to those who do not fear. Similarly, Cain receives from his "Voice" harsh truths comprehensible only to his heroic self. From his "Voice" he hears that "I must offer myself to be killed by every man if he can kill me. Without danger I cannot be great," or that "death is not really death: that it is the gate of another life: a life infinitely splendid and intense: a life of the soul alone: a life without clods or spades, hunger or fatigue."

But if the Siegfried which emerges in Cain-as-young-unconventionalist earns Shaw's respect and approval as a sort of human ideal, it is clear that Shaw would hardly endorse the cult of primitivism which attaches to his character. For this darker side of his "young forester" the civilized and inveterately civilizing Shaw had no use at all. Indeed, in *The Perfect Wagnerite* he had already disparaged precisely this type, remarking that among the "Siegfrieds of 1848" were such figures as Roeckel and Bakunin, whom he described as "romantic amateurs and theatrical dreamers." From this point of view, then, the splendid arrogance of Cain's most characteristic utterances ("There is something higher than man. There is hero and superman!") is to be taken as nothing more than romantic twaddle, the vain boast of an overgrown bully. In other words, the Siegfried in Cain is to be taken with a grain of salt.

This Shaw himself supplies in the pungent form of parody. Specifically, he re-enacts through Cain and Adam the *Siegfried* clash between the hero and Wanderer; only he witholds from Cain the victory granted his prototype. One critic, by the way, has hinted of the Wagnerian quality of this encounter. "The Preface to *Back to Methusaleh*," writes William Blissett, "... mentions Wagner's *Ring* among other 'reachings forward to the new vitalist art'; but in the play itself the stage is set again for a conflict between vital youth and authoritarian age, only for the effect to be deliberately dissipated. Young Cain holding a spear defies old Adam holding a spade but the future is with neither of them...."[18] Actually, Blissett finds only incidentally Wagnerian what Shaw seems to have introduced with deliberation, retaining in the clash of youth and age both the imagery and the emotional tenor of the original:

> *Siegfried:*
> THE WANDERER. Why then I must hinder your way! For still do I hold the mighty haft. The sword that you swing once broke upon this shaft: yet once again let it splinter upon this spear!
> SIEGFRIED. So my father's foe faces me here? Sweet is the vengeance that comes my way! Swing with your sword and let it split on my sword!
>
> *In the Beginning:*
> ADAM [in a sullen rage]. I have half a mind to show you that my spade can split your undutiful head open, in spite of your spear.
> CAIN. Undutiful! Ha! Ha! [Flourishing his spear] Try it, old everybody's father. Try a taste of fighting.

In place of victory, Shaw provides his Siegfried with a stiff dose of ironic deflation through Eve's intrusive, "Peace, peace, you two fools." The tenor of the incident as a whole clearly expresses Shaw's dissatisfaction with Wagner's heroic type; it suggests that the Siegfried of this first of the *Methusaleh* plays, though a figure to be preferred over the timid Mime in Adam, is but a primitive foreshadowing of Shaw's ideal. Thus, *In the Beginning* concludes (as did the second act of *Major Barbara*) with the true Hero conceived but not yet manifest.

It is left to the second and third plays of the cycle to produce a legitimate Shavian Siegfried, this in the person of the Archbishop of *The Thing Happens* and as prefigured in the youthful Haslam of *The Gospel of the Brothers Barnabas*. Although there is in fact nothing obstensibly "heroic" about this chattering, comical clergyman, Shaw has taken care to invest him with lineaments subtly suggestive of his Wagnerian pedigree. Like Siegfried (and like Cain), Haslam is infected with a case of filial resentment, remarking, "I wish my father had found some other shop for me." Also—a more explicit allusion—Haslam possesses the hero's unique talent for understanding the voice of birds: "Oh yes. Theres a bird there that keeps on singing 'Stick it or chuck it: stick it or chuck it'—just like that—for an hour on end in the spring." What it is that qualifies Shaw's clergyman for the role of Siegfried is difficult to say, although his breezy manner and *"frank schoolboyishness"* (both "frank" and "schoolboy" are qualities associated, in *The Perfect Wagnerite,* with Siegfried) do suggest the sort of clear-sighted freedom from convention which Shaw includes among the attributes of the Hero.

Only in his reappearance as the grave and long-lived Archbishop of *The Thing Happens* does Haslam blossom into the Siegfried of Shaw's ideal. In the first place, like Cain and then Haslam, the Archbishop retains unmistakable traces of his Wagnerian lineage. Like them, he acts in opposition to a Mime whose affairs he holds in contempt. "What higher employments," he scoffs at President Burge-Lubin, "are you capable of?" Like them—and especially like Siegfried as celebrated in *The Perfect Wagnerite*—he retains a healthy streak of anarchism. Shaw's hero, "who destroys only to clear the ground for creation," returns in the Archbishop's remark that "I persuaded the authorities to knock down all our towns and rebuild them from the foundations, or move them. . . ."

What in fact the Archbishop represents is the emergence into full stature of the Siegfried which in Cain and Haslam is only stillborn; and in this respect the qualities which distinguish him from his predecessors are significant of the evolutionary gap between them. Unlike Haslam, for example, whose healthy freedom and clearsightedness remain merely comic attributes in a character little more than a "schoolboy," the Archbishop appears in *The Thing Happens* with "his boyishness of manner . . . quite gone." He stands rather as a gravely mature figure, a former President and General—a figure who corresponds in fact to Shaw's own conception of the modern Siegfried, who is to "learn Alberic's trade and shoulder Alberic's burden." The advance of the Siegfried in the Archbishop over the hero in Cain is equally pronounced. Whereas Cain dissipated his strength in actively obstructing the work of life ("nothing but death or the dread of death makes life worth living"), and who, indeed, had not strength enough to bear its burden ("You see, life is too long. One tires of everything."), the Archbishop remains appalled at the waste of life around him ("We die in boyhood: the maturity that should make us the greatest of nations lies beyond the grave for us.") and actively seeks to further it ("We must will to live longer.").

The question, of course, inevitably arises: how has the Archbishop done it? As a result of what process have the attributes which he shares with Cain and Haslam before him coalesced to form in him a clearly superior human type? And the answer, of course, is—long life. It is length of years which have transformed the bellicose Cains and the boyish Haslams of the world of *Methusaleh* into the mature, capable Siegfried which is the Archbishop, a figure in whom the heroic ideal of *The Perfect Wagnerite* comes to fruition. And with his arrival is brought to completion this second of Shaw's major revisions of Wagner, the *Ring* receiving here what might be called a biological update as it had earlier, in *Major Barbara*, a sociological one.

There once was a warrior who, following a path dictated by a certain esoteric voice, was led to penetrate through a certain fire and emerge unscathed and even revitalized. That warrior is, of course, Siegfried— and also Joan of Arc. There once was a warrior the story of whose courageous penetration through fire Bernard Shaw associated with the rise of Protestantism. That warrior is, of course, the "Siegfried as Protestant" of *The Perfect Wagnerite;* it is also the Saint Joan to whom, in his preface to the play of the same name, Shaw refers as "one of the first of the Protestant martyrs." Of the hero of *Saint Joan*, J. L. Wisenthal has written that her "personality reminds one strongly of Siegfried. . . . Some of the music given to Wagner's innocent, impudent, self-assured, conquering hero (who is slain by his enemies) would be very appropriate for Joan."[19] All of which tempts the supposition that in Joan the Wagnerite Shaw might well have fashioned once again a new Siegfried.

We turn to the play itself and are not disappointed. As the Epilogue opens, Ladvenu intrudes upon the reclining Charles to bring him news of Joan's posthumous acquittal. The gist of his report is that out of the lies and falsehoods which sent Joan to the fire has emerged the truth and with it a new hero:

> At the trial which sent a saint to the stake as a heretic and a sorceress, the truth was told; the law was upheld; mercy was shown beyond all custom; no wrong was done but the final and dreadful wrong of the lying sentence and the pitiless fire. . . . Yet out of this insult to justice, this defamation of the Church, this orgy of lying and foolishness, the truth is set in the noonday sun on the hilltop, . . . the true heart that lived through the flame is consecrated; a great lie is silenced forever; and a great wrong is set right before all men.

Now this is certainly a familiar scenario: the emergence through fire as emblematic of the victory of truth over falsehood. Where in Shaw have we seen it last? In *The Perfect Wagnerite*, where he wrote,

> Those frightful flames which have scared mankind for centuries from the Truth, have not heat enough in them to make a child shut its eyes. They are mere phantasmagoria, highly creditable to Loki's imaginative stage management; but nothing has ever perished or will perish eter-

nally in them except the Churches which have been so poor and faithless as to trade their power on the lies of a romancer.

The parallels between these excerpts suggest that underlying Ladvenu's speech are allusions of distinctly Wagnerian nature. Indeed, included is a "hilltop," and beyond this a reference to the "true heart that lived through the flame" as a result of which "a great lie is silenced forever." Are we then to take Joan as the Siegfried which has accomplished all this?

Details of setting and dialogue make quite clear that, yes, it is as a triumphant Siegfried that Joan returns in the Epilogue, the whole of which resonates richly of the hero's association with fire. In the first place, the room to which Joan returns in the Epilogue suggests the Wagnerian sleeping chamber encircled by fire, this latter element provided symbolically by Shaw in a dextrous manipulation of set: "*The walls are hung from ceiling to floor with painted curtains which stir at times in the draughts. At first glance the prevailing yellow and red in these hanging pictures is somewhat flamelike when the folds breathe in the wind.*" Shaw insists, moreover, that precisely as Joan enters these flames are to be invoked, her intrusion causing "*a rush of wind through the open door* [that] *sets the walls swaying agitatedly.*" Among the Wagnerian accoutrements of this scene is even a sleeping Brunnhild in poor King Charles, whose prototype Shaw suggests by a neat turn of dialogue: Joan's query, "Did I make a man of thee after all, Charlie?" is after all the near gender-switch which Siegfried, startled upon finding Brunnhild, visits upon her in his humorous "That is no man!"

The hero's penetration through fire and awakening of Brunnhild represents the climactic incident not only of *Siegfried* but of the *Ring* as a whole; it signifies for Shaw the victory of truth and the dawn of a new, heroic humanity. For the parallel incident enacted in *Saint Joan* Shaw makes no such lofty claims. In fact, he deliberately alters the terms of the "awakening" to illustrate that Joan's victory over illusion and falsehood is hers alone, isolated and, ultimately, isolating. Wagner's hero can plunge through the flame to awaken the vital Brunnhild, but Joan's equally triumphant return fails to elicit a like response from the super-somnolent Brunnhild in Charles ("Easy, Charlie, easy.... Thourt asleep."). Indeed, this indomitable sleep of humanity within the fires of illusion Shaw makes even more explicit a bit further along. Toward the end of her visit, Joan offers to return to earth in her new identity as saint—"I bid you to remember that I am a saint, and that saints can work miracles. And now tell me: shall I rise from the dead, and come back to you a living woman?" With this gesture coincides "*A sudden darkness* [which] *blots out the walls of the room.*" Clearly implicit in Joan's offer is a determination to dispel the illusory flames which encircle her audience. Contented Brunnhilds, they respond only in "*consternation*," and request only to be allowed to slumber complacently on:

> DUNOIS. Forgive us, Joan: we are not yet good enough for you. I shall go back to bed.
> . . . .
> CHARLES. And what can I do but follow Jack Dunois' example, and go back to bed too?

It is evident therefore that if, as The Soldier affirms, "the fire that is not quenched is a holy fire," then that which can be quenched is the unholy element in which humanity still slumbers. It is in this regard supremely ironic that only this refugee from hell (a seasoned veteran, presumably, of the fire which truly scorches) lingers at last, alone responsive to the Saint and her message.

The final line of the play, Joan's "How long, O Lord, how long?" is a saint's lament for an earth still unsanctified. It is additionally the hero's lament for a humanity unwilling to rise to a sense of its own dignity. But perhaps more than these, it may be taken as an expression of Shaw's own disillusionment; for with this play of 1923 the Siegfried type, hitherto so prominent a feature of his most serious plays, and emblem of an almost inveterate confidence in humanity, disappears at last and utterly from his work.

Notes

1. Bernard Shaw, *The Perfect Wagnerite* (New York: Dover Publications, Inc., 1967), p. 60. All subsequent references taken from this edition.

2. Wagnerian motifs occur frequently in Shaw. For an extended discussion see J. L. Wisenthal, "The Underside of Undershaft: A Wagnerian Motif in 'Major Barbara'," *The Shaw Review*, 15, no. 2 (May 1972), 56–61; Arthur Ganz, "The Playwright as Perfect Wagnerite: Motifs from the Music Dramas in the Theatre of Bernard Shaw," *Comparative Drama*, 13 (Fall 1979), 187–207.

3. One other major play, *Heartbreak House*, includes a good deal of material inspired by *Siegfried*. It is, however, woven within a dramatic pattern too rich to be unravelled in this short paper.

4. From the Stanley Rypins transcription of Shaw's shorthand. The original diary is in the London Library of Economics and Political Science.

5. *Widowers' Houses* was initiated as the collaborative effort of Shaw and William Archer, who has written that "it was to be called *Rhinegold*, was to open, as *Widowers' Houses* actually does, in a hotel-garden on the Rhine, and was to have two heroines, a

sentimental one and a comic one, according to the accepted Robertson, Byron, Carton formula." See Preface to *Widowers' Houses* (1893 edition), most readily available in *The Bodley Head Bernard Shaw*, I, p. 37.

6. *The Bodley Head Bernard Shaw, Collected Plays with Their Prefaces* (London: The Bodley Head, 1971), I, p. 104. All subsequent references to the plays taken from this edition.

7. Wisenthal and Ganz have both pointed to the following *Die Walküre* prototypes: in Undershaft, Wotan; in Barbara, Brunnhild; in Bill Walker, Siegmund; in Britomart, Fricka. In a recent article ("Wagner and Shaw: Rheingold Motifs in *Major Barbara*," *Comparative Drama* [Spring 1980], 70–73) I have identified the following *Rheingold* prototypes: in Barbara, Freia; in Undershaft, Wotan; in Price, Shirley, and Mitchens, Giants; in Walker, Loge.

8. Alfred Turco, Jr., *Shaw's Moral Vision* (Ithaca: Cornell University Press, 1976), p. 217.

9. Richard Wagner, *The Ring of the Nibelung*, trans. Stewart Robb (New York: E. P. Dutton, 1960), p. 110. All subsequent references to Wagner's dramas taken from this edition. [For convenience's sake, I have presented Wagner's verse in the form of prose.]

10. Robert Jordan, "Theme and Character in *Major Barbara*," *Texas Studies in Literature and Language*, 12 (1970), 473.

11. Wisenthal, "The Underside of Undershaft," p. 59.

12. Ganz, "The Playwright as Perfect Wagnerite," pp. 199–200.

13. Wisenthal, p. 57.

14. Ganz, p. 200.

15. The phrase "metabiological pentateuch" is used in "A Postscript: After Twentyfive Years" (*The Bodley Head Bernard Shaw*, V, 690). Shaw's reference to *Back to Methusaleh* as his "*Ring*" appears in a letter of 1919 to Siegfried Trebitsch (Maurice Valency, *The Cart and the Trumpet* [New York: Oxford University Press, 1973], p. 349.)

16. J. L. Wisenthal, *The Marriage of Contraries* (Cambridge: Harvard University Press, 1974), p. 207.

17. Louis Crompton, *Shaw the Dramatist* (Lincoln: Univ. of Nebraska Press, 1969), p. 172.

18. William Blissett, "Bernard Shaw: Imperfect Wagnerite," *University of Toronto Quarterly*, 27 (1958), 196.

19. Wisenthal, *The Marriage of Contaries*, p. 249.

Robert Wexelblatt

EPICURUS AND ARISTOTLE—
AND SATAN AND JUAN

George Bernard Shaw subtitled *Man and Superman* "A Comedy and a Philosophy." The subtitle is a little redundant since all of Shaw's comedies are, by his own lights, philosophical. To Shaw, for a writer to be philosophical is a very good thing indeed. It is on the criterion of philosophical purpose—by which the determinedly didactic Shaw meant *moral* purpose—that he cantankerously assigns John Bunyan a higher literary rank than Shakespeare in the long "Epistle Dedicatory" to this play. However, the subtitle is still apropos. Formally, it describes the conjunction of *Man and Superman*'s Acts I, II, and IV (the comedy) with Act III's extended debate in Hell (the philosophy). Beyond serving as a concise table of contents, however, Shaw's subtitle reflects the fact that in Act III of this play he directly relates comedy and philosophy. Among quite a few other things, in the long dream-sequence Shaw sets forth his views on the philosophical implications of his chosen genre, the meaning conveyed by comedy itself. He could scarcely have done otherwise, given the subject he chose to explore and the generalized Mozartian types he selected to conduct the discussion.

In drama, if not in life, biology is destiny; for what underlies dramatic writing from the Greeks on up is one of the two universal biological experiences: sex for comedy, death for tragedy. In Act III of *Man and Superman,* Shaw wrote about what Aldous Huxley would later call, in similar terms but in a different tone, "the really revolutionary revolution"; that is, the methodical breeding of the human species. So the grand subject of *Man and Superman* is reproduction. Because of this Shaw had to touch on the foundations of comedy—what endings are "happy," and what sort of happiness constitutes an "ending." The conclusions of tragedies are unhappy because an order ends, a family dies; the endings of comedies are happy because these are saved and continued. Shaw understood this quite as well as Aristophanes. Classic comedy is not based on what he called "novelet-made love" sublimated into courtship and engagement. Thus, in the "Epistle Dedicatory" he complains, "... we have no modern English plays in which the natural attraction of the sexes for one another is made the mainspring of the action."

As the dedication goes on to make clear, Shaw's examination of sex in terms of evolutionary biology was prompted by political frustration. The public hysteria accompanying the outbreak of the Boer War had suddenly revealed to him the futility of an entire decade of reasonable Fabian lecturing to the British public. But Shaw was not disillusioned. Unwilling to surrender his political ideals in the face of a recalcitrant human nature, he simply chose, like a good modern Utopian, to suggest the necessary changes in human nature which would suit his ideals. Like Bunyan and unlike Shakespeare, he loved life at this moment less than its meaning. Besides, Shaw was very fond of the technological progress on which modern Utopianism is based; that is, the Procrustean fitting of life to theory. Henry Straker's role in the play is in part to make the point that engineering—mechanical now, genetic later—will certainly take charge of the future. But Shaw's technical, political, and historical concerns—even his having prophesied the birth control pill and nuclear weaponry—are, surprisingly, of less importance to us now than what he has to say about the most ancient and classical of philosophical questions: what constitutes a good life? It is Shaw's comedy and his philosophy rather than either his biology or his politics that are likely to last.

The influences of Henri Bergson and Friedrich Nietzsche on the philosophy of this particular comedy are easy and highly tempting to exaggerate. After all, the "Life-Force" of Shaw can immediately be identified with the former's *élan vital,* while Shaw's Superman seems an explicit translation into English of the latter's *Übermensch.* Moreover, Juan's opinion that evolution is "driving at brains" can be taken as Shaw's specification of Bergson's general concept of "Creative Evolution." Ana's overwhelming urge at the end of Act III to find and seduce a father for the Superbaby would seem to echo Nietzsche's insistent cry that the will is primary, Ana's representative Feminine Will being identified with that of "Life" itself. The echoes are indeed very numerous. Juan's clever attacks on morality and its pleasing illusions seem to be precisely those of Nietzsche (along with a bit of Ibsen) filtered through Shaw's splendid Irish wit; and even the Devil's negative vision of man, with his "heart in his weapons," might have been culled from the more sanguinary passages of *Beyond Good and Evil.* Shaw's views on the sexes are likewise in the Teutonic line of Goethe ("*das Ewig Weiblich*"), Schopenhauer, and Nietzsche. No doubt the catalogue could be protracted to the point where Shaw would appear to have acted only the part of an exceptionally gifted paraphraser and plagiarist.

But all these parallels and echoes notwithstanding, I would still like to suggest that they amount to a tally of superficialities; that, while Bergson and Nietzsche were clearly authors Shaw had been reading with profit around the turn of the century, the real foundations of the dialectic of Act III of *Man and Superman* are both different from and older than the terms laid down by Shaw's French and German-Polish contemporaries.

In proposing that Shaw's Satan be regarded as an Epicurean and Don Juan as an Aristotelean, I do not mean to argue for a different set of "sources." It is unnecessary to say that Shaw was *copying* anyone at all. What is more likely is that the argument itself, the classic argument about whether life has any purpose, of its own accord took Shaw back to the Greeks and especially to the fourth century B.C., when both Athens and philosophy were in decline and the question took on considerable importance.

The landscape of Shaw's after-life really is that of secular philosophy. Heaven and Hell are only "two ways of looking at things," as the Statue says. The philosophical model for Hell—the *locus classicus* of *that* way of looking—is the Garden of Epicurus. The enormous popularity of Epicureanism with the Ancients lay in its capacity to eliminate fear, in its defensiveness, and not its hedonism. So far as that goes, Epicurus was an ascetic who accounted prudence the highest of virtues and recommended a diet of fruit, bread, and water, eschewing all "unnatural and unnecessary desires." Shaw instinctively grasps the defensiveness of the Hellish, or Epicurean, temperament by turning a memorable joke on the fearsome Dantesque inscription over the Infernal portals, "Abandon hope, all ye who enter here." "Just think what a relief!" observes the Statue, fresh from the moral strenuousness of Heaven. The absence of hope is the absence of responsibility, and the absence of responsibility is the prerequisite of a defensive hedonism. Likewise, for Epicurus to rid man of the fear of the gods he had to prove that there is nothing to be hoped from them. Shaw's Hell, like Epicureanism, is less a pleasure-dome than a colossal defense-mechanism; it is not aimed at the enjoyment of pleasures, but at the avoidance of pains. "I have anticipated Thee, Fortune, and entrenched myself against all Thy secret attacks," wrote Epicurus in summary of his efforts.[1] The metaphor from defensive strategy could not be more revealing. Epicurus, having witnessed the crushing of the Athenian uprising against the Macedonians in 323 B.C., having observed the omnipresent fear of death and irrational anxiety about the supernatural which haunted his superstitious generation, devised an elaborate mental system founded on the unstated view that any threat to one's serenity is intolerable. The recommendation to avoid pain rather than to pursue pleasure is clearly defensive—a defense against hangovers, the gout, the Law. In Epicureanism, the Greeks found the theory behind the general pulling in of horns that accompanied the deaths of Alexander the Great and his tutor, Aristotle.

Each of Epicurus' philosophical doctrines can be understood as furthering the purpose of securing happiness (modestly defined as *ataraxia,* meaning "without pain in the body or disturbance in the mind") from one threat or another, yielding perhaps the grandest historical illustration of that process Freud called "rationalization." With Epicurus philosophy itself is redefined. No longer is it aimed at searching out wisdom, but only at consolation: "Vain is the word of a philosopher which does not heal any suffering of man."[2] To heal suffering was also to eliminate risk, and to do that it was essential for Epicurus to eradicate the notion that life is purposive or meaningful. Where there is a purpose to achieve, there is a duty to fulfill and thus a chance of failure or disappointment. Thus, Epicurus chose moderate or passive hedonism, Democritean materialism, and Protagorean moral relativism as the doctrines most suitable to his ends. In effect, Epicurean philosophy prescribes the best way of killing time. Shaw's Devil merely goes the Greek one better by arranging a pleasant way to kill eternity. The fact that Satan's Infernal Amusement Park offers positive pleasures, while Epicurus' Garden is a place to avoid pains, is accounted for by the reflection Juan at once makes to Ana, that those in Hell have no bodies to age, to contract diseases, or to suffer hangovers. Epicureans would have been Cyrenaic hedonists (eating, drinking, and being merry) but for the risky consequences of doing so. In Hell Satan has already achieved what he claims our brains would sooner or later make possible on earth; with the invention of contraceptives we could have all the pleasure with none of the consequences.

It is interesting to note that Shaw throws in a dash of Nietzsche to fortify the Satanic-Epicurean position. For it is in Satan's mouth, not Juan's, that he puts the concept of Eternal Recurrence, an idea of futility so upsetting to Nietzsche himself that he bragged only the *Übermensch* could stand to face it. In this regard, at least, Shaw's Superman cannot be identical to Nietzsche's *Übermensch;* for we are led to believe that he will resemble Juan, his prototype, and thus refuse to see all of life as a pointless and tediously repetitive circle. Moreover, Shaw's version of the next stage of human evolution will not be *less* rational than *homo sapiens,* like Nietzsche's resurgently Dionysian "blond brute" and "healthy bird of prey," but a man leading a life of purposive contemplation.

So the real model for the Shavian Superman, and by extension the inspiration for Shaw's Heaven, must be sought elsewhere than in Nietzsche. It is, I think, to be found in the great philosophic tradition against which Epicurus himself rebelled. Just as Satan went to school in Heaven and dropped out, so Epicurus is reported to have studied with both Platonists and Aristoteleans before breaking with both and setting up his Garden.[3] The sort of "philosophic man" Juan so eloquently extols in *Man and Superman* is obviously not an Epicurean, but a Socratic, a Platonist, and, pre-eminently, an Aristotelean.

One way of distinguishing the nature of the tradition of these last-named philosophers from that which followed in Epicurus is to look at where each sort of philosophy begins. Epicurus sets up first his idea of, or requisites for, happiness. Happiness must be above all secure, inviolable, inalienable. From this he proceeds to his rationalizations—a procedure very much in the line of Shaw's Satan. First the Devil "organized this place," then he invented its Constitution. The method of the Socratic tradition is just the opposite. One starts off with a thoroughgoing inquiry into the nature of reality (or, in the case of Socrates himself, an unending inquiry) and only afterwards attempts to formulate an idea of the good life, or of happiness, which must be constructed to accord with what has been learned of reality. This is what Juan fundamentally seeks to do; it is the meaning of the "redemption" which is, after all, the sole *action* of Act III. Hell bores him; pursuing pleasure and avoiding pain bore him; the absence of risk bores him; pleasant illusions bore him; manners and fun bore him; ladies and gentlemen bore him. But what *really* bores him is the underlying hellish idea that life has no purpose, that "killing eternity" by a total immersion in insubstantial entertainments is all there is to do. For if that were so, Shakespeare would indeed be superior to Bunyan (though for the wrong reasons), the Sophists to Socrates, Epicurus to Aristotle, and what hope would there be for George Bernard Shaw with *his* grand purpose of changing the world?

So "Hell" is where we escape to; it is "the way of seeing things" by which we defend ourselves against reality and against the risk of attempting to alter it. Hell is not only negative and defensive philosophy, of course, but also bad art, hollow fantasy, the abode not of authentic men and women but of ladies and gentlemen. Heaven, however, is where reality is "mastered." It is the natural habitat, certainly, of great artists like Rembrandt and Mozart, but most especially the eternal home of "the philosophic man." This is why Shaw spends so much time talking about talking, or rather has Satan complain to Juan about the enormous quantity he does of it. In placing the philosopher above all others Shaw has flown in the face of the popular view of philosophers as abstracted and absent-minded jaw-wavers, producers of *"mere* talk." The point he wishes to make is that talking, to be redeemed, must not only be *about* reality (Juan does so very effectively in Hell), but must actually *direct* reality. "Heaven'" is that place where the "clever men" become the "pilots." Hell is a state of contented drifting; Heaven is the condition of heroically driving. After all, Socrates died to prove that all his philosophizing was not mere talk, but rather directed the course of his life and dictated his death.

In the end, the best attack on Epicureanism was actually that of its contemporary rivals, the Stoics, which Shaw adopts—that it is a philosophy suited only to a shallow, dull, and dishonorable existence. Satan, for all that he sounds like a master-of-revels, is still the Prince of Darkness and Lies, tempting men away from their purpose through the corrosive spirit of defensiveness and the universal negation it produces.

The positive vision of the Life-Force described by Juan is Aristotelean. At the core of Aristotle's comprehensive philosophy of virtually everything is his idea of *entelechy*. This word, coined by the philosopher himself, means "the end or purpose within the self"; it is the potential within the acorn through which—given soil, light, and water—it can become an oak tree. Aristotle is a vitalist. No matter the subject, his point of view is invariably that of the Life-Sciences which he loved and at which he excelled. Whatever he looks at—from the development of a chicken embryo to the construction of a tragic drama—he finds in it the principle of purposive development of what is unique to the organism. While the atomized and mechanistic Nature of Epicurus is essentially dead, Nature to Aristotle is everywhere living, changing, growing, or decaying. As *entelechy* is the living form within matter, human virtue and happiness are to be found in achieving our unique form in our material lives; that is, in self-realization. For Aristotle, as for Juan, the best and happiest human life lies in the cultivation of reason and the assimilation of knowledge, for reason is unique to our species and constitutes our special excellence. For Aristotle reason and virtue are practical as well as intellectual. Juan says much the same thing and, just as Aristotle had done, contrasts the life of the philosopher pursuing wisdom to that of the soldier pursuing glory:

> I sing not arms and the hero but the philosophic man: He who seeks in contemplation to discover the inner will of the world, in invention to discover the means of fulfilling that will, and in action to do that will by the so-discovered means.

The "will of the world," alias the Life-Force, is essentially a cosmic expansion of the idea of *entelechy*. True, it also resembles Bergson's Creative Evolution in being purposive and Nietzsche's violent Will-to-

Power in its ability to overwhelm all the conditions men seek to impose upon it, all that Nietzsche dismissed as "Slave Morality." But in the end, Shaw's views of this Force or Will are closer to Aristotle's than to either of these for the reason that he finds in the Life-Force a basis for morality and not a denial of it; a foundation upon which reason can build its stately mansion, not that which demolishes reason; a desire for ever more awareness, not a brutalizing diminution of sensitivity. Shaw does not so much share the anti-rationalism of his contemporaries as he borrows it. Indeed, he borrows it in the process of building upon it.

What Shaw learned from his readings of Ibsen and Nietzsche was not only *that* the truth must be faced, but which truths. As Juan succinctly puts them: "Nature is a pimp. Time is a wrecker. Death is a murderer." The Hellish, Epicurean, or Victorian response to such blunt verities is to evade them, to cover them over, to seek to hedge them in by any means available. According to Satan, to do so is only to be "polite." But while Shaw impolitely insists on honesty, he is never quite *ruthlessly* honest. Unlike Nietzsche, he has no objection to *real* kindness or to genuine compassion. Shaw is, after all, a comedian talking about eugenics and not, despite his posturing in the "Epistle Dedicatory," a humorless Social Darwinist or fanatic would-be sterilizer of "inferiors." Indeed, the key difference between Shaw's Superman and Nietzsche's *Übermensch* may lie precisely with Shaw's sense of humor. The Superman, we suppose, will be capable of smiling, perhaps even, like Don Juan, of smiling at himself. The *Übermensch*, however, is the most humorless of all human conceptions. To acknowledge humor is to acknowledge limitations. Socrates is the most human of philosophers because he is the funniest. It is also on the point of human limitations, incidentally, that Shaw transcends and departs from his mouthpiece, Juan, albeit that he does so through the Devil. Indeed, at the end of the scene, after Don Juan has laid out his final solution of selective breeding and taken off for Heaven, there is an extraordinary moment when it looks very much as if Shaw has reversed the meaning of the whole dialogue and has given the Devil that last word after all. Satan says to the Statue:

> There is something unnatural about these fellows. Do not listen to their gospel, Señor Commander: it is dangerous. Beware the pursuit of the Superhuman: it leads to an indiscriminate contempt for the Human.

The dangerous twentieth century grows old apace. Were it not for this little speech, this human caution, Juan's final tendency toward fanaticism might have been ascribable to Shaw as well. He might have looked, in fact, rather like Nietzsche, with his perpetual complaints about the "human, all-too-human." In his prefaces, Epistles, Handbooks, and notoriously prolix stage directions, Shaw often seems anxious to redeem his comedy by philosophizing; but in *Man and Superman* it is the comedy which has redeemed the philosophy.

There is an irony about Shaw's pleas for the selective breeding of supermen and elimination of the "Yahoos" which comes from the nature of the plea itself. In having Juan argue against Satan in the way he does, Shaw invokes the highest tradition of Western secular philosophy, the tradition which runs from Socrates through Plato to Aristotle, one begetting the other. Its firm sense of life as purposeful, or teleological, is essentially what drew Shaw to it in answering not just Epicurus' irresponsibility but also the lingering Tennysonian despair over Evolution ("O life as futile, then, as frail!"). But Shaw's inveterate and frequently admirable desire to change the world led him, from time to time, into saying some silly things, occasionally things that would be dangerously silly were they to be taken up and acted upon. Some of these things are said in *Man and Superman* and its considerable surrounding apparatus—the "Epistle" and the "Handbook." This question of the dangerousness of Shaw's meliorism is a general one about his work and is related to what he is aiming to improve. In *Man and Superman* we have to do with more than the hypocrisy of Victorian sexual, economic, or political morality. The playwright here takes on a profounder theme and argues for nothing less than an upgrading of the biological nature of our species. Shaw was never a petty reformer. At the end of his life—or at least in his last Will and Testament—he gave his fortune to the task of replacing the English language. In each case, biologically and linguistically, what he had in mind was a more rational alternative. This is not at all illogical or even particularly quixotic for such a committed and long-lived reformer as Shaw was. Language and biology are indeed the two most intransigent of reactionaries, one being the repository of ancient cultural attitudes, the other the reserve bank of our genetic heritage. Even more than the irrational jingoism of the British at the time of the Boer War, language and biology were immovable objects at once challenging and frustrating the irresistible force of Shaw's moral audacity. Like the English public, however, they were impervious to persuasion. Shaw, therefore, sat himself down in the camp of those who, as Valéry once said, "wish to make reality more like their dreams and their dreams more like reality." But the dream here is rather like the one etched into our consciousness by Goya; it is the dream which fills the sleep of reason and that, at least occasionally, breeds monsters.

In the end, it is Shaw's devotion to reason that defines him as a thinker. This devotion may also account for him as a reader, a reader of works by men like Nietzsche, Ibsen, or Bergson. What he seized upon in them was the one handle of social criticism, and what he did not choose to pick up was the other handle of anti-rationalism and anti-humanism. Shaw's faith in reason, at its best, returned him to the finest tradition of rational, humanistic, and ethical discourse in Western culture; and, at its worst, it led him to anticipate some of the outrages already plotted or committed in the name of a New Order or a classless Utopia. His desire to go beyond Marx's idea of rearranging an economic substructure to recreating a biological and linguistic one as well—a pleasant revolutionary dream in 1903–seems a disturbing nightmare in 1980. Perhaps, then, the last word really is the Devil's.

Notes

1. *Fragments* (Vatican Collection), Letter to Menoeceus, 135. From *Epicurus: The Extant Remains*, trans. Cyril Bailey (Oxford: Clarendon Press, 1926).
2. *Fragments*, 54.
3. See Norman W. DeWitt, *Epicurus and His Philosophy* (Minneapolis: Univ. of Minnesota Press, 1954), 15.

Thomas F. Hale

BERNARD SHAW: THE EMERGENCE OF A REPUBLICAN ROYALIST

Among the many categories of dramatis personae which appear in Bernard Shaw's works, one of the most persistently recurring types is the monarchical hero or heroine. Even a casual perusal of Shaw's plays will yield a significant list of such dramatic characters and any Shaw enthusiast will readily recognize many of them: Cleopatra in *Caesar and Cleopatra*, the Dauphin (Charles VII) in *Saint Joan*, Catherine the Great in *Great Catherine*, Napoleon in *The Man of Destiny*, the Kaiser in *The Inca of Perusalem*, Annajanska, the Bolshevik Empress, in the play by the same name, King Magnus in *The Apple Cart*, Edward III in *The Six of Calais*, Charles II in "*In Good King Charles's Golden Days*," and William III in *Playlet on the British Party System*.[1] Yet despite this conspicuous procession of royalty through the pages of Shaw's writings, no one has as yet dealt with these monarchs in relation to Shaw's own views concerning socialism, monarchism and republicanism. Indeed, there is a good deal of confusion about Shaw's credentials as a republican or a royalist. For example, Joseph Percy Smith in *The Unrepentant Pilgrim* says that Shaw and the Fabians advocated the disestablishment of the House of Lords, but then points out that "whether Shaw would in fact have been in favour of going the rest of the way to republicanism is less clear."[2] Similarly, Alick West in *A Good Man Fallen among Fabians* asserts that Shaw did not believe in republicanism.[3]

Actually Shaw claimed to be a republican during most of his career even though his actions at times belied his words. Analysis of his republican opinions is therefore difficult and the problem is compounded by the fact that during some stages of his political development he was an ardent and outspoken republican while at other times his anti-monarchical sentiment became so latent as to seem almost negligible. He even came close to styling himself a royalist at one point. What obscures the matter even more is that Shaw's pronouncements on the subject could sometimes lead one to believe that he was simultaneously a republican and a royalist.

The origins of Shaw's republican and monarchical ideas might, in a broad Shavian sense, be hereditary. Though his family had no monetary legacy with which to endow him, Shaw nevertheless seems to have been the legatee of the Shaw family's republican heirlooms. This inheritance included the claim, wrongly asserted, that the Shaws were descendants of Oliver Cromwell, British regicide par excellence.[4] This family fiction of possessing the finest republican blood by pedigree was very likely augmented by Shaw's second cousin and uncle by marrige, the Reverend William George Carroll, "first minister of the Episcopal Church of Ireland to become a Home Ruler and a Republican, a conversion which required a great deal of moral courage in a man of his creed and cloth, and one, Mr. Shaw told his son, which cost him a bishopric to which he could reasonably expect to have been appointed." This clerical relation was "intimately associated" with Shaw's early years in Dublin and taught his cousin Bernard his first Latin, which, following the traditional pattern of such instruction, may have stressed the republican writers of ancient Rome.[5] Too much, however, can be made of this, as Shaw does not deal directly with the ideal of republican virtue in his pronouncements on the subject of republicanism. The linkage here is admittedly not direct; however, it is safe to assume that Shaw did indeed adopt and use ideas which he shared with his family as is revealed in the brief publication efforts of his older sister Lucy. Interestingly, Lucy, very much like her brother, described a plutocrat as "a Railway King, Coal Oil Emperor or Canned Meat Monarch."[6]

The republican inclination which Shaw inherited was no doubt abetted during his Dublin years and later by the freethinking atmosphere created by his family. After he left for London in 1876, Shaw was drawn quite naturally to meetings of the National Secular Society whose president, Charles Bradlaugh, had also been the charismatic leader of the brief, but important, republican movement of the 1870s. As Bradlaugh's biographer has pointed out, Shaw was among the many future notables at this time who "joined the regulars at Bradlaugh's feet."[7] Much impressed by Bradlaugh, who was one of Victorian England's finest orator-radicals, Shaw, in his later years would not only chair the 1913 Bradlaugh memorial dinner, but also choose Bradlaugh as the archetype for "the right sort of dictator" who could give England the leadership she needed.[8] This association with Bradlaugh's National Secular Society led in turn to a relationship with Annie Besant which continued Shaw's exposure to secularists as well as republicans, for as Mrs. Besant has stated (perhaps unknowingly echoing the all too prophetic sentiment of James I, "No bishops, no king!") republicanism was just as much a part of secularism as was atheism.[9] Indeed Mrs. Besant's own "Republican Song," set to the tune of the French national anthem and eventually known as the "English Marseillaise," was printed in *The Secular Song and Hymn Book* and was a standard part of the repertoire of Secularist Halls for a long time.[10] Since Mrs. Besant would sometimes render a solo of her musical creation,[11] it is entirely possible that Shaw himself sang this republican hymn and may actually have joined Mrs. Besant in a parlor duet.

Shaw eventually may have disassociated himself from the secularists for reasons he disassociated himself from radical republicans; that is, the espousal of "heterodoxies" which distracted converts from overriding issues of general importance. In this instance, the Bradlaugh-Besant campaign for birth control, setting off as it did an internecine fight among secularists, may have disenchanted the young pre-Fabian Shaw. Be that as it may, Shaw's association with the secularist-republicans would reinforce his republican egalitarianism.

Another source of republican sentiment which is easier to identify would be Shelleyolatry, a phase of Shaw's intellectual and political development which can be traced back to about 1876, the period of Shaw's late teens and early twenties—the time he left Dublin and settled in London with his mother and sisters. As Shaw later stated in a letter to Molly Tompkins, it was then, when he was nearly twenty, that he came under the influence of the arch-republican poet Shelley.[12] Shaw's infatuation with Shelley was so deep that Hesketh Pearson has written that Shaw was going through a phase of "Shelley worship."[13] That Shelley himself was a most ardent republican is attested to by his poem *Queen Mab* and Shelley's famous plea, "Oh, that the free would stamp the impious name of king into the dust."[14] A young, impressionable person, as Shaw was at that time, could have hardly been a Shelley enthusiast without becoming imbued with the republican ardor of his mentor. As Shaw later stated in his preface to *Immaturity*,

> I had read much poetry; but only one poet was sacred to me: Shelley. I had read his works from end to end, and was in my negations atheist and republican to the backbone. I say in my negations; for I had not reached any affirmative position.[15]

Though Shaw's enthusiasm for Shelley the poet did not wane during the 1880s, Shaw was not a "republican to the backbone" throughout this decade. At a meeting of the Shelley Society held in 1886 and in an

1892 article in the *Albemarle,* Shaw continued to express his admiration for *Queen Mab,* and also said in general terms that he supported Shelley's heterodoxies. But when Shaw compared himself to Shelley he made significant omissions, as in such remarks as "Like Shelley, I am a Socialist, an Atheist and a Vegetarian."[16] By not specifically labelling himself a republican, Shaw suggested his possible departure from the complete Shelleyan creed. It seems, at least, that Shaw now discounted the exigency of the republican cause.

What had happened in the period between the late 1870s and the mid 1880s is that Shaw's "negative" position on republicanism had been replaced by what Shaw thought of as the affirmative outlook of socialism. In 1883 Shaw became one of the few persons who had, up to then, digested *Das Kapital,* and "From that hour," he says, "I became a man with some business in the world."[17] His conversion to socialism convinced him that the old measures of Liberal-Republicanism were insufficient to meet the needs of society for reform. Shaw's fifth novel, *An Unsocial Socialist* (1883), reveals that his frame of mind in regard to the monarchy had indeed changed. The influence of Marx in this novel explains why Shaw no longer subscribed to the urgent necessity for republicanism. To Marx, and now to Shaw, the enemy of the people was not the queen of England but rather King Capital.

Shaw's self-proclaimed Damascus Road conversion to socialism via Marx inspired the writing of *An Unsocial Socialist.* It is not therefore surprising that the neophyte adopted the Marxist view that there was no pressing need for the establishment of a republican form of government as long as capitalism persisted in its inevitable exploitation and oppression. Indeed, Sidney Trefusis, the novel's main character, is "Marx in Shaw's clothing," and as such has no enthusiasm for the toppling of thrones.[18] In the closing chapters of *An Unsocial Socialist,* Chichester Erskine represents the old style Liberal-Republican-Radical and acts as a foil for the Marxian Trefusis' critique of the insufficiency of the old politics. Erskine fully expects concurrence from Trefusis when he asks, "Is it not absurd to hear a nation boasting of its freedom and tolerating a king? . . . I admire a man that kills a king. You will agree with me there, Trefusis, won't you?" But to Erskine's surprise and chagrin, Trefusis replies, "A king nowadays is only a dummy put up to draw fire off the real oppressors of society . . . no more accountable for the manifold evils and abominations that exist in his realm than the Lord Mayor is accountable for the thefts of the pickpockets who follow his show on the ninth of November."[19]

In a further amplification of Shaw's views on the issue of republicanism, which is contained in the appendix to *An Unsocial Socialist,* Trefusis says,

> What king's son would not exchange [places] with me—the son of the Great Employer—the Merchant Prince?... Industrial kingship, the only real kingship of our century, was his by divine right of his turn for business; and I, his son, bid you respect the crown whose revenues I inherit.[20]

As Trefusis had pointed out to Erskine earlier, the history of the United States provided ample evidence of the inconsequential benefits derived from mere republicanism when un-coupled with socialism. To Trefusis, who is here Shaw's mouthpiece, the American republic was the "... home of liberty, theatre of manhood suffrage, kingless and lordless land of Protection, Republicanism, and the realized Radical Programme, where all the black chattel slaves were turned into wage slaves (like my father's white fellows) at a cost of 800,000 lives and wealth incalculable."[21]

Even though Shaw now viewed republicanism as a red herring which distracted the truly thoughtful socialist, he still evidenced no reverence for royalty in general. In discussing the physical appearance of various groups of persons in his photograph collection, Trefusis refers to the socialists and Communards as "tolerably intelligent and thoughtful looking," whereas "these other poor devils, worried, stiff, strumous, awkward, vapid, and rather coarse, with here and there a passably pretty woman, are European kings, queens, grand-dukes and the like."[22] Trefusis is not just critical of royal physiognomies, for he also deprecates the minds behind the faces; "The son of a millionaire, like the son of a king, is seldom free from mental disease."[23]

Despite these faults and foibles which Trefusis detects in royal personages, a certain amount of compassion reveals itself when monarchs are considered on the plane of shared human experience. Curiously, Trefusis makes a plea for the consideration of the plight of kings:

> What private man in England is worse off than the constitutional monarch? We deny him all privacy; he may not marry whom he chooses, consort with whom he prefers, dress according to his tastes, or live where he pleases. I don't believe he may even eat and drink what he likes best; a taste for tripe and onions on his part would provoke a remonstrance from the Privy Council.... He must smile and bow and maintain an expression of gracious enjoyment whilst the mayor and corporation inflict upon him the twaddling address he has heard a thousand times before. I do not ask you to be loyal, Erskine; but I expect you, in common humanity, to sympathize with the chief figure in the pageant.... [24]

Despite these kind words for monarchs who had to endure the drudgery of their office, Shaw, as represented by Trefusis, should not be mistaken for a turncoat republican. Shaw now placed a low priority on republicanism, but he had not embraced royalism. Shaw's republicanism had merely become Fabianized.

Shaw's infatuation with Karl Marx *in toto* was short-lived. Within a year after he had written *An Unsocial Socialist,* he had become, as Lenin chose to describe him, "a good man fallen among Fabians." In the summer of 1884 Shaw was elected to membership in the Fabian Society and was soon writing his first, and the society's second, Fabian Tract. In this short pamphlet, entitled *A Manifesto,* Shaw indulged in what the historian A. M. McBriar calls the "polite republicanism" which was characteristic of the Fabian Society during its early years.[25] Shaw's reference to republicanism in this work is contained in the stipulation, "That no individual should enjoy any Privilege in consideration of services rendered to the state by his or her parents or other relations."[26] Other examples of ambiguous Shavian anti-royalism are contained in Tract 3, *To Provident Landlords and Capitalists* (1885), wherein Shaw states that "the establishment of Socialism in England means nothing less than the compulsion of all members of the upper class, without regard to sex or condition, to work for their own living,"[27] and also in Tract 40, *Fabian Election Manifesto, 1892,* in which Shaw rather indelicately refers to the privileges of the lords and crown as "detestable."[28]

Despite Shaw's generally polite references to royalty, not all Fabians observed a sense of decorum when discussing the monarchy. Indeed, it was partly on account of the fact that Queen Victoria was referred to as "a vulgar old German lady" during a meeting of the society that the Fabians were denied use of the Dr. Williams Library for their future meetings.[29] Most members of the society were, however, willing to follow the pragmatic lead of Shaw and the Webbs, and during the 1890s Fabian interest in republicanism waned even further.[30]

An obvious illustration of the general Fabian acceptance of the monarchy and their willingness to work within the framework of constitutional monarchy would be "The Queen's Speech" which Shaw drafted for the mock government meetings of the Fabian-sponsored "Charing Cross Parliament" in the summer of 1887. Despite the celebrations then occurring for Queen Victoria's Jubilee, which might have been expected to be repellent to Socialists, Shaw throughout the speech he wrote for the occasion seems to have been comfortable with the incongruity of a self-proclaimed republican socialist putting words in the mouth of a reactionary queen. In the context of our interests here, the subtance of the speech, dealing as it did with measures of Fabian reform, is not germane. Except for a reference to "a revision of the Civil List" (the budget for the royal family), there is no hint of republican or egalitarian thinking and it should be remembered that even stalwart monarchists like Gladstone thought of the Victorian Civil List as a fiscal item in need of retrenchment. The Shavian "Queen's Speech" is approached as if it were to be delivered by a Platonic Philosopher Queen rather than a republican socialist.[31]

The growing accommodation between Fabian socialism and the monarchy was apparent not just in Shaw's shift of opinion, but also in the decisions of the society itself. During the preparations for the celebration of the wedding of the future George V and Queen Mary in 1893, the Fabian Executive, of which Shaw was a member, won approval from the membership for its decision to rent its office window space to the highest bidder who cared to view the royal procession as it passed below.[32] Interestingly, Shaw may have shortly thereafter wished, for personal journalistic reasons, that his fellow Fabians had not rented their window space, as he was assigned to cover the royal wedding procession for *The Star*.[33] The unsigned account of the procession which Shaw prepared for the press no doubt forced him to give some thought to the whole issue of monarchism and republicanism, and therefore his rather long article is significant. Right from the lead paragraph, it is clear that Shaw accepted his job without republican objections and that he may have taken some delight in this bit of reportage. Though Shaw is good-natured throughout, he is nonetheless critical. His commentary on the decorations and illuminations is based not on the expression of loyalty which each represented, but rather on an aesthetic concern for good taste. Displays are described as ranging from the gorgeous to the garish, while certain aspects of the festivities are rated as brilliant and affording a "kaleidoscope of splendours." Perhaps as a means of creating newsprint filler or to occupy slack time waiting for the parade to begin, Shaw concocted a number of scenarios to enliven his task. He reports that "his dream of being the first loyalist in Fleet Street to throw his cap for the royal couple was shattered by a number of thoughtless wassailers who stayed up all night." Later in the day, "*The Star* man," as Shaw referred to himself, was driven by the July heat to contemplate a faked anarchist attack on the royal carriages so that the police would rescue him from the stifling embrace of the dense crowds in which there was hardly room even to faint. In a more serious vein, *The Star* man felt that Queen Victoria, as she passed by and was greeted with considerable applause, was positively "radiant" though she had not always looked so cheerful before. His sentiments were reportedly supported by a clerical dignitary on the grandstand nearby (perhaps a literary invention) who was overheard to say that "the cheering will begin in earnest when she gets out into the streets, into the hearts of her people." The indulged temptation to make such editorial remarks, even indirectly, demonstrates the influence of Shaw's quiescent republican sentiments or at least his inability to ignore the political and social significance of even ceremonial occasions. Yet, by and large, Shaw managed to give his readers the newscopy they wanted, as most of the article centered on traditional matters of concern, even down to the details of who-wore-what and what-colors-were-chosen. Like Trefusis in *An Unsocial Socialist,* Shaw did genuinely sympathize with the royal actors in the pageant, whose share of drudgery that day was far greater than his own. He thus predicted that after such a "microscopic inspection" their royal Highnesses would be glad to leave their "effusive worshippers" behind. Indeed, Shaw's willingness to see the lighter side and engage in a bit of merriment basically reflected and anticipated the attitude of the Fabians in general. A few years after this, for example, Hubert Bland, one of the founding fathers of Fabianism, asserted, "a monarchy will be no obstacle for the next three centuries. Therefore on certain fitting occasions, and in festive moods, we are quite willing to sing 'God Save the Queen.' "[34] Interestingly, Shaw in his later years went so far as to supply new words for the second stanza of the national anthem at the behest of Sir Edward Elgar,[35] the very creator of "Pomp and Circumstance" itself.

The accommodation between socialism and the monarchism which Shaw's report for *The Star* illustrates, could, however, be pushed too far to suit the tastes of the Fabian membership. During the Diamond Jubilee celebrations in 1897, the premises were again rented to persons wanting to view the royal procession, but only after a heated debate and the resignation of three members.[36] It was a further embarrassment to the Executive that the £35 rental fee was later reneged on and the Fabians' solicitors took legal action to uphold the contract between the Fabian Society and the royalist spectators.[37] When, however, it was also proposed in 1897 that funds be contributed for a subscription to illuminate the Strand for the festivities which were a part of the Diamond Jubilee festivities, the rank and file rose in revolt against the Executive Committee which had agreed by a vote of eight to two to subscribe one guinea.[38] Shaw and Sidney Webb summoned up their powers of persuasion, but to no avail; the majority had its way in one of the few instances when the Executive failed to carry its point of view.[39] What is clear from this is that Shaw was ambivalent in his attitude to the royal family after his conversion to socialism; in other words, Shaw the pragmatist and hedger was in the ascendant on this issue. In any case, the Executive learned its lesson, as the rental of window space and related issues did not arise at the future meetings of the Fabian Society.

No doubt as a response to the republican sentiments of the rank and file, the Executive Committee prepared a draft scheme of lectures for the autumn of the Jubilee year which listed such topics as "The Relations of Republicanism and Socialism" and "The Republican Movement in Great Britain," and gave as possible speakers for the republican position H. G. Salt and G. Standring, and Hubert Bland for the opposing point of view.[40] The Executive also had to contend with draft propositions "that the health of the Queen be not drunk" at the annual dinner and "that morning dress be permissible." Perhaps as a further sop to the younger Fabians who had risen in revolt, the notorious republican Radical, Sir Charles Dilke, was invited late in the Jubilee year to give a public lecture on the "British Empire" which included the topic of the "Possibility of a Combination of Indian Autocracy and Colonial Democracy, with British Constitutional Monarchy, in Any National Union."[41] (Dilke is also memorable for his notions of imperial federation which may have had some influence on Shaw's similar proposals in his 1917 Republican Manifesto.) It was, however, R. Wherry Anderson who ultimately addressed the issue directly on the topic, "Socialism and Monarchy," on November 26, 1897.[42]

In what might appear to be true Pickwickian fashion, Shaw continued to style himself a republican during the decades preceding the First World War. But as we have seen, Shaw's republican sails were trimmed too severely for the royal family to worry on his account. During the Shelley centennial celebrations in 1892, Shaw claimed that he agreed "unreservedly" with all of Shelley's opinions, but surely Shaw was aware that he was overstating his position.[43] Trefusis's remarks about republicanism in *An Unsocial Socialist* clearly indicated that Shaw had reservations about Shelley's brand of anti-royalist beliefs. In 1902 while Britain's struggle with the South African Boers was still in progress, Shaw made another of his bald assertions of adherence to republicanism in a then-unpublished draft article on the Boer War:

> I can quite understand the Englishman who says that he hopes that Boers may win.... There is so much to be said for that view that I myself should not regard our defeat as an unmixed evil even for us, much less the world. I am even biased against loyal England because I am a republican by conviction and by birth an Irishman....[44]

What Shaw could have meant by his claim to be "a republican by conviction" is difficult to fathom, for he did not elaborate on his position. Obviously his willingness to temporize and equivocate about this issue demonstrates that Shaw's supposed conviction was actually a notion of republicanism so abstract that it was in practical terms quiescent. One wonders at times if Shaw was just using republican credentials as a strategy to get the attention of his audience. Nevertheless Shaw applied this same type of description to himself in his 1906 preface to *John Bull's Other Island*. In language which was very similar to his pronouncement about the Boer War, he said, "I am violently and arrogantly

Protestant by family tradition; but let no English Government therefore count on my allegiance: I am English enough to be an inveterate Republican and Home Ruler."[45] How a person can reconcile "inveterate" republicanism with the desire to lend financial support to the celebration of Queen Victoria's Jubilee presents a problem in verbal gymnastics which even fanciers of Shavian paradox would have difficulty in resolving. Suffice it to say that it was not unusual for Shaw to place his own very special construction on words.

In any case, Shaw himself made light of what little republican sentiment he did possess at this time. When he was informed of the upcoming attendance of Edward VII at the staging of *John Bull's Other Island* in 1905, Shaw's humorous response was, "Short of organizing a revolution I have no remedy."[46] But perhaps this is a clue to what Shaw meant by calling himself a confirmed republican when his actions belied his words. He presumably decided not to concern himself with the issue of the monarchy until all the other Herculean tasks of the socialist had been performed after the revolution. Until then Shaw apparently refused to be bothered by the inconsistency involved in his republican declaration of faith and his seemingly royalist activities. His republicanism was not abandoned—it had merely ceased to be a matter of ideology: "I prefer Democracy to Autocracy, again, not on principle, but because on looking about me I find that it is a good deal better to be a Swiss than a Russian, and I attribute the superiority of life in Switzerland to her democratic institutions."[47] Shaw still agreed with Shelley about republicanism, but he was no longer a Shelleyolator, and in Shaw's mind this was the preferred attitude as Shelley, like Karl Marx, "deserved something worthier from his pupil than idolatry."[48]

Despite these less firm protestations of loyalty to the republican cause, Shaw did not entirely cease to criticize the activities of the royal family on an *ad hoc* basis. Shaw never railed against the monarchy as Shelley had done, but from time to time he would register his objections to things which he found amiss.

One cause for personal complaint against the British monarchy had to do with the control which the royal family exercised over the staging of his plays; that is, the right of the king's appointee, the Lord Chamberlain, to prohibit the performance of dramatic productions. Ever since *Mrs Warren's Profession* (1893) had been banned by the royal censor, it had been a sore point with Shaw that the Lord Chamberlain was accountable solely to the sovereign and not to public opinion or even the Cabinet. When a parliamentary committee was finally set up in 1909 to enquire into the feasibility of censoring the censors, Shaw was even more piqued by the thought that the committee's investigation would probably come to naught because of "the fear of displeasing the king by any proposal to abolish the censorship of the Lord Chamberlain.... All the lords on the Committee and some of the commoners could have been wiped out of society (in their sense of the word) by the slightest intimation that the king would prefer not to meet them...."[49] This was no exaggeration on Shaw's part. Just one year prior to this, Keir Hardie and Arthur Ponsonby suffered such a fate in a blatantly public maneuver by Edward VII to intimidate M.P.s who protested against one of the king's meetings with the autocratic czar of all the Russias.[50] Shaw was also irritated by the absurd attempts of the king's appointee to protect supposedly hallowed institutions like the monarchy. In pointing this up, Shaw claimed that the Lord Chamberlain

> would refuse to license Hamlet if it were submitted to him as a new play.... He would disallow the incestuous relationship between the King and Queen. He would probably insist on the substitution of some ficticious country for Denmark in deference to the near relations of our reigning house with that realm.[51]

To an iconoclast, such a state of affairs was intolerable, and it is not surprising that Shaw pleaded for the abolition of royal censorship, which continued nevertheless to be one of the last vestiges of the king's once great prerogative until 1968, long after Shaw died. In fairness to the royal family, Shaw was, however, willing to admit that the damage done to his reputation by royal proclamations that his plays were unfit for public performance, was to some extent counterbalanced by the fact that "the British Court, in the course of its private playgoing, paid no regard to the bad character given me by the chief officer of its household."[52] Actually, Prime Minister Arthur Balfour was so impressed with *John Bull's Other Island* that he persuaded his eminent friends to see it, which was at least partly responsible for a special performance for King Edward VII, who supposedly laughed so hard he broke his chair.[53] Perhaps Shaw's irritation at the Lord Chamberlain was strictly a matter of principle rather than personal pique. The irony of the censorship quagmire may have even appealed to Shaw's sense of humor. As he pointed out in a letter to W. B. Yeats, the Lord Lieutenant of Ireland had greater powers of censorship than the Lord Chamberlain for the simple reason that the Lord Lieutenant's powers were conferred by an 1843 Act of Parliament and consequently, if the king himself wrote a play, the Lord Lieutenant could ban it and probably would if the play were serious or if the king signed Shaw's name rather than his own. Exaggerating to Yeats a bit more, Shaw claimed that by implication Edward VII himself liked *The Shewing-Up of Blanco Posnet* because the king had knighted Sir Herbert Beerbohm Tree after Sir Herbert had spoken up in defense of Shaw's play—a clear indication of a difference of opinion between the king and his censors.[54]

Censorship by the king's household was not the only object of Shaw's criticism of the monarchy. His socialist conscience, and perhaps his latent republican instinct, were pricked by the manner in which court life was conducted and by the way in which royal ceremonies were carried out. The luxuries and extravagances of the upper classes and members of the court were, he objected, unconscionable in that

> armies of clever servants, court dressmakers, jewellers, gamekeepers, and the like are organized for the amusement of persons who were already satiated with amusement, and for the care and nurture of their pets, dogs, cats, and birds, whilst the bitterest needs of thousands of hard workers are left unsatisfied.[55]

As for court life itself, Shaw felt that it was "contemptible" because it was shrouded in the sort of sham which emphasized "every foolish unreality and insincerity."[56]

The critic in Shaw could also be brought out by certain features of monarchical rituals which did not suit his taste. As was discussed earlier, Shaw favored a Fabian contribution to the illumination of the Strand for Victoria's Jubilee in 1897, yet he did not approve of all aspects of the celebration which took place. The "silly" gushings of the press and "the noisiest of her subjects" were to Shaw but "impertinent and senseless Jubilee odes such as their perpetrators dare not, for fear of domestic scorn and ridicule, address to their own wives and mothers."[57] Four years later the funeral arrangements for Queen Victoria elicited a restrained sense of outrage over what Shaw described as "the suspension of commonsense." To Shaw, with his belief in cremation, the exhibition of the queen's corpse in a sealed lead coffin for a whole fortnight was an "insanitary and superstitious" spectacle of "intolerable ignorance" which was "socially deplorable." His unsolicited advice for the occasion was that if the royal family would "bring its customs into some sort of decent harmony with modern civilization, they would make loyalty much easier for twentieth-century Englishmen."[58]

It appears that such irrational spectacles and exhibitions by royalty could at times almost get the best of Shaw in his calculated attempt to forget republicanism in order to concentrate on the spread of socialism. This comes out in an unpublished draft of an article written in 1902 in which he defended his reluctant support for British imperialism during the Boer War by citing examples of past imperialisms which were beneficial to civilization in terms of their consequences. "Napoleon," Shaw wrote, "had no 'right' to propose to invade England; but when our feudal relics become more than usually exasperating, we are occasionally sorry that he did not."[59] Thus Shaw was not completely blind to the social and economic consequences of retaining the monarchy. His remark about "feudal relics" would even seem to indicate that he still had a trace of the old Shelleyan republican in him. Shaw's hackles could also be raised by foreign despots who were treated with sycophancy. For example, in a 1908 letter to Herbert Gladstone, the Liberal Home Secretary, Shaw complained of the prosecution of a man for blasphemous libel and the handling of the recent Denshawi episode, and went on to ask why tribute had been paid to the late king of Portugal without any attempt to distinguish between an appropriate condemnation of political assassination and the attempt, by a constitutional monarch, to become a despot by systematic destruction of popular liberties and democratic institutions. A Unionist cabinet, he observed wryly, could not have done so without outraging Liberals.

Another opportunity for an expression of Shaw's distaste for irrational royal spectacles and gushings about royalty occurred during the obsequies for Edward VII in 1910. Writing for *The New Age*, Shaw reiterated some of the points he made concerning Queen Victoria's death. His article, "The General Mourning," declared at the outset the biases which shaped Shaw's commentary, for he, as an Irishman, had no particular concern for English kings and being devoid of idolatry had "not the very faintest respect for royalty as such" except that he was concerned for them as his fellow creatures and was therefore troubled with "all sorts of kindlinesses and delicacies."[60] Claiming that his thoughts represented "a large body of public opinion" Shaw nevertheless pointed out that he, unlike most royal subjects, was an "inveterate republican" whose only chance meeting with Kind Edward four years before had provoked "some remorse in the presence of a man whom I thought it desirable, on general grounds, to behead. . . ."[61] Speaking for himself and others, Shaw claimed no objection to the wallowing in the pageantries, but did most strenuously object to the distortion of all reality about the late monarch:

> The articles which have filled the papers about him since his death are clearly worthless: first, because they represent, not a man, but a paragon impossibly combining the wisdom of a deity, the kindliness of a saviour, the statecraft of a Charlemagne, and the infallibility of a Pope in one person; and second, because I know, as everyone knows, that they would have been word for word the same if he had been George IV, or James I, or Henry VIII, or Richard III, or John Lackland, or Timour the Tartar. The English people get huge enjoyment out of a death (as Oscar Wilde said, they have a vocation for funerals), partly

because the taste for death is a thoroughly vulgar one, and partly because it sets them free to indulge without stint in the amusement they love most in the world, which is writing and saying nice, good-natured, grateful, enthusiastic things that everybody knows to be utter nonsense, or virtuously indignant things that everybody knows to be hypocritical.[62]

Shaw found idolatry which caused such outpourings of nonsense to be harmful because it distracted the reading public from such "vulgar items of mere news" as the recent deaths of 130 men in a burning mine.[63] The unseemly quality of this adulation of royalty was all the more inappropriate and ironic in Shaw's view since Edward's popularity was based on his ordinariness, that he was in no apparent way exceptional, and accordingly, it was easy for Tom, Dick, and Harry to identify with him as a jovial, cigar-smoking figure who might have been "an admirable sporting publican." Shaw took particular issue with the poetic requiem written for *The Times* by Rudyard Kipling as the worst example of a distorted portrayal of a do-nothing king, even though it was "not true, not a word of it," for if Kipling's gushings were accurate, then Edward would have been responsible for such things as the Denshawi atrocity, and as a consequence the English would have to fight the civil war battle of Naseby all over again, pack the king off, and offer the crown "under crushing limitations" to Theodore Roosevelt. In Shaw's opinion, Kipling could have just as accurately given King Edward the credit for the appearance of Halley's comet that year as attribute other forms of drivelling accomplishments to him. Kipling, who Shaw pointed out was the author of "Lest We Forget," should not have fallen into such absurd error because even "Kaiser William, for all his mailed fist and his ancestors' statues, is no longer allowed to utter a word to his loyal subjects: he must publicly take the written words from the hands of his minister and repeat them obediently."[64] On a more personal level, Shaw, again pressing his interest in cremation, objected to the Lying-in-State as a "morbid and superstitious rite" that had properly been abandoned at the death of George III in 1820. Also, Shaw agreed with Robert Blatchford, the editor of *The Clarion,* that the cost of such ceremonies should not be indulged in until England had clothed and fed all its children. Although Shaw laced his remarks with his characteristic humor, his readers were not all amused. Mr. C. Hughes Davies wrote in a letter to the editor that the vulgarity of the English taste for death was not vulgar and no more abnormal than a taste for life.[65] An approving reader, using phraseology suspiciously similar to Shaw's went to the trouble of compiling two columns of sentiments similar to Shaw's by writers such as Shakespeare, Pope, Dryden, Swift, Byron, Cowper, and Thackeray. Quoting William Cobbett's *Reign of George IV,* the correspondent, styling himself "Plain

Speaking," offered these lines to support Shaw: "We are, however, permitted to write, and speak, to our heart's content, in praise of kings, dead or alive, without any liability to punishment; we may in praise of them not only say the whole truth, but may add as many, and as monstrous, lies as we please."[66] Presumably Shaw found it reassuring to find that his critique of royalty placed him in such illustrious company.

In spite of the fact that Shaw could at times be critical of the institution of the monarchy and the general activities of the court, he nevertheless drew short of personal criticism of royal personages. The reasons for this were probably grounded in the advice which Shaw gave to his fellow socialists in an 1895 article entitled, "Illusions of Socialism." He warned his comrades against indulging in the illusion that their opponents were villains and fiends, and admonished them to develop "more and more of that quality which was the primal republican material—that sense of the sacredness of life which made a man respect his fellows without regard to his social rank or intellectual class. . . ."[67]

For royal persons as individuals, Shaw had a certain amount of compassion prompted by what he thought of as the inane duties which were inflicted upon them. No doubt at some time or another, Shaw, like most people, had projected himself into the shoes of royalty and had discovered that he would not have enjoyed a role analagous to that of the fainéant long-haired kings of Merovingian France who had little control over their lives and were exhibited like puppets for the sake of inspiring loyalty. To Shaw, the desire to become a monarch was "on the face of it a fool's notion. It is at bottom the folly of the ignorant simpletons who long to be kings and chiefs because they imagine that a king or chief is an idle voluptuary with lots of money, leisure, and power over others, to use irresponsibly for his own amusement."[68] In a passage from *Great Catherine*, which is reminiscent of Good Queen Bess's plaint that "The Crown is more a joy to them that see it than to them that wear it," Shaw puts into the mouth of Catherine the Great the words:

> . . . what maddens me about all this ceremony is that I am the only person in Russia who gets no fun out of my being Empress. You all glory in me: you bask in my smiles: you get titles and honors and favors from me: you are dazzled by my crown and my robes. . . . But what do I get out of it? Nothing. Nothing!! I wear a crown until my head aches: I stand looking majestic until I am ready to drop: I have to smile at ugly and old ambassadors and frown and turn my back on young and handsome ones. Nobody gives me anything.[69]

Shaw was not implying that monarchs should be given special consideration, however. His empathy for kings was no different from his sympathy for anyone who had to contend with distasteful taskwork, of which Shaw himself had had a bellyful when he was a young clerk.

It was a point of principle with Shaw that all men, and especially all socialists, should conduct themselves toward royalty in a manner which was no different from that accorded to fellow creatures of whatever status. As he said in 1897 during the anniversary celebration of Queen Victoria's accession to the throne, "I am myself cut off by my profession from Jubilees; for loyalty in a critic is corruption. But if I am to avoid idolizing kings and queens in the ordinary human way, I must carefully realize them as fellow-creatures."[70] This is just what Shaw attempted to do in his plays.

Notes

1. William III appears in the playlet from Chapter III of *Everybody's Political What's What?*

2. Joseph Percy Smith, *The Unrepentant Pilgrim: A Study of the Development of Bernard Shaw* (Boston: Houghton Mifflin Co., 1965), p. 118.

3. Alick West, *A Good Man Fallen among Fabians* (London: Lawrence & Wishart, 1950), p. 156.

4. St. John Ervine, *Bernard Shaw: His Life, Work and Friends* (New York: William Morrow & Co., 1956), p. 7.

5. Ibid.

6. Ibid., pp. 119–200. Also, B. C. Rosset, *Shaw of Dublin: The Formative Years* (University Park: Pennsylvania State University Press, 1964), p. 308.

7. David Tribe, *President Charles Bradlaugh, M.P.* (London: Elek Books, 1971), p. 114. See also, G. B. Shaw, *An Unfinished Novel,* edited with an introduction by Stanley Weintraub (New York: Dodd, Mead, 1958), pp. 11–12. Shaw also met about this time Sir Charles Dilke, the other major figure in the republican agitation of the 1870s. See Hesketh Pearson, *George Bernard Shaw: His Life and Personality* (New York: Atheneum, 1963), p. 112.

8. Bernard Shaw to Charlotte Payne Townshend Shaw, typescript letter, October 13, 1913, British Museum ADD. MSS. 465018. Allen Chappelow, *Shaw—"The Chucker-Out": A Biographical Exposition and Critique* (London: George Allen & Unwin, 1969), p. 175.

9. Annie Besant (ed.), *The Secular Song and Hymn Book* (London: C. Watts, n.d.), p. iii.

10. Ibid., pp. 82–84.

11. Arthur H. Nethercot, *The First Five Lives of Annie Besant* (London: Rupert Hart-Davis, 1961), p. 97.

12. Roland A. Duerksen, "Shelley and Shaw," *PMLA,* LXXVIII (March, 1963), p. 114. Shaw claimed, however, that he had already read Shelley from beginning to end while in his late teens, i.e., his Dublin years. See Bernard Shaw, *Sixteen Self-Sketches* (London, Constable, 1949), pp. 69–70. Shaw, in a letter to Ivor Brown of September 7, 1949, also said that, "Before I was twenty, I was a Shelleyolator." See British Museum, ADD. MSS. 50526, Pt. 2, f. 461.

13. Hesketh Pearson, *George Bernard Shaw*, p. 47.
14. Kingsley Martin, *The Crown and the Establishment* (London: Hutchinson, 1962), p. 30.
15. Duerksen, "Shelley and Shaw," p. 115.
16. Archibald Henderson, *George Bernard Shaw: Man of the Century* (New York: Appleton-Century-Crofts, 1956), p. 151. Dan H. Laurence (ed.), *Selected Non-Dramatic Writings of Bernard Shaw* (Boston: Houghton-Mifflin, 1965), p. 321.
17. Henderson, *G.B.S.: Man of the Century*, p. 219.
18. Ibid., p. 107.
19. G. B. Shaw, *An Unsocial Socialist* (New York: Boni & Liveright, 1917), pp. 189–190.
20. Ibid., p. 247.
21. Ibid., p. 195.
22. Ibid., p. 195. It is worthy of note that the Queen Mother Elizabeth has an Augustus John portrait of Shaw in her collection, which was presumably included as a collector's piece rather than as an indication of interest in Shaw.
23. Shaw, *An Unsocial Socialist*, p. 101.
24. Ibid., pp. 189–190.
25. A. M. McBriar, *Fabianism and English Politics, 1884–1918* (Cambridge: University Press, 1966), p. 25.
26. Edward Pease, *The History of the Fabian Society* (New York: International Publishers, 1926), p. 43.
27. Ibid., p. 47.
28. Smith, *The Unrepentant Pilgrim*, p. 118.
29. Pearson, *G.B.S.: His Life and Personality*, p. 86.
30. McBriar, *Fabianism and English Politics*, p. 79.
31. See Bernard Shaw, "The Queen's Speech," reprinted from *Our Corner*, August 1887, pp. 125–127, in *The Shaw Review*, XXIII, no. 3 (September, 1980), pp. 135–138.
32. Margaret I. Cole, *The Story of Fabian Socialism* (London: Heinemann, 1961), p. 60.
33. *The Star* (London), July 6, 1893.
34. *Saturday Review*, XC (November 10, 1900), p. 586.
35. Pearson, *G.B.S.: His Life and Personality*, pp. 126, 148.
36. Fabian Society, Minutes, June 11, 1897.
37. Fabian Society, Executive Committee, Minutes, September 24, 1899.
38. Fabian Society, Minutes, May 28, 1897. Interestingly, Ramsay MacDonald was more of a republican than Shaw, over this issue at least.
39. Cole, *The Story of Fabian Socialism*, p. 60.
40. Fabian Society, Executive Committee Minutes, June 25, 1897.
41. Fabian Society, Executive Committee Minutes, October 29, 1897.
42. Fabian Society, Minutes, November 12, 1897.
43. Duerksen, "Shelley and Shaw," p. 117.
44. Chappelow, *Shaw—"The Chucker-Out,"* p. 410.
45. Bernard Shaw, *Collected Plays with Their Prefaces* (New York: Dodd, Mead & Co., 1975), II, p. 811.
46. Pearson, *G.B.S.: His Life and Personality*, p. 231.
47. Bernard Shaw, "I Am a Social Democrat," *Liberty*, January, 1894, p. 5. British Museum, ADD. MSS., 50693, f. 5.
48. Ibid.
49. Shaw, Preface to *The Shewing-Up of Blanco Posnet, Collected Plays*, III, p. 679.
50. Frank Hardie, *The Political Influence of the British Monarchy, 1868–1952* (London: B.T. Batsford, 1970), p. 87.
51. Shaw, Preface to *The Shewing-Up of Blanco Posnet, Collected Plays*, III, p. 720.

52. Shaw, Preface to *Heartbreak House, Collected Plays*, V, p. 50.
53. Ervine, *Bernard Shaw*, pp. 337, 346.
54. Bernard Shaw to W. B. Yeats, n.d. (c. 1909–1910), British Museum, ADD. MSS. 50553.
55. Chappelow, *Shaw—"The Chucker-Out,"* p. 273.
56. Bernard Shaw, *Collected Letters*, Vol. II: *1898–1910*, ed. Dan H. Laurence (London: Max Reinhardt,1972), p. 217.
57. Bernard Shaw, *Plays and Players: Essays on the Theatre*, selected with an introduction by A. C. Ward (New York: Oxford University Press, 1952), pp. 257, 259.
58. Shaw, *Collected Letters*, Vol. II: *1898–1910*, pp. 216–217.
59. Chappelow, *Shaw—"The Chucker-Out,"* p. 410.
60. Bernard Shaw, "The General Mourning," *The New Age* (June 2, 1910), p. 100.
61. Interestingly, Shaw may have been technically guilty of *lese majeste* by uttering these remarks, as old statutes from the Tudor period proscribed even the "compassing" of the king's death.
62. Shaw, "The General Mourning," *The New Age* (June 2, 1910), p. 100.
63. Keir Hardie had made just this same argument when the future Edward VIII was born in 1894. Perhaps Shaw was influenced by Hardie in this regard. See Owen Peterson, "Keir Hardie: The Absolutely Independent M.P.," *Quarterly Journal of Speech*, LX (April, 1969), pp. 142–150.
64. Shaw was in error in this particular concerning the constitutional status of the Kaiser, however.
65. *The New Age*, June 16, 1893, p. 104.
66. *The New Age*, June 23, 1910, pp. 189–190. It was not a rare occurrence for Shaw to write letters under pseudonyms in reply to his own articles.
67. This is a paraphrase of Shaw in Chappelow, *Shaw—"The Chucker-Out,"* p. 226.
68. Shaw, Preface to *John Bull's Other Island, Collected Plays*, II, p. 883.
69. Shaw, *Collected Plays*, IV, p. 921.
70. Shaw, *Plays and Players*, p. 257.

Philip Klass

"THE LADY AUTOMATON" BY E.E. KELLETT: A *PYGMALION* SOURCE?

Shaw's first suggestion of *Pygmalion* occurs in a letter to Ellen Terry dated September 8, 1897. A passing reference to a "rapscallionly flower girl" and the producer Richard Mansfield deflects him into a digression:

> "Caesar & Cleopatra" has been driven clean out of my head by a play I want to write for them in which he shall be a west end gentleman and she [Mrs. Patrick Campbell] an east end dona in an apron and three orange and red ostrich feathers.[1]

These are thin lines indeed when compared to the richness of the play that was to emerge fifteen years later. Where, for example, is the all-important connecting strand, phonetics, that the gentleman is to use to pull the "east end dona" out of her gutter—and that Shaw claimed, in his preface, had interested him "towards the end of the eighteen-seventies"?[2] Where is the character of the justly conceited but nevertheless irritating Henry Higgins, the fictional scientist whose origin in the personality of a real scientist Shaw pointed to a few lines later in the same preface?

> Henry Sweet, then a young man, lacked their sweetness of character: he was about as conciliatory to conventional mortals as Ibsen or Samuel Butler. His great ability as a phonetician (he was, I think, the best of them all at this job) would have entitled him to high official recognition, and perhaps enabled him to popularize his subject, but for his Satanic contempt for all academic dignitaries. . . .

Elements similar to these and remarkably suggestive of others in the play—the preoccupation with the phonograph (or gramophone); the counterplot involving a male social butterfly; the ending that was *not*, as

Shaw insisted almost violently, a resolution into forever-after connubial bliss; above all, the Pygmalion *motif* itself, with its testing of the manufactured female at a great social occasion—all these may be noted in a short story, "The Lady Automaton," by E. E. Kellett, which appeared in *Pearson's Magazine* for June, 1901, about one-fourth of the way in time from conception to completion of Shaw's drama.

We have nothing that might pass for proof anywhere that Shaw actually read the story, but even if we had, the great distance of eleven years from publication of the short story to final draft of the play makes clear that, at most, any borrowing would have been on the unconscious level, that an idea mentioned to Ellen Terry could have lain beside a hazily recollected bit of reading for a long time until *something*—whatever happens in a great, creative mind—stimulated both of them to combine with other ideas and suggestions in a new and most remarkable growth.

If we don't have proof, is there anything close to circumstantial evidence? How likely is it that Shaw read that issue of that magazine? Well, we do know that Shaw was a great reader, that he read enormously, omnivorously, almost miscellaneously. We do know that Shaw and H. G. Wells had met, some six years before the story's publication, on the opening night of Henry James's *Guy Domville*, January 5, 1895. In his *Experiment in Autobiography*, Wells not only says, "On that eventful evening I scraped acquaintance with another interesting contemporary, Bernard Shaw,"[3] but also reminisces about the leading character and ending of James's play in terms that again—almost incredibly—evoke similar matter in *Pygmalion* and its epilogue:

Wells on James's Play	*Shaw's Epilogue*
Guy Domville was one of those rare ripe exquisite Catholic Englishmen of ancient family conceivable only by an American mind, who gave up the woman he loved to an altogether coarser cousin, because his religious vocation was stronger than his passion.[4]	The word passion means nothing else to them [uncultivated people]; and that Higgins could have a passion for phonetics and idealize his mother instead of Eliza, would seem to them absurd and unnatural. Even had there been no mother-rival, she [Eliza] would still have refused to accept an interest in herself that was secondary to philosophic interests. Had Mrs Higgins died, there would still have been Milton and the Universal Alphabet.

The year 1895, of course, was the one in which Wells's first science fiction novel, *The Time Machine*, was to be published in its final, book-length form. *Pearson's Magazine* carried a good deal of science fiction (then known as "scientific romances") by H. G. Wells and other acquaintances and contemporaries of Shaw's. It was certainly sparkling and provocative enough to have attracted the attention of anyone with a hearty reading appetite and a taste for the very latest ideas; Shaw, the author of five rather unsuccessful novels, would likely have been especially interested in the most recent productions of the successful fictionwriters he knew and whom he would be encountering quite often around London. And would anyone as involved with speech and phonetics as he had been for over twenty years not be *told* of a story—assuming it had not already been part of his casual reading—like E. E. Kellett's "The Lady Automaton,"[5] with its emphasis on speech patterns and artificial voice and intriguing uses of the newly invented phonograph?

That story was one of Ernest Edward Kellett's few pieces of published fiction. He was born eight years after Shaw, in 1864; but both men died in the same year—1950. Kellett was an Oxford man and, besides being a successful school teacher, edited *The Book of Cambridge Verse* in 1911; he published two collections of essays, as well as volumes of criticism, translations, and memoirs. And *this* unexpected tale.

One can only say that if the gods saw fit to suggest the most famous male monster of all time to a mere slip of a runaway English girl in Switzerland, the least they could do was to provide the most ladylike equivalent imaginable to the senior English master at Leys School. Neither narrative comes close to being great literature: while *Frankenstein* clanks into our consciousness as perhaps the best bad novel ever written, "The Lady Automaton" whirrs much more smoothly along its mediocre way. Neither writer is truly capable of emerging from the problems of individuals that their stories set into the larger issues of science fiction, the apocalyptic heights, say, of the young H. G. Wells; but both are terribly alert to rumbling scientific consequences that others hear only as a tinkle; both writers will influence perhaps much more than they achieve. And if Kellett's story about the social success of a female robot affected the evolving plot of Shaw's *Pygmalion*, that is an achievement itself.

The precipitating plot element in both works is remarkably similar: a modern Pygmalion—a scientist, not a sculptor—accepts a challenge to create not a mere woman, but a lady, a counterfeit lady who will fool all.

Kellett's Inventor
"And I want her to be a lady that would deceive anyone ... —in fact, perform the part of a society lady as well as the best bred of them all."

Shaw's Phonetician
"Yes: in six months—in three if she has a good ear and a quick tongue—I'll take her anywhere and pass her off as anything."

In both works the commitment is made to a foil character, someone who is already awed by the scientist's achievements and will be further awed by the success of this particular achievement. Kellett's foil character, coming earlier in time than Shaw's Pickering, is of the same profession as the greatest foil character of them all, Sir Arthur Conan Doyle's Dr. Watson, who made his first appearance in 1887. Stephen Leacock described the type as the "Poor Sap," and said the character's only function was to play surrogate for the reader and to be overwhelmed constantly by what his brighter companion thought and said and did. In addition, in these works, both Pickering and Kellett's narrator-physician express the audience's unease as well as its admiration at what is being done.

The use of the phonograph is another essential narrative device to both Shaw and Kellett. It is one of the most important items in Higgins's laboratory in Wimpole Street, and not only does Eliza learn by it, but when she leaves Higgins, she says to him of her voice and appearance, "Well, you have both of them on your gramophone and in your book of photographs. When you feel lonely without me, you can turn the machine on. It's got no feelings to hurt."

While Kellett begins a paragraph with "Though Amelia certainly could not feel," and underlines the Lady Automaton's lack of emotional as well as physical response throughout, it is more notable that he points to the phonograph as an instrument which his inventor has perfected and now uses to create the Automaton's "sweet and beautifully modulated feminine voice" well before he assembles the rest of her. The quality of the voice and the "walking phonograph" nature of the Automaton is never lost sight of (hearing of?) throughout the tale.

Similarly, in Mrs. Higgins's at-home scene, Eliza is described by the playwright as "*speaking with pedantic correctness of pronunciation and great beauty of tone,*" and Pickering chatters enthusiastically of "dozens of gramophone disks." The machine that could reproduce the human voice and its relationship to a living human was apparently as fascinating to Shaw as phonetics itself, and as interesting to Kellett as automatons in general.

For that matter, Shaw is almost as interested in automatons as is Kellett. There are many glancing references throughout the play: "Woman: do you not understand that I have *made* you [italics mine] a consort for a king?" Higgins asks Eliza in their last scene together. And "She's a triumph of your art and of her dressmaker's," Mrs. Higgins tells her son.

Most remarkably, Mrs. Higgins's role as early outside consultant—"I've a job for you," her son tells her. "A phonetic job," just as he asks her later, "Well? Is Eliza presentable?"—can be seen as paralleled in "The Lady Automaton" with that of the Countess of Lorimer, who "undertook to pilot her [the Automaton] through the first shoals of real life." The two older, upper-class women are needed relatively early in the two experiments to do a job that the male creators simply cannot do themselves.

Perhaps the most intriguing plot parallel of all, more colorful and more memorable even than the impeccably spoken Billingsgate of Eliza or the tantalizingly repetitious small talk of the Lady Automaton, is the embassy reception in *Pygmalion* and the ball at Mrs. Vandeleur's in "The Lady Automaton." Both scenes could easily come under the same heading—"Tryout of Mechanical Contrivance at a Major Social Event." Both are suspenseful as well as funny; both prove the success of their respective experiments; and in both the final unraveling may be said to begin.

Nor is that all. In each case, how is the success of the "contrivance" described?

"The Lady Automaton"	*Pygmalion*
Exquisitely dressed, with a proud demeanor, with the step of a queen, she swept into the ball-room. "Who is she?" said young Harry Burton to me. "By Jove, she looks like a born queen."	NEPOMMUCK. Instinct, maestro, instinct. Only the Magyar races can produce that air of the divine right, those resolute eyes. She is a princess. HOSTESS. Oh, of course I agree with Nepommuck. She must be a princess at least.

But this born queen—or princess—acquires a consort, a young man who is a native of the aristocratic world where she has scored such a smashing success: a Freddy. Actually, while there is only one Freddy in *Pygmalion*—and it is his proposal of marriage which provides the leverage for Shaw's ending—there are two Freddies in "The Lady Automaton," and *both* offer impossible marriage. Again, the ending derives from these proposals, or rather the consequent wedding ceremony attempted with one of them. The very existence of these characters, the two Freddies (Burton and Calder) on the one hand, and the lone Freddy ("Pickering! Nonsense: she's going to marry Freddy. Ha ha! Freddy! Freddy!!") on the other, not to mention their crucial relationship in each case with the resolution of the plot, makes it quite possible that the similarities between the play and the short story are something more than coincidental.

The similarities do abound. Kellett's narrator describes his involvement ("I was carried away in a kind of drunken enthusiasm, and almost as feverishly excited as Moore himself.") in terms that *must* evoke Higgins and Pickering gabbling in a kind of chorus to Higgins's mother about the wonders of their experiment with Eliza.

And there is the curious matter of parallel vocabularies. Did both Kellett and Shaw always refer to "dolls" in their daily speech? Were their thought processes relative to creator and created so much alike?

"The Lady Automaton"	*Pygmalion*
"I am determined that she shall be the beauty of the season. She shall eclipse them all, I tell you. What are they but dolls? and she is more than a doll; she is *me*."	MRS HIGGINS. You certainly are a pretty pair of babies, playing with your live doll.
....	HIGGINS. You let her alone, mother. Let her speak for herself. You will jolly soon see whether she has an idea that I haven't put into her head or a word that I haven't put into her mouth. I tell you I have created this thing out of the squashed cabbage leaves of Covent Garden; and now she pretends to play the fine lady with me.
The plain fact dawned on me that Moore's extraordinary success had turned his brain. He had put so much of himself into his automaton that he had positively begun to regard her as a real living being, in whose veins flowed his own blood, in whose nostrils was his own breath. Eve was not more truly bone of Adam's bone than this Amelia was part and parcel of Moore's life.	

The resemblances—in plot development, in character types, in vocabulary—are quite striking. Even the differences are significant of some sort of connection—for example, while there is an unbridgeable gulf between the raw material, a "bedraggled guttersnipe" and a boxful of machine parts, the end products, the two "ladies," are both not much more than surface achievements. (Eliza realizes, she tells her creator, that she cannot maintain her "lady" status herself.) And, while Arthur Moore and Henry Higgins are totally different human beings, interested in different *kinds* of science (not just different sciences), both are more or less tranquil about the prospect of their creations passing through marriage and into the possession of other men.

But if Shaw did borrow from Kellett—immediately when he read the story, or later and unconsciously when he had all but forgotten the story and was working on the play, or later and unknowingly when someone who had read the story worked some parts of it into a conversation with him—if Shaw *did* borrow, how much does *Pygmalion* really owe to "The Lady Automaton"?

E. E. Kellett's story is about a fine prank with a piece of machinery, a prank that succeeds up to a point and then ends in so much sawdust. Bernard Shaw's play is about a girl imprisoned in gutters and back alleys because of a lack of education and because of the speech patterns produced by that lack, about what just one shred of education—in speech—could do to make her an acceptable lady; and it ends with her giving up that fake ladyhood for genuine womanhood. *Pygmalion*, it happens, relates to the best kind of science fiction: its science is involved with large social issues and affects human beings in important new ways. "The Lady Automaton" is simple, gadget-happy science fiction; there are no significant social issues and no noticeable human beings; the inventor dies in what we would now call the Hollywood mad-scientist finale, when "his wonderful toy was broken"—and even the narrator goes insane in an entirely gratuitous, pseudo-Poe farewell paragraph.

Even if Shaw overtly, consciously, with utterly Shavian malice aforethought, borrowed large quantities of fictional paraphernalia from Kellett's short story, certain precedents obtain. How much do Shakespeare's *Macbeth* and *Lear* and *Cymbeline* really owe to Holinshed? And is Plutarch in any real sense the author of *Coriolanus*, of *Julius Caesar*, of *Antony and Cleopatra*? Is Shakespeare's *Hamlet,* with all of its complexity and internalized drama, in any sense a plagiarism of the bangety-bang version of the play of the same name which had appeared a couple of decades earlier and which was mined of its plot to produce the later masterpiece?

Nevertheless, the fairly clear relationships between the short story and Shaw's play raise all sort of questions. How interested was Shaw in science fiction (not yet named as such), and how often did he attempt it only to discover again that his interest in immediate social questions was stronger than his interest in scientific possibility? Many writers who wrote science fiction read him; and many writers who influenced writers of science fiction read him.[6]

One of the best-known of the robot stories after the landmark plays of Joseph and Karel Capek in the 1920s (the Capeks admired Shaw, who by no coincidence wrote a robot-maker named Pygmalion into his 1921 futuristic play-cycle *Back to Methuselah*) is that of Helen O'Loy. Created by Lester del Rey in 1938, "Helen O'Loy" is now considered a minor classic in the field. It deals with the construction of a female robot—the term automaton having pretty much gone out with the nineteenth century—very much on the order of E. E. Kellett's seductive piece of clockwork.

Better, though. Far too much better. So much better, in fact, that, in an inversion of the mythic Pygmalion, she falls in love with her owner:

> Dave wasn't a prude, but he remembered that she was only a robot, after all. The fact that she felt, acted, and looked like a young goddess in his arms didn't mean much. With some effort, he untangled her and dragged her off to supper, where he made her eat with him to divert her attention.[7]

It does him no good. Robot or woman, she's quite persistent:

> No woman ever made a lovelier bride or a sweeter wife. Helen never lost her flair for cooking and making a home.

I think both Kellett and Shaw would have enjoyed this story. Kellett because Helen is a lovely piece of machinery and even more successful at getting away with her deception than his Lady Automaton. And Shaw—well, Shaw because of Shaw's views on the relative strengths of female and male personalities. You see, the only way the man in this story can get away from the female robot is by dying.

The Lady Automaton

By E.E. Kellett

"Yes," said Arthur, "I feel very much inclined to try it."

The speaker, Arthur Moore, was a man whom I was proud to call my friend. Early in life he had distinguished himself by many wonderful inventions. When a boy he had adorned his bedroom with all sorts of curious mechanical contrivances; pulleys for lifting unheard-of weights; rattraps which, by cunning devices, provided the captured animal with a silent and painless end; locomotives, which, when once wound up, would run for a day; and numberless other treasures, which, if hardly useful or even ornamental, had yet the effect of inspiring the housemaid who made the bed with a mortal terror of everything in the room.

As he grew older he lost none of his skill. At the age of fifteen he had successfully emulated most of the feats of Vaucanson; his mechanical ducks gobbled and digested their food so naturally that even the

The LADY AUTOMATON.

By E. E. Kellett.

"YES," said Arthur, "I feel very much inclined to try it."

The speaker, Arthur Moore, was a man whom I was proud to call my friend. Early in life he had distinguished himself by many wonderful inventions. When a boy he had adorned his bedroom with all sorts of curious mechanical contrivances; pulleys for lifting unheard-of weights; rat-traps which, by cunning devices, provided the captured animal with a silent and painless end; locomotives which, when once wound up, would run for a day; and numberless other treasures, which, if hardly useful or even ornamental, had yet the effect of inspiring the housemaid who made the bed with a mortal terror of everything in the room.

As he grew older he lost none of his skill. At the age of fifteen he had successfully emulated most of the feats of Vaucanson; his mechanical ducks gobbled and digested their food so naturally that even the famous scientist, the Rev. Henry Forest, was for a moment taken in. He had been to College, but, after a year of University life, he had wearied of the dull routine, and had begged his father to let him start life on his own account.

His father need have had no fear for the result. Within a year young Moore's automatic chess player, that had played a draw with Steinitz himself, had attracted the awe-struck attention of the civilised world by the simplicity and daring of its mechanism. The chess player was followed in two years by a whist player, still more simply and boldly conceived; and after that time scarcely a year passed without being signalised by the appearance of new wonders from Moore's fertile brain and dexterous hand.

His last achievement had been a phonograph so perfectly constructed that people began to think that even Edison must soon begin to look to his laurels, or he would be eclipsed by the rising fame of this young man of thirty.

I had known him since he was a boy; and had kept my acquaintance with him in spite

The title page of Kellett's story as it appeared in *Pearson's Magazine* in 1901.

famous scientist, the Rev. Henry Forest, was for a moment taken in. He had been to College, but, after a year of University life, he had wearied of the dull routine, and had begged his father to let him start life on his own account.

His father need have had no fear for the result. Within a year young Moore's automatic chess player, that had played a draw with Steinitz himself, had attracted the awe-struck attention of the civilised world by the simplicity and daring of its mechanism. The chess player was followed in two years by a whist player, still more simply and boldly conceived; and after that time scarcely a year passed without being signalised by the appearance of new wonders from Moore's fertile brain and dexterous hand.

His last achievement had been a phonograph so perfectly constructed that people began to think that even Edison must soon begin to look to his laurels, or he would be eclipsed by the rising fame of this young man of thirty.

I had known him since he was a boy; and had kept my acquaintance with him in spite of the ever-widening difference between our paths and our beliefs. I had chosen the medical profession, and was already a fashionable doctor, pretty well known by the public.

It was just after the new phonograph had appeared that I had with Arthur the memorable and unfortunate conversation which I shall regret to the very end of my life.

"Well," I said, "a new and great success again. You will be one of the greatest benefactors of the century in a few years."

"Yes," he answered, for he had no false modesty. "I believe the phonograph is about as perfect as I can make it. Suppose we listen to it now."

He produced the instrument, and I had the pleasure of listening to a speech of Lord Rosebery with the familiar tones and inflections of the great orator reproduced to the life. I could have believed I saw the Prime Minister before me.

"Wonderful," I said. "It is indeed perfect. What a strange and almost uncanny thing it is! We shall soon have to be very careful what we say; for a bird of the air shall carry the voice, and that which hath wings shall tell the matter. Fancy what a preventive of crime a phonograph fastened on every lamp-post would be! It would be a kind of Magic Flute, forcing people to tell the truth whether they would or no. Jones might say, 'I said this,' but the phonograph would say 'You said that.' Mere human fallible creatures will soon be banished from the witness-box; judges and juries will content themselves with taking the evidence of unerring, unlying phonographs."

"Heaven save us," Moore replied; "all of us say many things that will hardly bear repeating; and if they are all to be recorded how dreadful it would be."

"Yes, you see you are after all but a doubtful benefactor of the human race; it is not everybody, who, like Job, can wish that his words were now written."

"Nor Job himself at all times," he answered; "perhaps he would hardly have wished to have recorded the words he used when he cursed his day."

"In fact," I said, "what is a phonograph after all but a tattling old woman, repeating whatever it hears without discrimination or tact?"

"Exactly," he said; "but with this difference; that the phonograph repeats what it hears without alteration or addition, whereas the old woman repeats it just as it suits her."

At this moment the fatal idea struck me, which now I would give worlds to have forgotten or suppressed before it came to the birth. Alas, we know not the result of our least words.

"Why," I said, "don't you try to make a kind of complement of a phonograph?"

"What do you mean?"

"Why, this. Your phonograph only repeats what it hears. Why not make an instrument which should not *repeat* words, but speak out the suitable answer to them? If, for instance, I were to say to it 'Good morning; have you used So-and-so's Soap?' then why should it not answer 'No, I use somebody else's,' instead of merely reiterating my words? At present your machine is nothing but an echo; glorious, I grant; a triumph of civilisation; but what an achievement it would be to contrive a sort of anti-phonograph, that should give the appropriate *answer* to each question I like to put!"

"Why, a thing that could do that would be nothing less than man."

"Well," I said, "what is man but a bundle of sensations—a machine that answers pretty accurately to the questions daily put to it?" For I was, or pretended to be, a full-blown materialist.

"It may be so," he answered, "yet it seems to me that he is a very complex machine for all that. He has taken thousands of years to evolve, if what Darwin says is true; you ask me to make him in at most a year or two."

"Listen to me," I said, half in irony, half in earnest. "When you made your whist player, what did you do but calculate on a certain number of actions, all theoretically possible, and arrange that the machine should give the proper answer to them?"

"True."

"And with your chess player, was it not the same?"

"Exactly."

"Well, then, the general principle is granted. Are there not practically infinite varieties of hands at whist? Yet your automaton never made a mistake. Are there not infinite varieties of number? Yet did that puzzle Babbage's calculating machine?"

"You may be right, Phillips," he said, smiling at my earnestness. "I will think of it."

I took my leave, little dreaming that I had set in motion a mighty force which would bring misery to more than a few. Indeed, I completely forgot the whole conversation. It was not till several months later that, happening to meet Moore in the street, I was suddenly startled by hearing the words I have already mentioned.

"Yes, I feel very much inclined to try it."

"To try what?" I said, completely bewildered.

"Why, the thing we were talking of some months ago. Listen. Words are nothing but air-vibrations, are they?"

"Nothing," I answered.

"Well, then, it follows that words, if put in the proper positions, can generate motion."

"I follow you; a molecular windmill."

"Well," he said, "this is the idea of my machine. Words are spoken into the ear of my automaton. Passing through the ear they enter a machine you would call an anti-phonograph, and set in motion various processes which in a very short time produce the words constituting the proper answer."

"Wonderful," I said, "if true."

"Come and see then," he rejoined, "if you will be so sceptical."

I followed him to his workshop, and saw a small instrument, in its main external details exactly like a phonograph.

"This," said Moore, "is the centre of my automaton. Try it yourself. Ask it a question—anything you like."

Wondering, I did as he suggested. There was a tube on each side of the instrument, communicating with its centre, which I supposed would form the "ear" of the automaton when finished. I was at a loss how to begin the conversation, so called the weather to my aid.

"A very cold day," I remarked.

A sweet and beautifully modulated feminine voice answered.

"Yes; but hardly so cold as yesterday."

I started, as though I had seen a ghost. Had I not been a doctor, old as I was, I should have precipitately fled. But it takes a good deal to shake the nerves of a physician. In an instant I recovered myself.

"Moore," I said, "you can't play with me. You are ventriloquising."

He was very indignant.

"What do you think of me?" he said. "I to go playing the tricks of a strolling mountebank!"

"Try it again. I will not open my mouth."

I tried again, a certain uncanny feeling still possessing me. Oh, for the inventive powers of a Frenchman, in order to begin the conversation naturally!

"That was a fine speech by Mr. Chamberlain yesterday evening."

"Yes," the delicate feminine voice again replied; "I didn't read it all, but the beginning and the end were very good, weren't they?"

Again the same eerie feeling came over me, followed as before by the conviction that some trickery must be at the bottom of this most unparalleled experience.

I tried yet a third time, determined to watch Moore's face during the whole operation.

"It looks as if there'll be war between China and Japan," I said rather inanely.

"Yes, and I fancy Japan will win," replied the voice, *precisely at the same moment as Moore was saying:*

"Two to one on the little 'un."

I was convinced by that. No human being ever spoke two sentences precisely at the same instance. Either there was somebody else in the room, or Moore had succeeded, marvellously succeeded. He had made an instrument that could not only imitate the tones of the human voice, but could keep up a conversation as constantly, if not as wittily, as Miss Notable and Mr. Neverout in Swift's "Polite Conversation."

"Satisfied, old fellow?" said Moore, rising from his chair and coming toward me.

"My dear fellow," I said, "I know you are incapable of deception. But this is extraordinary. I never heard anything like it."

"No, more did I," he replied with pardonable vanity, "until a week or so ago. I had tried all kinds of devices to make the thing answer sensibly; she would answer, of course, long ago, but I wanted her to behave like a lady, not like a lunatic."

"So you mean your automaton to be a lady, do you?"

"Yes," he replied, drawing closer. "And I want her to be a lady that would deceive anyone. Not a thing that can only act when lifted into a chair, or stuck up on a platform; but a creature that will guide herself, answer questions, talk and eat like a rational being—in fact, perform the part of a society lady as well as the best bred of them all."

"Moore," I said, "you must be mad."

"Mad or not, I mean to try it. See here. Here is another automaton that can walk, eat, turn its head, shut its eyes. That is common enough.

Here is the brain power, the 'anti-phonograph' that can speak and hear—indeed, do anything but think. What is wanted but that the two should be combined?"

"My dear fellow," I answered, "it is easy to talk like that. I am a materialist, and would grant you more than most; but even in my view the brain is more than a mere machine. A man guides himself; you have to guide this automaton. How are you to get inside her and make her do all these things together at the proper time?

"Take a very simple example; your thing has to be sure to open its mouth when it speaks. How are you to insure that the process which causes it to open its mouth, and the process which causes certain words to be uttered, shall take place simultaneously? Suppose the thing to say, 'I will sit down,' how are you to insure that, at the proper moment, she shall go through the proper motions involved in sitting down? Remember, an error of half a second in your mysterious clockwork may make all the difference between your lady occupying a dignified position in a chair and sprawling ingloriously on the floor.

'Why, think of the actions of but five minutes, She rises from a chair, she avoids the toes of the ladies and gentlemen in the room, she bows to a gentleman, she smiles—more or less hypocritically—at a lady, she makes a *bon-mot,* she laughs at somebody else's *bon-mots;* she even blows her nose. What countless simultaneous processes, not one of which must go wrong!"

Moore heard me through.

"Plausible enough," he said, when I had finished; "we shall soon see who is right."

"Who was it," he went on, "who lectured so vigorously on the folly of certain women of our time, and talked so largely about their utter inanity? 'The Society woman of our time,' you proclaimed, 'what is she but a doll? Her second-hand opinions, so daintily expressed, would not a parrot speak them as well?' You meant that for metaphor and eloquence, old fellow, and yet you object to my proving that it is all literal truth."

"Prove it first," I said.

"Only give me time," he answered. "But before you go," he said, with a sudden impulse, as he saw me nearing the door, "for Heaven's sake not a word of this until I give you leave."

"Make your mind easy," I replied, "a doctor knows how to keep a secret. When your lady goes out of order, send for a bottle of my emulsion, and I'll engage she'll trouble you no more."

During the next few months, I often thought of Moore and his hallucination; the picture of the poor fellow engaged on a hopelessly mad task often rose before my mind. I pitied him greatly. "Another fine brain wasted," I used to say. "A man that more than rivalled Edison spending the best years of his life over a mad chimera!"

I urged rest, a sea voyage, anything to cure him of his brain-sick folly. But he met me always with one reply: "Rest *then;* not before." Rest in the grave, poor fellow, I thought, as I noted his hectic cheek and staring bones. His fiery soul was fretting his body to decay.

At last, more than a year after our last conversation, amid the heap of letters lying on my table at breakfast, I came upon one that startled me. It was from Arthur Moore, short, but to the point.

"Success at last; come when you can."

As soon as my round of visits was finished, I drove to his rooms. Mounting the stairs, I was ushered into the room by the most beautiful girl I had ever seen; a creature with fair hair, bright eyes, and a doll-like childishness of expression.

"Can he have married?" I thought, as I looked at her. "How is Mr. Moore?" I said aloud.

"Poorly to-day," she replied. "He will be here in a minute."

Where and when had I heard that voice before? I seemed to know it, and yet I could not associate it with anybody. But I had no time to be perplexed, for in two or three seconds Moore appeared, looking ghastly and deathlike in his pallor.

"You are ill," I said, when the first greeting was over. "You have been overstraining yourself. You must really rest, or you will kill yourself."

"Yes, I must," he replied; "and I think I shall. It has been toilsome work. But I think it was worth it, don't you?"

"How should I know?" I answered. "I haven't seen it yet."

"Yes, you have," he said, smiling in spite of the pain that he must have been feeling.

I looked around, bewildered. I could see nothing but the same old room, and the strange girl sitting in an easy chair in the corner.

"You are mysterious," I said.

"Wait a moment," said Moore. Then, turning to the girl, he spoke a little louder.

"It looks as if there *has* been war between China and Japan," he said.

Again those clear, distinct, delicate tones, as the answer came.

"Yes, and I fancy Japan *has* won."

I saw it all now. That beautiful, lady-like girl that had ushered me into the room, whom I had taken for his wife, was an automaton! That doll-like expression was due to the fact that she *was* a doll. I was utterly astounded. Moore sat by, enjoying my bewilderment; for a moment his weakness left him.

"Come here," he said to the automaton.

The lady arose, after one second of apparent indecision, and approached him.

"Let me introduce to you Dr. Phillips," he said.

The lady smiled approval. (To this day I have never understood how Moore had managed to produce that smile—that fatal monotonous, fascinating smile.)

"Dr. Phillips, Miss Amelia Brooke."

The lady bowed, and extended her hand.

"I am most happy to meet one of whom I have so often heard," she said.

Could it be a reality? I felt more and more staggered. The lady stood perfectly still, her hands clasped before her. This fair creature not of flesh and blood? Impossible!

"You may go," said Moore.

The thing moved back to her place, and sat down.

"What do you think of her?" he said aloud.

Before answering, I looked round to see where she was.

"Don't mind," he said laughing; "she can't hear. I often have that feeling myself. You may discuss her as you please, and she won't be offended. She has one merit other women haven't; she is not touchy; but she has a failing the best of them have not; she can't blush. On the whole, however, I prefer her."

"I am still almost incredulous," I replied; "indeed, until I have dissected her, and found pulleys instead of a liver, and eccentrics instead of a spleen, I shall hardly believe she isn't a woman in reality."

"You can easily do so," he said. "Come here, Amelia."

The creature rose, and came forward.

"Let Dr. Phillips see your arm," he said.

The lady showed me her arm, and turned up her sleeve. It did not need a moment's inspection to show me that this was not an arm of flesh and blood. What it actually was made of Moore would not tell me.

"Better than a waxwork figure, isn't it?" he said.

"Much better," I replied. "Might deceive anyone but a doctor."

Passing my hand down to her wrist, I noted an exactly-moving pulse. So wonderfully was the human pulse imitated, that I believe anybody but one, like myself, trained to accurate discrimination would have been deluded. I could not refrain from expressing my admiration.

"Yes," said Moore, "she will often have her arms bare, and there may be a good deal of hand-pressing and that sort of thing; so that I thought I ought to have everything right."

"Does her heart beat, too?" I asked.

"No," he said; "I wanted the space for other mechanism, so she has to do without a heart altogether. Besides," he added, smilingly, "I wanted her to be a Society lady."

"The thing will be worth thousands to you," I said when I had finished the examination of the creature's cutaneous covering. "It is uncanny enough, and I can't say I like it, but it will draw. What a pity Barnum has gone! He would have given you a million pounds for it."

Moore rose angrily.

"Do you think I will sell my own life-power for money?" he cried. "That thing has cost me at least ten years of my life, and she shall never be exhibited like a two-headed nightingale, or a creature with its legs growing out of its pockets! She shall walk drawing-rooms like a lady, or I will break her to pieces myself!"

"My dear fellow," I said, "you are overexcited and ill. Surely you cannot know what you are saying?"

"I know well enough," he answered doggedly. "I have made a lady, you can't deny it; and a lady she shall be.

"Phillips," he went on, all the force of his character coming out in his face, "I am determined that she shall be the beauty of the season. She shall eclipse them all, I tell you. What are they but dolls? and she is more than a doll; she is ME. I have breathed into her myself, and she all but lives; she understands and knows! Come, promise me you will not betray me."

"Of course I will not," I said; "but you must give up this mad scheme. Consider, as an automaton she will make you for life; as a lady she will be found out in five minutes, and you will be laughed at. For your own sake pause."

"Listen," he said fiercely. "You call her an automaton. I tell you she is alive. See!"

He called the thing to him.

"Amelia," he said, "I have made you, and you are mine. Are you grateful?"

The creature smiled—the one smile she possessed, which she had, as I knew afterwards, for prince or peasant, man or maid.

"I can never forget what I owe you," she replied.

"Kiss me, then," he said.

The thing bent down and kissed him obediently.

"You see," he cried, "is *that* an automaton? Now, will you introduce her to Society as a lady?

"For the present she is perfect. I have taught her French—drawing-room French, I mean—and three songs. She can enter a room, bow, smile, and dance. If, with these accomplishments, she can't oust the other dolls and turn them green with jealousy for one season, I am much surprised. Now, will you help me?"

I tried to enter a feeble protest, but he overbore me. You ask how; I cannot tell. Call it magic—anything you like; but it overbore me. I yielded; I promised my assistance.

We sat like two mischief-making children far into the small hours of the night, plotting how we could carry out the plan best. Moore had enslaved me, body and mind; I was carried away in a kind of drunken enthusiasm, and almost as feverishly excited as Moore himself. Nothing would now have stopped me. Would Frankenstein have paused the very hour before his creature took life? As for Moore, I believe he would have gone on with his designs in the very midst of the thunders of the Judgment Day itself.

Why should I linger over the early triumphs of our Phantasm? I was a fashionable doctor; I brought Miss Amelia Brooke out as a niece of mine. The Countess of Lorimer, one of my patients, undertook to pilot her through the first shoals of real life.

Never shall I forget that first evening. Scarcely had she entered the room—it was at Mrs. Vandeleur's—when the eyes of all seemed, as if by magic, to be turned towards her. Exquisitely dressed, with a proud demeanour, with the step of a queen, she swept into the ball-room. She was my niece; I ought to have been proud of her, but I hated her with an intense loathing. Moore could do much with me, but he could not make me like this creature. Yet I was bound in nature to do all I could for her.

"Who is she?" said young Harry Burton to me. "By Jove, she looks like a born queen."

"You flatter me," I replied. "She is my niece. Good Heavens," I went on to myself, "would that she were a born anything, instead of a made doll!"

"Oh," rejoined Burton, "lucky man that you are! Introduce me, will you?"

"With pleasure," I answered.

I took him up and introduced him. During the ceremony I watched the creature carefully. No, there was no doubt about it. Such acting would deceive the Master of the Ceremonies in the Court of Louis XIV himself. Every motion, every word, was exactly as it should be. How on earth had Moore managed it? I was almost deceived myself. Could this be after all a real creature of flesh and blood, substituted for the Phantasm? No; that detestable, beautiful smile was there—a smile which no woman ever wore, yet which none the less would be the bane of more than one man's existence.

Harry Burton danced many dances with her that night. When it closed, he was head over ears in love.

"Phillips," he said in a brief interval, "she is divine."

"Fiendish, rather," I thought. "Yes," I said aloud, "I think she is good looking.

"Good looking!" he cried. "What are all these painted dolls to her? *They* have nothing to say for themselves, *they* are mere bundles of conventionality; but *she*—she is all soul."

"My boy," I said warningly, "you are evidently all heart. Be careful. Don't do anything rash. Dance with her, talk to her—do anything but fall in love with her."

"Who talked of falling in love?" he said, astonished at my earnestness. "I said nothing but that she was the finest girl in the room, and so she is, by Jove!"

At this moment a new dance began, and Burton ran off to claim his partner. I remained, absorbed in not very pleasant reflections. Things were getting involved already. Moore had only told me he was making a woman; I had never calculated that he would make a coquette. What would come of it? I sat and watched her as she danced, dancing beautifully but a little mechanically, I thought, saying always the right things, answering questions always in the same way, and wearing at pretty regular intervals the same detestable smile.

If I hated her before. I hated her tenfold now. I would speak to Moore, and put an end to it. A sudden cold—ordered to the South of France—and never let her come back. Good Heavens, this creature never had a cold, never had a headache, never felt out of sorts; yet Moore said he had made a woman.

Slowly the evening dragged to its close—the most wearisome evening I had ever spent. The creature did not seem to tire; one dance or twenty was the same to her. The monotony of it all became at length intolerable to me. At the earliest decent opportunity I took my leave.

Moore had never been a Society man. Even to witness his own triumph he had refused to be drawn out of his retirement, and it was with a feverish eagerness that he waited for the story of her successes from my lips.

"How did it go off?" he said anxiously, as I made my promised call to tell him.

"As an experiment, very well," I answered. "There was no hitch, no failure. The success was only too monotonous. Human beings sometimes put their foot in it; she never. Would to Heaven she might show now and then a little proneness to error!"

"You are queer," Moore answered. "Why should you grudge her her victories?"

"Arthur," I said, "the joke has gone quite far enough. Put a stop to it. Why go further? Think of the chances of detection—no, think of the far worse chances of success! Can't you see that the more skilful the deception the more dangerous will its consequences be? Already, more than one young fellow has fallen head over ears in love with her. It is horrible to think of!"

'The fools!" he said, with a rather cynical smile. "That is just the way with young fellows—never looking below the surface, looking only at the face. Why, Phillips, if they are taken in in that way they deserve to be taken in. I shall do nothing."

So the thing went on, new developments constantly arising. I hasten to the fatal ending.

Among the many deserters from the shrines of other goddesses who thronged to pay their court to this new and strange divinity, two seemed to hold the divided first place in her favour. One was my young friend Harry Burton; the other was handsome, impulsive, universally-liked Dick Calder. These two had been firm friends before, in spite of the fact that they had often flirted with the same girl. But it was impossible for two young fellows to love Amelia and continue to love each other.

To do Amelia, justice, she was rigidly impartial between Burton and Calder. For both she had the same silvery tones, for both the same fascinating smile. To both, if they asked the same questions, she returned identically the same answers. To both she sang the same songs, with the crescendo on the same passages, and both, at the conclusion of the songs, received the same languishing, irresistible smile over the right shoulder, which made them her slaves on the spot.

One evening, a curious incident happened. Burton and Calder were as usual basking in the rays of their divinity, when by some mischance Amelia's brooch fell to the ground. Both the swains stooped to pick it up, but Burton was successful. Delighted at his triumph over his rival, he solicited the honour of refastening it. Calder watched him with jealous eyes. Suddenly a clumsy pair of waltzers, not looking where they were going, came hard into Burton. The brooch pin was driven deep into the fair throat of Amelia. Burton started in horror; he began a savage oath, but stopping in time he pulled out the pin. Amelia had not uttered a sound.

Burton, speechless with dismay, was taking out his handkerchief to staunch the blood; a little crowd was gathering round them; when I, suddenly recollecting myself, rushed in. With the speed of lightning I slipped out my handkerchief and tied it round Amelia's neck.

"Stand back, all of you!" I said in a tone of command. Even Burton and Calder fell back a little.

"My niece is very sensitive," I said. "the hurt is not great, but it would be as well that she should go home at once." A terror had possessed me; an overmastering fear of detection held me as in a vice.

"I assure you, uncle, that I am not hurt at all," said Amelia.

"Come along," I said sternly.

I hurried her off, finding just time to bid my adieus to my hostess, and to console the dumfounded Burton by saying there was no danger.

We drove, not home, but direct to Moore's lodgings. Hurriedly we went upstairs. Moore was still up. He seemed surprised to see us.

"What do you want," he said.

"Fools that we are," I answered. "Why we were within a hair's breadth of detection. *The creature can't bleed.*"

"Why, what need has she to bleed?" he said.

"Every need," I answered. "Doesn't a girl bleed when a pin is driven a good inch into her throat?"

"What do you mean?"

I explained the circumstances, and how I hoped I had for this once staved off discovery. I had been just in time.

"No," he said, when I finished. "I never thought she would need to bleed. Strange that I should have forgotten that. They say that murderers always forget just one thing, just one little thing. But *they* take pains to get rid of the blood, and I ought to take pains to have it there."

"Give it up, Moore," I said.

"Give it up! Never!" he shouted. "Give it up for a few drops of blood! Rather would I drain my own veins into hers. Rather go out and kill somebody. What did Mephistopheles say? 'Blood is a peculiar sort of juice.' But I will make it."

Miss Brooke was "ill" for a few weeks from "shock to the system." At the end of that time I saw Moore again. He and the Phantasm were in the room together. He gave me a pin.

"Prick her," he said.

I obeyed, not unwillingly; and to my horror something very like bleeding began.

"Yes," said Moore, "I have done it. I have looked up Shakespeare. Do you remember what Shylock says, to prove that a Jew is, after all, a man? 'Hath not a Jew eyes? Hath not a Jew hands, organs, dimensions, senses, affections, passions? fed with the same food, hurt with the same weapons, subject to the same diseases, healed by the same means, warmed and cooled by the same winter and summer, as a Christian is? If you prick us, do we not bleed? If you tickle us, do we not laugh? If you poison us, do we not die?' Now everyone of these marks my Amelia has; so I say she is a genuine woman. Why, if you tickle her, she will laugh!"

"No one is likely to tickle her," I said.

"No; but after our last experience it is well to be prepared for all emergencies."

In this case, however, I did not make an experiment. Moore's word was enough. If the creature's smile was so detestable, what must her laugh be like?

After her time of seclusion, Amelia again appeared in Society, and was again the cynosure of all eyes, chiefly, however, of the four owned by Burton and Calder. These latter had never ceased to make inquiries after her health.

I had often wondered whether Burton had noticed that the scratch of the pin had drawn no blood; but his conduct afterwards set me at ease. If he had seen it he had probably thought that his Venus was too ethereal to bleed even the thinnest celestial ichor.

Though Amelia certainly could not feel, yet there was no doubt that in the future she would bleed if pricked, and I was free from anxiety on that score. But there was one thing which caused me considerable uneasiness. She was a girl of originality—indeed, I venture to think that there has never been a girl quite like her—yet there was a sameness, an artificiality, about her which puzzled and alarmed me. To the same question she always and inevitably returned the same answer. On topics of the day she always had the same opinion, expressed in the same words. My rival, Sir John Bolas, who didn't like her for some reason or other, used to say that in her company he always felt as if talking to a very well-trained parrot. She uttered her opinions as if they had been learnt verbatim from someone else.

The time drew near for Calder and Burton to declare themselves. I need not say that, closely as I watched the doings of Amelia, I was not present on these auspicious occasions. But I can distinctly assert, nevertheless, from my knowledge of human nature, that the language of Calder, who came second, was almost precisely the same as that of Burton, who had the first chance. Hence it followed, with mathematical certainly, that Amelia's reply would be the same to both.

Here was a pretty predicament! What I had blamed in her was her unwomanly constancy; but this very constancy had led—as I was sure both *a priori* and from the happy faces of the two young men—to a display of fickleness unparalleled in the whole history of womankind. Within an hour after accepting Burton the faithless creature accepted Calder in almost identically the same terms. Even the most heartless of coquettes had surely never been guilty of such conduct as this.

All this, however, was for the present merely a plausible conjecture, based upon a more or less certain knowledge of character. To make sure of it, I determined to ask. The result but too sadly confirmed my fears. Burton was almost delirious with joy.

"She is mine," he said; "and that beast Calder was never in it with her. To think that I should ever have been afraid of a cad like that!"

I congratulated him, as in duty bound, and spent an hour with him, which may have been pleasant to him, but became very tedious to me, so difficult was it to get him off his one eternal topic and induce him to talk like a rational being. At last, however, I managed to effect my escape, and made my way to Calder. He also received me very graciously.

"Old man," he said, "I have good news to tell you. Amelia has just consented to be engaged to me."

"Indeed!" I replied; "I am very pleased to hear it. You are a happy man, Dick."

"Yes," he said, "happier than I deserve. But what delights me almost as much as having won her is that she never gave a thought to that fellow Burton. If I had had any sense I must have seen that a girl like her could never be taken in by a wretched fellow like him; but somehow I managed to be jealous of him. Well, *that's* all over, thank goodness. I really believe I shall get to like him now I'm sure he can do me no harm."

And so the young fellow chatted on, cutting me to the heart with almost every sentence that he uttered. What a dreadful awakening I was preparing for him! For of course, the awful truth must be told him, that he and his rival had fallen in love with a sham. It would be an awkward moment for both of us. Should I tell him now, and get it over? On the whole I preferred to put it off, and consult Moore first. His fertile brain would suggest a way out of the difficulty. Perhaps he would make a second automaton that would do for one of the rival suitors, while the other kept to Amelia. At any rate, I preferred to get his advice before acting. He had made the Phantasm bleed; might he not get us out of this still more unpleasant position?

I told him of the new complication. To my surprise he made light of it.

"Well?" he said, when I had finished my recital.

"Well?" I replied, "I should think that was enough."

"Why," he said, "I can see nothing wonderful in that. The wonder would be if they *hadn't* proposed to her. Women have had offers before now."

"But you can't intend to let things go on as they are?" I cried.

"That's exactly what I *do* intend," he answered. "Why should I interfere?"

"But think of it for one moment," I said. "Two men in love with the same automaton; two men in the position of accepted lovers at the same moment! Think of even *one* man in that position! How awful it is—why, it is too dreadful to think of!"

"Then I shan't think of it," he answered coolly. "My dear fellow, what is there so strange in it all? Men have been in love with stone-like women before this. Men have given themselves up to heartless and soulless abstractions before this. Anyone who gets my Amelia will get *something,* at any rate, not a mere doll."

The plain fact dawned on me that Moore's extraordinary success had turned his brain. He had put so much of himself into his automaton that he had positively begun to regard her as a real living being, in whose veins flowed his own blood, in whose nostrils was his own breath. Eve was not more truly bone of Adam's bone than this Amelia was part and parcel of Moore's life.

There was a mysterious union between them which gave me an uncanny feeling of sorcery. Could it be that by some unholy means Moore had succeeded in conveying some portion of his own life to this creature of his brain? I tried to dismiss the thought, for I am a man of science; yet it recurred again and again.

Burton and Calder were engaged to Amelia. It may be easily understood that now and then they came into collision. Sometimes things looked strange to them. Calder once demanded an explanation of his *fiancée* as to the frequency of Burton's visits. She gave him an account that satisfied him, and sealed it with a smile and a kiss that made him feel like a villain for ever doubting her.

People wondered at the confidence with which both the young men asserted that they were the favoured suitors, and admired the daring skill with which Amelia played off one against the other. No one warned the young men; it was none of our business to interfere with them.

In such matters one young man is remarkably similar to another. Their very modes of speech tend to become the same. In asking Amelia to fix the day, need it be wondered at that they used precisely the same terms as have been used by all young men from the day when the nameless suitor of "pretty Jane" promised to buy the ring for his beloved? The result may be easily foreseen. Amelia, by some hidden law of her being, for which not she but perhaps Moore was to blame, could not help fixing the same day for both. Had a third candidate appeared on the scene, she would have fixed the same day for him also.

When I had heard this fatal *dénouement,* I confess that even Moore's influence could not keep me from taking a step on my own account. I would not destroy Amelia, much as I hated her for the trouble she had caused me. Something seemed to tell me that her death would be the certain death of Moore, whose life was bound up in hers as closely as the life of Jacob was bound up in that of Benjamin.

By some subtle process, every time danger threatened Amelia, Moore's spirits seemed to sink; every time she surmounted the danger his spirits rose again. He had put himself into her. I would not destroy her; but I went to Calder and I gave him a pretty plain hint as to the position of affairs between her and Burton. He would not believe me.

"If I thought she was false," he said, "I would stab her where she stood, were it at the very altar. But it cannot be. She has pledged herself to me, and mine she is!"

"I know it for a fact," I answered, "that she has promised to marry Burton on the 29th of February."

"The twenty-ninth," he cried. "Why, that is *my* day, the day on which she promised to marry me."

"Precisely so," I said. "What she means to do I don't know."

"But I know what I mean to do," he answered gloomily. "I will have it out with her."

"No violence."

"None at all. Don't fear me. By Heaven, what a heartless creature. But it can't be true. You are deceiving me."

"Too true. But find out for yourself."

I took my leave, and went home.

I afterwards ascertained what Calder's plan was. He made no inquiry from Amelia; he simply went and begged her to put off the day of his marriage a month, from the twenty-ninth of February to the last day of March. She readily agreed. He then went off and bought a sharp Spanish dagger.

The day of the marriage drew near, and nearer. Every preparation was completed. It was to be fashionable. The church was got ready in expectation of a large assemblage of people. At length the eventful morning dawned. I was to give the bride away to Burton, as after the postponement of Calder's wedding he was the only bridegroom left in the race. We came out and stood before the altar.

As I passed along I noticed two figures in different parts of the building, both familiar to me. They were Moore and Calder. The former was untidy, evidently excited and restless. The latter was scrupulously neat; but he had a strangely determined look on his face. One hand was hidden under the breast of his frock coat.

The service proceeded. Fancy a girl like this being told she was a daughter of Abraham, so long as she was not afraid with any amazement! Certainly a cooler, less perturbed daughter of the patriarch I never saw. She gave the responses in a clear, musical voice. They came to the fatal question—"Wilt thou have this man to be thy husband?"

Before she could answer "I will," there was a sudden confusion; a man rushed forward, drew forth a dagger from his breast, and shouting, "You shall not!" stabbed Amelia to the heart—or rather through the left side of her bodice. She fell to the ground, striking her head heavily as she fell against the rail. There was a whirr, a rush. The anti-phonograph was broken. I bent over her, and opened her dress to staunch the wound. Moore had made no provision for her bleeding *there*. As I drew out the dagger, it was followed by a rush of sawdust.

In the confusion of the strange discovery, no one noticed that a real death was taking place not twenty feet away. As the sexton was clearing out the church, he noticed a man asleep in one of the pews, leaning against a pillar. He went up and touched him; but there was no answer. He shook him; but the man was as heedless as Baal. It was Arthur Moore, and he was dead. He had put his life into his masterpiece; his wonderful toy was broken, and the cord of Moore's life was broken with it.

And as for me, why, I am no longer a fashionable physician. As I write, there are men about me, who talk of me as a *patient*.

Notes

1. *Collected Letters*, I, ed. Dan H. Laurence (New York: Dodd, Mead, 1965), 803.
2. *Pygmalion*, from *Collected Plays with their Prefaces* (New York: Dodd, Mead, 1974). Further references to the play and preface are from this edition.
3. H. G. Wells, *Experiment in Autobiography* (New York: Macmillan, 1934), p. 454.
4. Wells, p. 451.
5. E. E. Kellett, "The Lady Automaton," *Pearson's Magazine* (June, 1901). Quotations are from this edition, which is reprinted here in its entirety.
6. See *Shaw Review*, XVI, 2 (May 1973), "G.B.S. and Science Fiction," ed. John R. Pfeiffer, for a survey of Shaw's interest in, and impact upon, the genre.
7. Lester del Rey, "Helen O'Loy," reprinted in Robert Silverberg, ed., *The Science Fiction Hall of Fame*, I (New York: Doubleday, 1970), 62–73.

Edgar Rosenberg

THE SHAW/DICKENS FILE: 1914 TO 1950. AN ANNOTATED CHECKLIST (CONCLUDED). ADDENDA: 1885 to 1919.

> Sir, Whoever makes an exhaustive search through my writings for quotable aphorisms will have to read a mass of articles, each containing 2000 words or upwards, which have appeared regularly for ten years past in the *Star, World,* and *Saturday Review,* totalling up to from 800,000 to a million words; not to mention my occasional magazine articles and published books. I will undertake the work, as a special favour to you, for the sum of £5000, payable in advance.—G. Bernard Shaw.

This from our sponsor, writing in 1898, ten years before he reached the middle of his journey. Shaw's letter (addressed to the editor of *The Eagle and the Serpent,* a "Journal of Egoistic Philosophy and Sociology") may serve as a warning to compilers, archaeologists, and excavators—in other words, to people like myself, who confidently assume that they can unearth nearly all of Shaw's allusions to a given subject—to Dickens, say—even without benefit of concordances and imperfectly indexed editions. In the headnote to the first instalment of this enterprise, I suggested that another search might yield "100 more allusions to Dickens," leaving the supercilious "but certainly no more than 100" to the reader's powers of inference. But as I have myself uncovered nearly 250 more such references since I began this project, my plea will have to stand as rash and premature. If therefore I now claim that the entries which comprise the bulk of this article conclude the Shaw/Dickens file, first sharpened in the September 1977 issue and continued in the January 1978 issue of *The Shaw Review,* the reader is asked to keep the distinction between "conclusion" and "completion" steadily in mind. For all I know, the job could go on and on like an escalator, and the only reasonable solution therefore is to pull the switch at a given point, and turn off the power once the more obtrusive vehicles have been brought to their destination.

Though the division of the checklist as a whole into three instalments is largely a matter of accident and a function of the two sovereign determinants of all things—Time and Space—in retrospect at least we may lay to our souls the flattering unction that the tri-partite division has a certain organic soundness and even canonical sanction. Of the hundred-odd entries (hyphen optional) which made up the first instalment, some three fourths were taken from the seven volumes of musical and dramatic criticism which Shaw—already a consummate stylist and radically opinionated *frondeur*—contributed between the late 1880s and late 1890s to the three journals he cites in his promotional blurb—by the time this sentence goes to press, the musical notations will have been perfected in Mr. Dan H. Laurence's new edition. Instalment No. 2 covered the twenty years spanning Shaw's most prolific period as a playwright—one of the most astonishingly fertile careers in modern literary history when we remind ourselves that between 1896 and 1915 Shaw wrote no fewer than 26 plays. Still to come, along with *Back to Methuselah, On the Rocks,* and a dozen ha'penny pieces of interest chiefly to people who are interested in everything about Shaw, were *Heartbreak House* and *Saint Joan*—and though it isn't a bibliographer's business to air his critical opinions, I may as well go on record, after doing all this homework, as reading these two late plays in the same radiant light in which Shaw read *Little Dorrit* and *Great Expectations* and in which Gounod heard *Don Giovanni:* as their composer's final and most magisterial artistic statements.

Saint Joan appeared in 1923, and still another 27 years were to pass before Shaw bought his ticket to the stall of night. But the final portion of the Shaw/Dickens checklist is no longer urgently concerned with Shaw the playwright. Instead, these nearly 200 entries, beginning with New Year's Day 1914 and ending a few weeks before Shaw's tumble at Shaw's Corner, give mouth to Shaw the political journalist, pamphleteer, crusader, and Wise Old Man, whose wisdom may grate on our political sensibilities and whose loquacity—strident, repetitious, bellicose—may betray, here and there, the mildly paranoid truculence of the very old (it was "the giant Goethe" who affirmed "*Ein alter Mann ist stets ein Koenig Lear*"), but whose mind, at 80, is keen enough to retrieve the Whole of Dickens in twenty pages and, at 94, tidy enough to tip a farewell wink towards Sloppy.

Those of us who, like the Duke in *As You Like It* and the Reverend Alexander Stewart in Shaw's review of Stewart's folkloric insanity, find sermons in stones and books in running brooks, may find plots in telephone directories; and the register which follows is no exception. Apart from occasional sallies into dramatic commentary, its plot is glued together by three or four pervasive themes: Shaw's problematic stance during World War I and its aftermath; his attitude towards the endless disturbances in Ireland; his blinkered fixation on the rise of Fascism and its eruption into World War II; and—to modern readers weariest, most stale, flat, and unprofitable—his hobbyhorsical ambles, tittups, and Dead Marches over the stubble fields of phonetics: sermons the more exasperating in their lithoid sameness when after all phonetics (not, one would think, one of the vital issues of the century nor on the face of it productive of romantic interest) had yielded Shaw's most popular and lucrative creative work. But these are the dominants only: the fact is that Shaw, of course, has something to say on every subject under the moon—now (rising to the imperative mood) defending traffic violations, provided that the traffic violation issues in nothing worse than canicide; now (lapsing into the subjunctive—or optative—mood) speculating on his provender while on a bombing mission over Tokyo at the recruiting age of 86. In less sanguinary intervals, he resumes his great debate with that friendly foe G.K.C. and with Saint Gilbert's acolytes, Cecil and Hilaire; elsewhere the political baggage is left behind and we are treated to snapshots of Ellen and of Stella.

The extracts from these compositions reveal some of Shaw's finest prose and some of his most arid stuff—as well as his unhappy Honey-thundering in Tyrant Adolf's Golden Days. The splendid evocation of Shaw's ride to the front near Ypres, for example, that journalistic glimpse of *Heartbreak House* in cameo, might have been written in a moment of inspired lunacy by essayists like Orwell or Graham Greene—had Orwell or Greene shared Shaw's blackening humor. Here are two slides. On the first, a headless soldier lies by the roadside while the Boche sends over his murderous percussion instruments. Then Shaw, with unparalleled impertinence, flashes the next slide on the screen: Mrs. Nickleby's mad suitor tossing cucumbers over the garden wall in one of Dickens's silliest lapses into adolescent horseplay. This is Shaw Pleasant, Shaw Our Contemporary. Shaw Unpleasant is the Shaw who in his lifelong battle against parliamentary babble found his music cure from Boodledom in nothing more uplifting than the lurid broadcasts from the Berlin Sportpalast by a more devilish Wagnerite disciple, and in the high-pitched noises of the fiddler on the Roman balcony; who palmed off Dickens as a proto-Fascist, and, in one of those mind-boggling *thulas* which give the whole reductive show away, kept trotting him onstage, goose-stepping across the boards in single file with Cromwell, Ruskin, Carlyle, Kemal, Hitler, Stalin, Mosley, Mussolini, the Mikado, and Pilsudski—any two of whom would have been at each other's throats the minute Shaw's back was turned. To claim that in his dalliance with dictatorships Shaw displayed a desperate predictability will not justify him to posterity; but his fierce reasonableness at least led him to pounce on racist theories as "pathological"—in one of his columns he packed off Hitler to an analyist—and kept him from succumbing to the mindless blood-and-soil humbug to which great men of Hamsun's stature drowsily succumbed. More surprising perhaps in the veteran of the War for Women's Liberation and Ibsen's chief apostle are the intermittently sardonic sexist noises by the aging Shaw—tinged, as they are, by a certain good-humoured tolerance. Why all this flimflam about women's suffrage in his feud with Joad and why (as late as '44) his gibes at Nancy Astor, Mrs. Pankhurst, and her sansculottist saboteuses? In view of these embattled matters, it would be tempting to ask Shaw's opinion of the League of Women Voters or of Equal Rights Employers—at worst, we may provoke a twitting reference to Mrs. Micawber's tag line or the bilious charge to consult Chapter 10 of *Little Dorrit*. Meanwhile, we may console ourselves with the reflection that until the day the ancient morsel finally gave in to the almighty evolutionary appetite, he provided enough answers (solicited or unsolicited) to see us through at least the next infidel half century.

I note lastly that the checklist which follows differs from the earlier ones in being markedly sparser and less far-ranging in its references, less exuberantly allusive, and that in general it lacks the "omniverous exultation" which Chesterton in mouthy wise ascribed to Whitman. Instead of drawing omniverously on the characters and on their verbal icons to point his moral and adorn his paragraphs, the older Shaw is increasingly fascinated by the example of Dickens the man and seeks out his instances not so much in the novels as in the Life: in Dickens's class status and class consciousness, his (alleged) political and economic ideologies, his view from the reporter's gallery, his domestic chagrins, his lethal American tour, his lethal public readings, his lethal dipsomania (not even Shaw is exempt from the tic which seems to afflict every Dickensian worth his salt, of writing out so many autopsy reports to Dickens that the imagination reels under these mortal blows)—and his failure to pose in the nude. And, of course, the calamity endured by any writer chained to the Phoenician alphabet, when 16 letters in addition would have been certain to produce more Pips and Dorrits.

The reader who finds a good many of these entries too gaunt and austere for his taste may skip ahead to the appended roster, in which I bring on Shaw in his ebullient nonage. Of the eighty entries or so which comprise the Appendix, the bulk are taken from the literary reviews which Shaw contributed to the *Pall Mall Gazette* between May

1885 and December 1888 and the art columns he wrote for *The World* between February 1886 and May 1889. They thus antedate the musical and dramatic criticism featured in Round One of the Shaw/Dickens roster; that is, the notes produced by Corno di Bassetto come in at the point at which the unsigned art notices leave off. Neither the matter in the *Gazette* nor in the *World* has been collected; a few of the book reviews have been published by Dan H. Laurence in earlier issues of *The Shaw Review,* and a dozen more, in which Shaw takes notice of some major and some major-minor novelists, have been conveniently assembled in Stanley Weintraub's volume of Shaw's non-dramatic literary criticism. But the entire caboodle really ought to be on display. Shaw "did" nearly 150 reviews for the *Gazette,* in which he applied his lens to easily twice as many books (I haven't counted them): a good many of the notices are in the nature of omnibus reviews, one of them embalming all of 22 volumes of poetry—or what might pass for poetry. Stylistically alone they seem to me as trenchant as the musical critiques which supplanted them, and though nine-tenths of the authors have been ground to dust by the tooth of time, their works not only reflect contemporary tastes but (more to our immediate purpose) have been dignified by Shaw's solicitude, deservedly or no. More often no—that goes without saying. Books on ectoplasmic hocus-pocus; inane political pamphlets; histories of music by tone-deaf musicologists; fake silver-spoon romances on which Mrs. Whititerly's granddaughters might have fed; chronicles of the nobility to edify Mrs. Pocket's feeble offspring—a gorgeous late-Victorian *Dunciad* in which it would be difficult to prophesy the election lights on any one, for virtually all of it seems hedged in by royalty-elect. Moreover, in this universal darkness Shaw discovers chinks of light: it is pleasant, for example, to come upon his scrupulously sporting judgment of Paul Heyse, the German Ibsenist playwright-novelist and translator of Leopardi, who preceded Shaw to Stockholm by 15 years.* The museum pieces are rather more perfunctory, but even they contain some wildly funny bits and pieces; and Shaw on Whistler or on Jan Van Beers or on a Mrs. Stillman, who paints Dante as a "moping, medieval Mrs. Gummidge," is at least worth an admission ticket at half price. Apart from the book reviews and art columns, the backpage entries offer some of Shaw's liveliest, most intimate and most prolonged encounters with Dickens: in things like the splendid article on *Pickwick;* the early fragment "From Dickens to Ibsen," unique in its sympathetic treatment of the very novels Shaw

---

*For a fuller view, the extracts from the *Gazette* should be implemented by the very few items (Nos. 2, 3, 9, 10, and 11) which I had in hand in time to run in the September '77 issue of *The Shaw Review.*

consistently dismissed in favor of the later books; the comprehensive letter to Kate Perugini of June 1903; and the delightful piece "Best Books for Children"—the best books, of course, being those which Shaw himself enjoyed in infancy.

Instalment No. 2 in January '78 concluded with an entry for December 1915; Instalment No. 3 picks up with January 1914. To purists who object to this highhanded disregard of the canonical proprieties, I should explain that of the entries for the years 1914–1916 easily half came to my notice only after the '78 manoeuvers, and it seemed reasonable to accommodate material which is substantively so much of a piece in the most nearly appropriate sequence. At that, my dating of the entries is not always Simon-pure. Unlike the extracts printed in the earlier issues, a good deal of the matter which appears below remains not only uncollected but unpublished, with the result that more than half a dozen entries can be dated only by approximation and conjecture; still a few others have to be dismissed with the last resource of the bibliographer: *n.d.*

In conformance with the restraint-of-trade rules set down by the Society of Authors and the Shaw Estate, I have had to curb my itch to quote from the unpublished materials, an act of heroic self-denial in view of the immensely quotable stuff to be found in Shaw's manuscripts and typescripts. The pertinent excerpts from the unpublished articles and correspondence therefore appear in synopsis, synopsis of a kind which (necessarily) deadens all Shavian nuances and inflections. But that, as Bertrand Russell said about the older mathematics, is not my fault. *En recompense,* or *en revanche,* within the limits of the *Shaw* annual, I have thrown temperance to the wind in cribbing from the published pieces and occasionally gone beyond the immediate reference to Dickens: either because the passage defies paraphrase or fragmentation or else because the Dickensian allusion, standing naked and alone, resists inspection unless the context invests it with a halfway intelligible appearance. Besides, the *longueurs* seem to me justified by the comparatively little known and largely inaccessible materials which are brought to market here, particularly those which are plundered from the journalism of the 1880s. At that, even the amplest entries, with their staccato editorial lead-offs, are bound to jar on anybody with an ounce of music in him. All these omissions of articles, pronouns, and modifiers ("Admits to horror of Pickwickian gluttony," etc.) promote a desperate Jinglery; and the abbreviated references to published works (WAYC, WWW) sound like radio stations. For the rest, I follow the editorial procedures outlined in my prefatory flourishes in '77: by marking what seem to me the more important entries with an asterisk; by assigning separate entries to transparently discrete passages from one and the same work; by following an entry with the letter (A) where the allusion seems too trifling to include or where allusions over and above those cited have been dropped; and by signalling in brackets the sources for the more recondite—and some more familiar—Dickens quotes, allusions, character-references. The unpublished matter in the main body of the checklist is taken from the Shaw Collection in the British Library, volumes BL Add. MS 50693 to 50699; the clippings from *The World* and *Pall Mall Gazette* appear in vols. 50691 and 50692, respectively.

I am indebted to Allan Chappelow for elucidating some of the undated passages in his volume *Shaw: "The Chucker-Out"*; to Stanley Weintraub for bringing half a dozen fugitive Shavings to my notice; to Scott McMillin for alerting me to Shaw's annotations to Bunyan's *Mr. Badman*; to Michael Slater for locating a few allusions to Dickens with which not even I was able to cope; to James Tyler, Librarian of the Shaw Collection, Cornell, for providing me with an easeful working base; and to the staff of the British Library, ditto. I owe a yet more substantial debt to Dan H. Laurence for verifying and (more often) correcting my helter-skelter assignment of publication-dates; whatever errors persist are confined to materials which my incurable diffidence kept me from palming off on him. My debt to Martin Quinn is incalculable and scarcely exhausted by the cryptic notation "Quinn," infra.: nearly half of the checklist is based on his research and steady submissions of extracts and clippings; in my perplexed meanderings through the Manuscript Room of the British Library, he played the friendliest Hermes; his name ought ot appear next to mine as co-author of this whole job; and he knows it. To Cornell University I owe thanks for a partial subvention of my musings in London—if not quite to the tune mandated by Shaw in his begging letter (nor payable in advance), at least in a sum proportionable to the difference in word count between his and mine.

Abbreviations for entries in this section as follows: unless otherwise indicated, page-references are to the volumes in the Standard Edition published by Constable & Co., London; in the case of the *Gazette* reviews, place of publication of the book under review is London and year is the year in which both book and review appeared. *AYC: Advice to a Young Critic: Letters 1894–1928* (London: Peter Owen, 1933), ed. E. J. West, 1956; *BH: The Bodley Head Collected Plays*, ed. Dan H. Laurence (7 vols., London: Max Reinhardt, 1970–74); Chappelow: Allan Chappelow, *Shaw: "The Chucker-Out"* (New York: A. M. S. Press, 1971); *CL: Collected Letters*, ed. Dan H. Laurence, 2 vols. I: 1874–97 (New York: Dodd, Mead, 1965); II: 1898–1910 (New York: Dodd, Mead, 1972); *CP: The Complete Prefaces of Bernard Shaw* (London: Paul Hamlyn, 1965); Crompton: Bernard Shaw, *The Road to Equality: Ten Unpublished Lectures and*

Essays, ed. Louis Crompton (Boston: Beacon, 1971); *D: The Dickensian* (London: The Dickens Fellowship, 1905–); *EP: Everybody's Political What's What?* (1944); *ETL: Ellen Terry and Bernard Shaw: A Correspondence*, ed. Christopher St. John (London: Constable, 1931); Hubenka: *Bernard Shaw: Practical Politics: Twentieth-Century Views on Politics and Economics*, ed. Lloyd J. Hubenka (Lincoln, Nebr.: Univ. of Nebraska Press, 1976); *IW: The Intelligent Woman's Guide to Socialism and Capitalism* (1928); *MCr: How to Become a Musical Critic*, ed. Dan H. Laurence (London: Rupert Hart-Davis, 1960); *MI: The Matter with Ireland*, ed. David H. Greene and Dan H. Laurence (London: Rupert Hart-Davis, 1962); *PCH: Peace Conference Hints* (1919), as Ch. 12 of *What I Really Wrote About the War* (1931); *PCL: Bernard Shaw and Mrs. Patrick Campbell: Their Correspondence*, ed. Alan Dent (London: Victor Gollancz, 1952); *PMG: Pall Mall Gazette* (London [1885–88]); *PP: Platform and Pulpit*, ed. Dan H. Laurence (London: Rupert Hart-Davis, 1962); *PPR: Pen Portraits and Reviews* (1932); Quinn: source supplied by Martin Quinn; *SA: Shaw: An Autobiography: Selected from His Writings by Stanley Weintraub*, 2 vols. I: 1856–98 (New York: Weybright & Talley, 1969), II: 1898–1950 (New York: Weybright & Talley, 1970); Smith: *Shaw on Religion*, ed. Warren Sylvester Smith (London: Constable, 1967); *SSS: Sixteen Self-Sketches* (London, 1949); Tauber: *George Bernard Shaw on Language*, ed. Abraham Tauber (New York: Philosophical Library, 1963); *TT:* Archibald Henderson, *Table-Talk of G.B.S.: Conversations . . . Between Shaw and His Biographer* (New York: Dodd, Mead, 1925); Weintraub: *Bernard Shaw's Nondramatic Literary Criticism*, ed. Stanley Weintraub (Lincoln, Nebr.: Univ. of Nebraska Press, 1972) West: *Shaw on Theatre: Sixty Years of Letters, Speeches, and Articles . . .* ed. E. J. West (New York: Hill & Wang, 1958); Wilson: *Shaw on Shakespeare: An Anthology of Bernard Shaw's Writings on the Plays and Production of Shakespeare*, ed. Edwin Wilson (London: Cassell, 1962); Wisenthal: *Shaw and Ibsen: Bernard Shaw's The Quintessence of Ibsenism and Related Writings*, ed. J. L. Wisenthal (Toronto: Univ. of Toronto Press, 1979); *World: The World* (London [1886–89]; *WWW: What I Really Wrote About the War* (1931).

III. 1914 to 1950

277. 1 Jan 1914, "The Peace of Europe and How to Attain It," *Daily News; WWW*, p. 16. Sardonically condones "the modern nostrum of hygienic war" so long as it isn't "forced upon foreigners nor made an obstacle to the business of the world. Let those who believe in it repair to Salisbury Plain and blaze away at one another. . . . They can then return to civil life purified by artillery fire and display those qualities which have made the title of Old Soldier so expressive that Dickens applied it even to a particular sort of woman" [Annie Strong's mother, Mrs. Markleham, *Copperfield*, ch. 16 and passim].

278. 22 Aug 14, "Mr. Shaw's Contribution to the 'Daily News,'" to the Editor of *The Saturday Review*. Agrees with the "miscreant" writing in *Daily News* that the violation of Belgian neutrality is a red herring and persists in maintaining "(naming no names, as Miss Squeers said when she, too, felt annoyed) ... that if Belgium had never been touched we should still have been bound to stand by France ... in its struggle against Prussian militarism ..." [*Nickleby*, but the words, though in character, nowhere to be found (by me)].

279. 14 Nov 14, "Are We Hypocrites?" in "Common Sense About the War," *New Statesman* Special Supplement; *WWW*, p. 34. On the "peculiar psychology of English statesmanship." The English a byword for "incorrigible hypocrisy." Just so: "The world has no greater interest in branding England with this particular vice ... than in branding France with it; yet the world does not cite Tartuffe as a typical Frenchman as it cites Angelo [*Measure for Measure*] and Pecksniff as typical Englishmen." Pecksniff not "so exceptional an Englishman in America as he is in England."

280. 19 Dec 14, "Nonsense About Neutrality," *WWW*, p. 141. Invasion of Belgium by Germany and Allies. English insistence on neutrality seems "forced and pompous on the continent." If Britons persist in their pious convictions, they'll find themselves "in the position of Mr. Pickwick when he was angry with Captain Boldwig for putting him in the pound. 'Perhaps,' said his candid friend, 'he might say that some of us had been taking too much milk punch' [Wardle to Pickwick, ch. 19]. And perhaps the Imperial Chancellor might remark slyly that for people who made the Opium War and sacked the Summer Palace, we are surprisingly particular."

281. 23 Jan 1915, "Chestertonism and the War," *New Statesman*; *WWW*, p. 178. Review of Cecil Chesterton's *The Prussian Hath Said in His Heart—*, "the readablest and quite the maddest book produced by the war." The Chestertons—G.K. and Cecil—like the Post Impressionists, are masters of the latest academic form, "intolerably hampered by so much ready-made ... thoughtstuff." Post Impressionist credo, "Unless you become as a cave man again, you can achieve nothing really alive in design and colour" adopted by G.K. and Cecil who "whilst retaining the technique of Scott, Dickens, and Macaulay, which they handle with careless ease ... disgorged [Copernicus, Galileo, and Bacon] readily enough, but could not give up Fielding and Dickens."

282. 23 Jan 15, "Chestertonism and the War," *WWW*, p. 179. Cecil's claim in public on the greater credibility of miracles than the fallibility of the Church: GBS "restrained only by [his] unfortunate shyness in rising like the elder Weller and giving three cheers for so heroic an act of modernist abnegation" [on Sam Weller's decision to remain in Pickwick's service, ch. 56].

283. 6 March 15, "To the Editor of *The Nation*," reply to a letter (*Nation*, 27 Feb signed by one "Buzfuz," Donegal, 21 Feb), "Buzfuz" insisting that the Belgians are entitled "to invite assistance from their neighbors...." Shaw: "'Buzfuz' gives his address as Donegal. Impossible. No Irishman could be so obtuse. I disposed of the figment of neutrality by the well-known Euclidian method of the *reductio ad absurdum*. 'Buzfuz' produces the additional absurdity that Belgium violated her own neutrality in resisting German invasion ... and then assumes that he has reduced *me* to absurdity. What are you to do with such people?" [*Pickwick*, ch. 34].

284. 15 May 15, to Mrs. Patrick Campbell, *PCL*, p. 175. The Censor's ghastly suspicions that Shaw's cablegram references to Jorkins and Spenlow "concealed military secrets to be transmitted to Germany" [*Copperfield*, esp. chs. 23, 35].

285. 13 March 1916, "The German War Book and the British Limit," *New Statesman*; *WWW*, p. 165. Rev. of *The German War Book* ... issued by the General Staff of the

German Army, trans. J. H. Morgan. "I opened [the book] with eager anticipation of having my blood raised to boiling point by a manual of such cynical perfidy and cruelty as only the stony heart and brazen forehead of the Prussian enemy could set down in print.... The publishers promised me [on the dust-jacket] to make my flesh creep" [Joe, *Pickwick*, ch. 8].

286. 13 March 16, "The German War Book," *WWW*, p. 171. February supplement of *Berliner Tageblatt* comments on the unprovoked seizure of the Danish fleet by the British in 1807; *Tageblatt* quotes debate in Parliament justifying its *coup de main* and "simply adds: 'Eines Kommentars werden diese Zitate kaum beduerfen' ['These quotations scarcely require commentary']." While the newspaper can't condemn Britain and Canning without condemning Germany and Chancellor Bethmann-Hollweg, by the same token Britain can't condemn Germany and her chancellor without convicting Britain and Canning. "Let Mr. Podsnap, at present distracting us from the serious work of beating the Germans by his blatant trumpetings of his moral superiorities, take needful note, and, in the happy phrase of Mr. H. G. Wells, 'cease flapping his mouth on the foe.' "

287. 13 May 16, "War Reputations," *To-day; WWW*, p. 212; earlier as "Scarecrows and Bluff Won't Frighten Germany," *New York American*, 7 May. Jingoism and distortions by the press and party leaders. Shaw's intimacy with the "people who are really running the war," whose contempt for the press and the party brass match his own, and in whose company he is "free from the asphyxiating vapors of spite and panic, greed and terror, Pecksniffery and Podsnappery, which rise and enfold us in paper clouds every morning and afternoon from Fleet Street."

*288. 13 May 16, "The Case Against Chesterton," *New Statesman* (pp. 133–36). Sustained debate with GKC, with constant reference to Dickens. Ostensibly a temperate review of Julius West's *G. K. Chesterton: A Critical Study*. But West encourages the "overdone" and reductive view of GKC as a Catholic Tory and GBS as an "utter Puritan.... Nor does Mr. Chesterton's outlook on politics resemble that of Sir Leicester Dedlock. I suggest ... that this use of Puritan and Catholic and Tory as abusive epithets, though exhilarating, is apt to mislead those who are not in on the family joke" (p. 133).

289. 13 May 16, "The Case Against Chesterton," p. 134. Chesterton's extravagantly "romantic imaginary public-house." *Per* Shaw, "he ekes out his taproom stories of Dickens and Jacobs with memories of one or two reluctant visits to saloon bars in the Strand to avoid hurting the feelings" of his hosts. Chesterton's delight "on a shiny night ... to *épater*, not *le bourgeois*, but the extreme left, the revolutionists, ... the Dwellers on the Threshold of the millennium." By all means, let him "pitch into the teetotallers, the Protestants, the Agnostics, the Scientists, ... the Jews, the Pacificos, the Eugenicans, the Suffragists, the Socialists, and, when the feeble-minded and the children are in question, into all the tribe of Mr. Honeythunder ..." [*Drood*, ch. 17 and passim].

290. 13 May 16, "The Case Against Chesterton," p. 135. Chesterton's sentimental solutions. As a "sound Dickensian," Chesterton objects to Jo's poverty; his hypothetical remedy: invest Jo's mother with the responsibility of rearing him decently. "Now that may solve the problem for Jo A ... whose mother is [one] in a thousand"; not for Jo B and C and D. "Will [Chesterton] say ... that he had rather see Jo free ... than inspected or torn from his mother's arms? Not without denying ... Dickens, who was always himself Honeythundering at 'my lords and right honourables and wrong honourables of every degree' to officiously make Jo their business [*Bleak House*, ch. 47]; to demolish Tom-All-Alone's; to endow and inspect and clean up; and to replace Mrs. Pardiggle and Bumble and Gradgrind, not by beer and jollity

and the fighting part of knighterrantry and medieval religion, but by the sworn enemy and destroyer of the accursed Poor Law: ... by Mr. Sidney Webb. He no sooner showed how Mrs. Pardiggle, fool and snob and self-elected irresponsible uninspected inspector, made the miserable savages she inspected worse [ch. 8], than he went on to show how the two decent ladies she brought with her made them better. The bond of sympathy between Mr. Sidney Webb and myself is that we were brought up on *Little Dorrit.* No use coming Dickens over us." [I find no record of Mrs. Pardiggle's two decent companions on a subsequent visit to the brickmaker's but am willing to pit Shaw's memory against mine.]

291. 13 May 16, "The Case Against Chesterton," p. 135. On Chesterton's anti-Modernism and ignorance "in the technical sphere" of politics and economics. If he is any less ignorant than Dickens on conversational subjects like "Evolution and Natural Selection ... and about Eugenics, about Darwin and Mendel, Bergson and Butler, Herz and Marconi" you would never guess it from his writings.

292. 13 May 16, "The Case Against Chesterton," p. 136. Chesterton's play *Magic,* in its omission of sexual intrigue and display of "all the essential tricks of the stage" fully "in the tradition of Shakespeare ... and Dickens, in which you must grip your character so masterfully that you can play with it in the most extravagant fashion ... The Duke in *Magic* is much better than Micawber or Mrs. Wilfer, neither of whom can bear the footlights because, like piping bullfinches, they have only one tune, whilst the Duke sets everything in the universe to the most ridiculous music. That is the Shakespearian touch."

293. 1 June 16, "To the Editor of *The New Witness.*" In answer to Gilbert Chesterton's "The Three Witnesses and the Law of Rent" in previous number of journal. [The 3 are Gilbert and Cecil Chesterton and Hilaire Belloc.] Largely restatement of the Jo problem (290, supra). "St. Gilbert's solution is ... [to] give some of the wealth to Jo's family, and then make it reasonably responsible to Jo.... Mrs. Webb deals with the cases in which Jo has no family, and those other cases in which Jo's family is so hopelessly incapable of being made reasonably responsible to anybody that it would be spiritual and perhaps physical murder to leave him in his family's hands.... As to the 'return to small properties,' that means Dedlock without his tradition of *noblesse oblige,* and Rouncewell, or rather Bounderby (the corrected version of Rouncewell) without a factory code.... St. Gilbert is a heroic highwayman of the royal road."

294. 10 June 16, "The Case Against Chesterton," to the Editor of *The New Statesman.* In reply to Chesterton's questions, who will restore any sort of liberty to Jo and Jo's mother once they have been divested of it, Shaw: either assure me that an "Act for the protection of Jo [is] passed ... enforced, [and] ... left unrepealed"; or keep Jo safe from Mother. "I do not want to deprive Jo's mother of self-direction: I am not a distiller. I want to deprive her of Jo-misdirection; and if Mr. Chesterton imagines that I long to restore it to her ... he little knows his man."

295. 10 June 16, "The Case Against Chesterton." Vs. Chesterton's bias in favor of private charity, which for Shaw "is the remedy of Sir Leicester Dedlock and of Snagsby. There is no more biting satire in literature than the story of [Snagsby] helplessly watching Jo dying of a socially preventible disease (lest his mother's self-direction should be compromised) and piling useless half-crowns on the table to relieve his futile compassion whilst he idiotically babbles '*Our* Father' to the child who is gasping his life out because nations have never been taught to say 'Our Children.' Mr. Chesterton 'sees himself,' as the actors say, as Snagsby. I do not. I feel like giving Mr. Chesterton a terrible lesson ..." [*Bleak House,* ch. 47. But the "babbling idiot" is Allan Woodcourt, not Snagsby].

296. 10 June 16, "The Case Against Chesterton." On the pragmatic vs. Chestertonian ways of reducing poverty. "... poverty can be got rid of only by legislators ... who are also very highly qualified as lawyers and economists, and ... just the sort of brainy, conscientious, 'dry' people the trueborn Englishman loathes from the bottom of his soul.... The battle of St. George with the Dragon is sordid and prosaic beside the battle of Mrs. Sidney Webb with Lord George Hamilton for the souls and bodies of the children of the poor.... It is true that Mrs. Webb is not like Esther Summerson. If she began to resemble that pre-Ibsenist ideal of her sex, Mr. Chesterton would be the first to implore her ... to retrace her steps ere it were too late. Esther left the brickmakers to their fate and to their freedom and to the ways of the poor. Even Mrs. Pardiggle had more social conscience than that. Esther's idea of helping them was to put her handkerchief over the face of a dead baby [*Bleak House*, ch. 8]. Its father subsequently sold the handkerchief to Esther's mother [*sic*] and drank the proceeds. Mrs. Webb keeps her handkerchiefs and looks the dead babies in the face, swearing that they shall not die if she can help it.... After all, it may be possible to combine the whirlwind social activity of Mrs. Pardiggle with the sympathy and goodwill of Esther. But no combination will be of any use without experience, an arduous study, and a tremendous documentation." [Another patch on Shaw: no such handkerchief sale on record; ch. 35 reveals that Lady Dedlock bought it from the wife in the drunken husband's absence—though he may well have drunk the proceeds.]

297. 15 June 16, "Mr. Belloc and Rent," to the Editor of *The New Witness*. Spars with Belloc on the problems of economic rent and diminishing returns. Belloc as an economist of the Gradgrind school.

298. 20 July 16, "A Reply on the Debate," *The New Witness*. On the distribution of economic rent: vs. Belloc and Cecil Chesterton. Disclaims any knowledge of the French peasantry beyond their depiction by Zola and Millet, but knows that "law or no law, primogeniture is a necessity to the present proprietor, and the younger son ... has to be got rid of as the gentlemen in the Fleet prison got rid of Mr. Pickwick when he was chummed on them" [ch. 42].

299. 20 July 16, "A Reply on the Debate." His nonage in the office of an Irish land agent, "playing the part of Pancks in cottages ... where old women cursed me for the deadly sin of oppressing the poor, and holding lordly collections of farmers' rents at the best hotel in the country town, being myself as helpless a wheel in the social machines as they" [*Dorrit*, I, 13 and passim].

300. 6 Jan 1917, "On British Squealing, and the Situation after the War," *New Republic; WWW*, p. 194. Rev. of Cecil Chesterton's *The Perils of Peace*, intro. Hilaire Belloc. Chesterton's pacifist but rabidly Germanophobe book applies "nursery morality to diplomacy and war." The imperative need for preparedness, habitually ignored at home and abroad. "Mr. Spenlow, who was so eloquent as to the positive wickedness of not making a will, died intestate [*Copperfield*, ch. 38]; and all these terrible Iron Chancellors and Brass Tamburlaines ... who, when the Kaiser rushes into their bedroom and cries 'War is declared' mumble 'Third portfolio on the left' and go to sleep again, are humbugs like Mr. Spenlow."

301. 24 Feb 17, "A Jester's Dilemma: Mr. Bernard Shaw's Reply," to the Editor of *The Morning Post*. Rebuttal to column (*Morning Post*, 13 Feb) entitled "The Jester's Dilemma," accusing Shaw of supporting E. D. Morel's denunciations of Belgian atrocities in the Congo and British atrocities elsewhere. "Fighting [Morel] by feeble insinuations that he is ... an agent of the Hohenzollerns is even worse business than fighting Germany by alleging that the Crown Prince purloins spoons ... for until the war is over it cannot be proved that the Crown Prince is not the Artful

Dodger in uniform, whereas Mr. Morel can stuff your own testimonials to his resplendent virtues down your throat at a moment's notice...."

302. 5 March 17, "I. Bombardment," *The Daily Chronicle;* WWW, p. 249. Shaw on the Western front near Ypres. "A man lying by the roadside was not a tramp taking a siesta, but a gentleman who had lost his head. There was no Belgian carillon, but plenty of German music: an imposing orchestration in which all the instruments were instruments of percussion. I cannot honestly say I disliked it: the big drum always excites me. I was not yet in the town; but I was unmistakeably in the Ypres salient; and the Boche was 'sending them over' as persistently as the gentleman next door to Mrs. Nickleby sent cucumbers and marrows over the garden wall [ch. 41]. I was reminded of him by the fact that in the whole countryside there was an extraordinary prevalence of gas and gaiters [ch. 49]. Boom! whizzzzzz!! Boom! whizzzzzz! ... all *fortissimo diminuendo;* then, *crescendo molto subito,* Whizzzzz—bang clatter! In such a bang and clatter had the gentleman by the roadside lost his head!"

303. 8 March 17, "The Shaw Worm Turns on Wells," to the Editor of *The New Witness.* Wells's misapplication in his *War and the Future* (1916) of Shaw's definition of Superman in *Man and Superman* and his popshots at "the megalomaniac school of Nietzsche and Shaw." Suggests that Wells modify the passage in his next edition; admits to presumptuousness in his attempt "to re-write anything for Mr. Wells; still, as Alfred Jingle said, 'Not presume to dictate; but boiled fowl and mushrooms capital thing ...' " [*Pickwick,* ch. 2].

304. 24 March 17, "Brogue-Shock," *The Nation* (London); *MI,* p. 138. On the Home Rule debate following the 1916 insurrection. "That is England all over: fighting millions of the most elaborately equipped ... soldiers in Europe with gigantic strength and unconquerable obstinacy, and jumping up on her chair with shrieks of terror when a mouse squeaks at her with an Irish brogue. What a people! ... One rather awkward consideration against [the Ulster proposal] is that there would be two parties to each transfer, and they might not always agree. Ulster, in her determination never to desert Mr. Micawber, has taken his welcome for granted; but it lacks confirmation" [*Copperfield,* ch. 12 and passim].

305. 22 June 1918, "Scotch Opera," *The Nation; MCr,* p. 302. Beecham's The Valkyrie ("Hunnishly known as Die Walkuere") at Drury Lane. Agnes Nicholls as Brynhild in excellent voice, "but I ask how any woman can be expected to look like a valkyrie, or feel like one, or move like one, in the skirt of an ultra-womanly woman of the period when a female who climbed to the top of an omnibus would have been handed [over] to the police as a disgrace to her sex? ... Why on earth does not Sir Thomas throw all this ragbag rubbish of fifty years ago into the dustbin, and make his valkyries look like valkyries and not like Mrs. Leo Hunter? The thing is beyond patience; I pass on" [*Pickwick,* ch. 15].

306. 4 Oct 18, to Alfred Cruikshank, acknowledging Cruikshank's monograph *The Truth About Hamlet,* Wilson, p. 79. "... you are too kind to Shakespear in trying to explain away the inky cloak scene. Shakespear, like Dickens, like Cervantes, like most geniuses of their type, made the acquaintance of their characters as they went along. Dick Swiveller on his first appearance is quite a loathsome stage villain from whom the heroine is to be rescued at the last moment. Pickwick and Don Quixote begin as mere contemptible butts.... But these puppets spring to life after the first two or three pulls of the strings and become ... very alive and real characters. I see no reason to doubt that the same thing happened during the writing of Hamlet."

307. 14 Oct 18, "Sir Edward Carson's Other Island," *Daily News* (London); *MI,* p. 187.

On Carson's opposition to Home Rule (expressed in an interview in *National News*, 13 Oct) on the grounds that separation would be disastrous both for England and Ireland. Shaw: "Home Rule for Ireland is not Separation: it is the alternative to Separation.... [England, Scotland, Ireland] suffer from the fact that their common Parliament... is nobody's Parliament.... It is pompous, windy, ignorant, despised, and *found out*. What Dickens knew about it fifty years ago the world knows now."

308. Nov 1918, "Is Dickens a 'Washout'?" Depositions by Gosse, Zangwill, GBS et al., *Strand* LVI, 340. "Mont Blanc is a 'washout' for anyone who has barely enough wind to climb Primrose Hill. Don't trouble about the 'authorities': try the booksellers."

309. 24 March 1919, "Are We Bolshevists?" *The Labour Leader*. "Well, of course, we are." GBS offers two definitions of bolshevism: socialism; government of the masses "by a mixture of cajolery and coercion...." British bolshevists differ from the native article in their aims; where "Lenin coerces and cajoles in the interests of those whom he coerces and cajoles... in the name of the prophet Marx" their British brethren "(Like Fanny Squeers I name no names and say 'Let them as the cap fits, wear it') coerce and cajole in the interests of property, without bothering about prophets. Profits are good enough for them" [*Nickleby*, see 278 supra].

310. 24 May 19, "How Frank Ought to Have Done It," *SSS*, p. 126. "Shaw [speaking of himself] is the greatest pedant alive. Dickens's man who ate crumpets on principle could not hold a candle to him..." [in Sam Weller's story in the Fleet, *Pickwick*, ch. 33].

311. 24 May 19, "How Frank Ought to Have Done It," *SSS*, p. 128. Chastity as powerful an incentive to the playwright as sex is; its suppression "on the scale on which the [sexual] instinct has been starved... would wreck any civilization." On intellectual passion: "the modern notion that passion means only sex is as crude... as the ploughman's idea that art is simply bawdiness." Efflorescence of art "when sex is barred, as it was... in the literature which produced Dickens."

312. June 1919, "Nature's Long Credits," Preface, *Heartbreak House*, BH V, 18; *CP*, p. 380. England's political hygiene before the war: "demoralize[d]... with long credits and... overdrafts" before erupting into "catastrophic bankruptcies." Not even CD's "prophetic works [foresaw] the evil of being slaughtered by a foreign foe on our own doorsteps."

313. June 1919, "Evil in the Throne of Good," Preface, *Hearbreak House*, BH V, 32; *CP*, p. 387. On the unprecedented waste of lives in the war, in which "Shakespears and Platos [would have been] killed outright.... Fools exulted in 'German losses.'... Imagine exulting in the death of Beethoven because Bill Sikes dealt him his death blow!"

314. Summer 1919, quoted in W. Walter Crotch, "The Decline—and After!" *D* XV, 124. GBS's claim to have pilfered characters from CD "with complete success": Jaggers popping up [as Bohun] in *You Never Call Tell;* "Lomax [in *Major Barbara*]... is technically a piece of pure Dickens."

315. 6 Sept 19, "Lord Grey, Shakespeare, Mr. Archer, and Others," *The Nation*. On Archer's cuts in performances of Ibsen. "Mr. Archer declares that I am in principle a liar for saying that he cut [Ibsen], and then goes on to explain that the cuts were only little ones, thus combining Marryatt and Dickens in a masterstroke of invective."

316. 17 Sept 19, in Frank Harris, *Bernard Shaw; D* XV, 71. Harris's "ignorance of Dickens is a frightful gap in [his] literary education." Urged to read late CD.

317. 11 Oct 19, "Wanted: A Strong Government," *The Irish Statesman; MI*, p. 193. "The

castle loves the old saying that the Irish conspirator is a figure of farce...." Comment is accurate if confined "to the Simon Tappertits who form secret brotherhoods and leagues, take oaths, drink out of a skull," etc. "Such conspirators are found everywhere among romantic *poseurs*. Simon Tappertit was an Englishman; and I have known men who held monthly meetings of Leagues of the Proletariats of the World ... with Presidents, minute books, registers of tyrants to be exterminated (after the taste of Madame Defarge).... The climaxes, when every police agent [under Napoleon III] threw off his wig and declaimed 'I am Hawkshaw the detective,' must have been thrilling. These conspiracies of playboys may win promotion for their promoters ... but they are only child's play...."

*318. 21 Nov 19, "Ruskin's Politics," Lecture Given at Ruskin Centenary Exhibition, Royal Academy of Arts; *PP*, pp. 139–40. Takes up the point developed in the Preface to *Hard Times* (1911, pub. 1912) that CD "always appeals to the aristocracy" for reform and allows the working classes to abdicate their powers to the governing bodies. But where Shaw seems to attack this attitude in the Preface, he here endorses it: "That is the attitude of Dickens, and the attitude of Ruskin, and that really is my attitude as well.... To tell the people to make their own laws is to mock them just as I should mock you if I said, 'Gentlemen: you are the people: write your own plays.' ... Ruskin, like Dickens, understood that the reconstruction of society must be the work of an energetic and conscientious minority."

319. ?Dec 1919, "The Drink Question" (BL Add. MS 50696, ff. 373–85, esp. 381). One of Shaw's amplest commentaries on the effects of drugs, caffeine, and alcohol on a dozen actors and writers. Ibsen, a model of sobriety, died of nothing worse than senility; Balzac succumbed to his negligent hygiene; Dickens gulped down doses of firewater the way ordinary creatures change clothes, though nobody would have thought him a bibbler. The Pickwickians are cited, with horror.

320. 24 Dec 19, to Henry Charles Duffin; as "Biographers' Blunders Corrected" [1947–48], *SSS*, p. 98. After reading proof of Duffin's *Quintessence of Bernard Shaw*, corrects Duffin's comment that GBS "[blames] Shakespear and Dickens for making drunkenness and shrewishness a matter of laughter" by repeating Keegan's epigram in *John Bull* and quoted again in *Ibsenism* that " 'every jest is an earnest in the womb of time.' " Evolution apparent in CD: "Mrs MacStinger ... is a joke. As Mrs Gargery ... she is no joke."

321. 24 Dec 19, to Henry Charles Duffin; as "Biographers' Blunders Corrected," *SSS*, p. 103. Claims to be "the only humanitarian writer" who condones child-beating so long as the child refuses to learn by experience; deplores flogging as a corrective to learning-by-rote. "I have insisted that if teaching is to mean nothing but beating a child if it does not give set answers to set questions, then Squeers and Creakle are fully qualified schoolmasters."

322. 1919, "Peace Conference Hints," *PCH* (as "Peace Conference Hints: Enter History: Exit Romance" forms ch. 12 of *What I Really Wrote* ...), *WWW*, p. 299. In *The Daily Chronicle*, Shaw had urged England's alliance with France in case of a German attack on France, and an alliance with Germany in case of a Russian or French or combined attack on Germany. "The dead silence which followed this proposal ... was inevitable; for as I was not a party politician, nor a famous cricketer, jockey, or glovefighter, neither the political columns nor the stunt columns ... were concerned with me: I might as well have been Fielding, Goldsmith, Blake, Dickens, Hardy, Wells, or Bennett for all the attention my political ideas received from the newspapers."

323. 1919, "Peace Conference Hints," *PCH*, *WWW*, pp. 335–36. Woodrow Wilson's demand for the abolition of conscription would be hopelessly circumlocutionized

by the English governing bodies. But GBS himself opposes "the pretence of abandoning warlike intentions" as pure sham. "It is the tragedy of the hypocrite that he is often held to his professions to such an extent that he has to confess to himself ruefully on his deathbed that he might just as well have been born an honest man." [GBS repeatedly views Wilson, his contemporary, as a tragic figure.] (A).

324. 1919, "Peace Conference Hints," *PCH, WWW*, p. 340. On "the national love of lecturing other people on their moral behaviour.... We revelled and wallowed in our superiority to the tearers up of scraps of paper... and to the violaters of the sacred covenant of neutrality. We then discovered that it was necessary... to seize certain Greek islands, and to send troops into Eastern territory.... These high-handed proceedings were quite inevitable. Moral recriminations about it are empty and idle.... But our action knocked the bottom out of all Mr Pecksniff's nonsense about scraps of paper and the sacredness of neutrality."

325. 1919, Introduction to *Trade Unionism for Clerks*, as "The Clerk and the Emperor of China" in *Hearst's* (Jan 1920); *SA* I, 74. GBS's flight from the lifelong drudgery of remaining a clerk: the avenue of escape barred to pathetic hirelings of the Newman Noggs variety [*Nickleby*, 2 and passim].

326. 5 Jan 1920, to Henry Charles Duffin (Univ. of Texas Library; Quinn). The old song: Jaggers as model for Bohun [314 supra; see entries below].

327. 10 Jan 20, "The Betrayal of Ulster," *The Irish Statesman; MI*, p. 240. On Lloyd George's bill (Dec 1919, enacted Dec 1920) providing home rule for 26 southern counties and 6 counties of Ulster. "We cannot deny that the wizard has succeeded. He has not coerced Ulster: he has offered her self-determination.... How simple! How just! How generous! And yet... what is Ulster to do with her self-determination?... Lord Birkenhead [the Lord Chancellor] no more will... raise the cry, 'Gallop apace, ye fiery-footed steeds,' to the defense of the Union: he is asking himself what the deuce he is to do when the Ulster Parliament declares that it never will desert Mr Micawber."

328. 18 Jan 20, to Mrs. Patrick Campbell, *PCL*, p. 202. "Your latest formula, as disclosed to me under threat of instant withdrawal of the play [*Pygmalion*], does not touch me; and I have no objection to it; but oh! what a silly old Mrs. Crummles you are to suppose that your name needs those trimmings!"

329. 31 Jan 20, "I Am a Classic, but Am I Shakespear's Thief?" *Arts Gazette* II; West, p. 131. Reply to C. G. L. DuCann's article "Bernard Shaw as Shakespear-Thief" in *Arts Gazette*, 24 Jan. Dissents from the commonplace, implicit in the title of Du-Cann's piece, that "evolution" is incompatible with literary pillage. Uncritical bias in favor of earlier writers provokes the reminder "that in some respects the work of the juniors makes the work of the seniors childish by comparison." E.g.: Giotto/Velazquez, Shakespear/Ibsen, Dickens/Strindberg, Tchekhov/Shaw.

330. 31 Jan 20, "I Am a Classic," West, p. 132. Limited number of available stage types; hence every writer necessarily a plagiarist. "Fiction is stiff with variants of Don Quixote. The clever servant who supplies the wordly wisdom which his [masters] lack (Sancho Panza, Scapin, Figaro, Sam Weller, Enry Straker) is always with us...."

331. April 1920, "Sir Edward Elgar," *Music and Letters, Harper's Bazaar; MCr*, p. 314. Elgar's lack of pretentiousness and deceptive resemblance to the "typical English country gentleman who does not know a fugue from a *fandango*. The landlady in Pickwick whose complaint of her husband was that 'Raddle ain't like a man' would have said, if destiny had led her to the altar with the composer of the great symphony in A flat, 'Elgar ain't like a musician.' The clique took Mrs. Raddle's view" [Mrs. Raddle to Mrs. Cluppins, *Pickwick*, ch. 46].

332. 23 Feb 1921, "Keats," *The John Keats Memorial Volume* (Keats House Committee, Hampstead); Weintraub, p. 136. Keats's towering geniality shows up the intermittent or debased geniality of his precursors and followers (A).
333. 6 Sept 21, "The British Officer," *The Daily News* (London); *MI*, p. 247. Triumph of the Irish Republican Army over the British military; De Valera's insistence on Irish independence vs Lloyd George's resolve to retain Ireland as military base: "The chronic panic of militarist Imperialism has obsessed him." GBS speculates the P.M.'s next move to lie in a deadly naval armaments race with America: "To such diplomatists [as Lloyd George and Lord Curzon] the difference between their dear friend Japan and their dear friend the United States is only the difference between Codlin and Short; and Mr. Lloyd George's effusive propaganda of gratitude to Japan . . . suggests that in his opinion Codlin's the friend, not Short" [*Old Curiosity Shop*, ch. 19]. Shaw concludes that the military union between Ireland and England will involve a suicidal Irish alliance with England against America for command of the seas.
334. 20 Nov 21, "Tolstoy: Tragedian or Comedian?" Extempore Speech at Tolstoy Commemoration, Kingsway Hall; *PPR*, pp. 261–62; Wilson, p. 243. Mixture of tragedy and comedy increasingly lawless after censorship forced dramatist to take up fiction: "it was practiced by Fielding and culminated in Dickens, whose extravagances would have been severely curbed if he had had to submit his Micawbers and Mrs. Wilfers to the test of representation on the stage, when it would have been discovered at once that their parts are mere repetitions of the same joke, and have none of that faculty of developing and advancing matters which constitutes stage action [cf. 292 supra]. . . . After Dickens, Comedy completed its development into the new species, which has been called tragi-comedy when any attempt has been made to define it." Since Dickens, only Anatole France ("Dickens's French double, disguised by culture") has managed to serve up this "salad of comedy and tragedy. . . ."
335. 20 Nov 21, "Tolstoy: Tragedian or Comedian?" *PPR*, pp. 263–64. Tolstoy the supreme modern tragi-comedian: witness the great opening chapter of "Ivan Ilyich." If CD's people are bombarded by a corkscrew, like the Orfling in *Copperfield* [ch. 11], the comic effect is momentary, whereas "Tolstoy could slay a soul with a corkscrew without letting you know either that he was a humorist or that you are laughing."
336. 11 Dec 21, "Shaw on the Play's Reception" [*Heartbreak House*], *Sunday Express*; *BH* V, 195. The failure of *HH* not due to the press notices but the mounting expense of running a theatre and the limited appeal of the play to sections of the public. "Twenty years ago I made a desperate effort to persuade several of our ablest writers of fiction to do something for the stage. They knew better. No one who is not daemonically urged by an irresistible inward force . . . practices my trade when he has already mastered the trade of Fielding and Dickens."
337. 1921, Preface, *Immaturity, CP*, p. 659. Preface to Shaw's first novel, written in 1879 and first published in 1930. "I sing my own class: the Shabby Genteel, the Poor Relation, the Gentlemen who are No Gentlemen." About his uncles, of whom "Two . . . emigrated to Tasmania, and, like Mr Micawber, made history there" [*Copperfield*, ch. 63].
338. 1921, Preface, *Immaturity, CP*, p. 673; *SA* I, 76; *MI*, p. 8. On his "breaking loose" from Ireland in 1876; his first exposure to cockney and difficulties with metropolitan vehicles. "I solemnly drove in a growler through the streets whose names Dickens had made familiar to me. . . ."
339. 1921, "The Dawn of Darwinism," The Infidel Half Century, Preface, *Back to*

Methuselah, BH V, 258; *CP*, pp. 501–2; *SA* II, 24. Unhistorical perspective by those who regard the pre-Darwinian as the Dark Age, "talked as if there had been no dramatic or descriptive music before Wagner; no impressionist painting before Whistler; whilst ... I was finding that the surest way to produce an effect of daring innovation and originality was ... to lift characters bodily out of the pages of Charles Dickens."

340. 1921, "Evolution in the Theatre," Preface, *Back to Methuselah, CP*, p. 543. Long tradition of dramatists "in revolt against falsehood and imposture." Tragedy glibly assumed mass slaughter in the last act; comedy assumed universal matrimony, as if "the last moment of the last act" determined the merit of the play. Hence the playwright's recourse to delightful "delineation of character" (A).

341. 1921, "Evolution in the Theatre," *CP*, pp. 544–45. Giants of contemporary drama, Ibsen and Strindberg, "refused us even the Shakespearean-Dickensian consolation of laughter at mischief, accurately called comic relief." Goethe alone rose above the mud in which the giants "are gnashing their teeth in impotent fury...."

342. Dec 1921–Jan 1922, "Blood Sports Disguised as Punishment are Less Cruel than Imprisonment but More Demoralizing to the Public," *Imprisonment, CP*, pp. 286–87. Spectators' brutal delight in public torture and execution. "For [the criminal] it would be far better to suffer in the public eye; for among the crowd of sightseers there might be a Victor Hugo or a Dickens able ... to make the sightseers think of what they are doing and ashamed of it."

343. Dec 1921–Jan 1922, "The History of Our Prisons," *Imprisonment, CP*, pp. 313–14. The Pickwickian innocence of prison conditions and the general apathy on the subject.

344. 9 Dec 1922, "Again the Dean Speaks Out," rev. of William Ralph Inge's *Outspoken Essays: 2nd Series, The Nation; PPR*, p. 155. Inge taken in by "that disastrously successful swindle which we call secondary education." On the débris instilled by Academe. Nontrained artists (Bunyan, Blake, Dickens) "point the way to the light whilst the educated are stumbling through a dense fog of inculcated falsehood...." These last are likened to "The gentleman who mistook Mr. Pickwick's lantern for a meteor and had his head 'knocked with a hollow sound' against the stable door by Sam Weller" [during Pickwick's romantic mission to Arabella Allen, ch. 39]. "The true Fall of Man occurred when he lost his intellectual innocence by trying to pluck the apple of knowledge from the upas trees of the teaching profession."

345. 11 Feb 1923, to G. K. Chesterton, in Maisie Ward, *Gilbert Keith Chesterton* (New York, 1943), pp. 414–15. Claiming Jingle's delicacy in refraining from dictation [*Pickwick*, ch. 2], GBS tries to dissuade GKC from calling his projected journal "Chesterton's Weekly." Cites the precedents of Defoe and Cobbett for using their own names as inapplicable.

346. 26 Feb 23, to G. K. Chesterton, Ward, loc. cit. Cautionary noises on Chesterton's journal. Urges him either to broaden his base of appeal or dispense with any base, as CD dispensed with it in *Household Words* and *All the Year Round*. Chesterton's difficulty: change in the character of journalism which in CD's day tolerated imaginative articles and stories and left politics and news to the daily press.

347. [1923] "The Unprotected Child and the Law," Pamphlet Issued by the Six Point Group, p. 8. Scores the failure "to protect children from the most detestable forms of molestation.... Both the opposition to legal protection and the advocacy of it are carried to rabid lengths by people who see either a prowling pest in every elderly gentleman who smiles at a child in the park or a prurient Mrs. Pardiggle in every police woman or welfare worker" [290, 296 supra].

348. 1 Feb 1924, "The Practical Man of Business," *The New Leader;* as "Burning the Candle at Both Ends," *WWW*, p. 392. Disastrous effects of running the House of Commons by "practical businessmen." "To keep the demobilized men quiet whilst their chances of employment are being destroyed, the practical business men handed out doles in all directions, and were afraid to withdraw them when the mischief was done lest they should provoke a revolution by men used to the sight and shedding of blood. Never was there such a romp in the history of Boodledom" [*Bleak House*, ch. 12 and passim].

349. 25 Feb 24, "To the Editor of *The Times*," *BH* V, 710. Shaw has been accused of " 'pouring scorn on a politician who actually allowed his own son to be killed in the war' " in Part II of *Back to Methuselah*. "In what sense did any man 'allow' his son to be killed in the war?" Defends his dramatic use of politicians; but "as far as it goes outside the public history of public men, [*Methuselah*] contains not a word against the private honour of any living person; and if I do not share the delicacy as to equally public and politically active women, which restrained Silas Wegg from going into details concerning the Decline and Fall of the Roman Empire, I can only say that my blue pencil is at the service of any lady who can find a single reference to herself which is not within the privilege of the friendliest good humour" [*Mutual Friend*, Bk. I, ch. 5].

350. May 1924, "The Maid in Literature," Preface, *Saint Joan*, *BH* VI, 41; *CP*, p. 616. Voltaire's *La Pucelle* intended to wipe out by ridicule contemporary institutions and fashions; free from any pretence at historical accuracy (A).

351. May 1924, "The Maid in Literature," *BH* VI, 42–43; *CP*, p. 617. "Mark Twain's Joan . . . with as many petticoats as Noah's wife in a toy ark, is an attempt to combine Bayard with Esther Summerson . . . into an unimpeachable American school teacher in armor. Like Esther . . . she makes her creator ridiculous, and yet, being the work of a man of genius, remains a credible human goodygoody in spite of her creator's infatuation."

352. Sept 1924, "The Drama, the Theatre, and the Films," *Fortnightly Review; Harper's; TT*, p. 47. Shaw on silent movies. Like novels, movies consist "of variations on a few plots." The "widest power of variation lies [in the language]. Take that away and you will soon be so hard up for a new variation that you will snatch at anything—even at a Dickens plot—to enable you to carry on."

353. Oct 1924, "Literature and Science," *Fortnightly Review;* as "Ulysses and Einstein," *Forum* (New York); *TT*, p. 98. Pornographic fiction churned out by "pitifully ignorant writers" for pitifully inexperienced readers. "Compare these novels with Ivanhoe and Pickwick. It is like comparing mince pies with apple tarts."

354. Oct 1924, "Literature and Science," *TT*, pp. 103–4. To Henderson's challenge to define a "sex novel": "I never used the expression. . . . If you called Wagner's 'Tristan' a sex opera or 'Romeo and Juliet' a sex tragedy, I should know what you meant, whereas if you called 'Dombey and Son' or 'Macbeth' sex stories I should conclude that you were mad."

355. Oct 1924, "Literature and Science," *TT*, p. 108; Weintraub, p. 214. *Ulysses* and its obscenities. "If Dickens or Thackeray had been told that a respectable author like myself would use the expletive 'bloody' in a play," Heaven help his disbelief. GBS "can find no interest in [Joyce's] clinical incontinences. . . . But if they were worth mentioning [he himself] would dress [them] up in a little Latinity."

356. 3 Nov 24, "Fiction and Drama," Lecture at Parkway Hall, Welwyn Garden; Chappelow, p. 49. Historical separation of drama from fiction; origin of fiction in spoken language. "The best story teller is the man who could give individuality to the characters, like the boy in Dickens who could read the police news in different

voices. This was the beginning of acting . . ." [Sloppy in *Mutual Friend*, Bk. I, ch. 16].

357. 26 Nov 1925, "The Impossibilities of Freedom," Portions of a lecture before the Fabian Society, Kingsway Hall; *New York Times*, 20 Dec 25; as "Shaw Foresees a Four-Hour Working Day," Hubenka, p. 185. Socialist idea of abolishing religion is unworkable: ". . . genuine religion is not quite so easily killed." Shaw anticipates "a tolerably stiff State religion which will be taught to children; and anybody endeavouring to teach the children anything else will probably be treated exactly as we should treat a person like Fagin in Oliver Twist, who deliberately taught children how to pick pockets."

358. 31 March 1926, "Stratford Must Not Wait," letter to the Editor of *The Evening Standard*, *BH* IV, 337. Appeal for a general subscription to restore Stratford. Failed attempt to subsidize a London-based National Shakespeare Theatre. "The 'Manchester Guardian,' like Mrs. Dombey's relatives, still calls on the committee to make an effort" [*Dombey*, ch. 1].

359. April 1926, "Bernard Shaw Self-Revealed," *Fortnightly Review; SA* II, 152. Evolution of literary figures. "Characters have to grow and define themselves as they go on: they may begin as mere dolls or even polliwogs. Pickwick . . . no more [to CD] at first than an elderly gentleman at whose hat an impudent street boy throws a snowball. Dick Swiveller began as a repulsive melodramatic villain whom the heroine was to be forced by her selfish relatives to marry. . . . [Shakespear and CD] wiped out characters which were meant to be more important: Poins and that futile relative of Little Nell's whose first name it is impossible to remember" [Master Humphrey, "The Single Gentleman" in *Old Curiosity Shop*, ch. 34 et seq.].

360. May 1926, "Bernard Shaw Self-Revealed," *Fortnightly Review; SA* II, 154. On his education. "All the instruction that was offered to me was either wrong absolutely or wrong for me. All the books that profess to show how to write plays are wrong from beginning to end and should be labelled How Not To Do It."

361. 25 July 26, "The Alleged Septuagenarianism of Bernard Shaw," *The Observer;* Henderson, p. 671. Sex. ". . . he would be a bold man who would declare that the literarily sexless Dickens was less virile than the literarily passionate Swinburne. The more real a man's sex is, the less likely he is to imagine that paper lovemaking is any better than paper fighting."

362. 1926, "How William Archer Impressed Bernard Shaw," *Three Plays by William Archer* (London, 1927), *PPR*, p. 22; *SA* I, 263. Unlike Archer, who defends the 19th-century drama, GBS finds Plot "the ruin of a story and therefore of a play": Shakespear and CD.

363. 1926, "How William Archer Impressed Bernard Shaw," *PPR*, p. 29. Archer's book on India useful because "resolutely unsympathetic." Wrote about Indians "as Dickens wrote about Americans"; CD's "honesty did not prevent his becoming more popular with them than any of their romantic flatterers. . . ."

364. 19 March 1928, "Ibsen—and After," Lecture delivered at the Royal Society of Arts, London, one of a series sponsored by the British Drama League to commemorate the Ibsen centenary. Conflation of reports in the *Manchester Guardian* of 20 March 28 and the British Drama League's publication *Drama* of April 28; Wisenthal, p. 254. Ibsen vs Dickens, and everyone else. "Ibsen . . . told stories that changed the mind of the world." Dickens and Scott, however delightful, didn't: "When one had done with them one's religion, social views, and prejudices remained the same as before." The only story-teller to rival Ibsen: Karl Marx.

365. June 1928, "The Middle Station in Life," *IW*, p. 174. Radical shift in the position of civil servants and unpropertied classes. CD's "futile propertyless gentlemen,

366. June 1928, "Sham Socalism," *IW*, p. 303. Nineteenth-century relief rules and Registrar General's census of death by starvation. "The lowest scale of relief which the Government ventured to propose would have seemed ruinously extravagant and demoralizing to the Gradgrinds and Bounderbys denounced by Dickens...."
367. June 1928, "Socialism and Children," *IW*, p. 414. Insists again that "those who have been 'educated' least know most.... Toots is not a mere figure of fun: [but] an authentic instance of a sort of imbecility that is dangerously prevalent in our public school and university products. Toots is no joke" [*Dombey*, ch. 11 and passim].
368. June 1928, "Appendix," *IW*, p. 469. For students of sociology, the 19th-century "poets and prophets" who trounced capitalism are "much more exciting than the economic theorists: Hard Times and Little Dorrit . . . [leave] the professed Socialists, even Karl Marx, miles behind in force of invective."
369. June 1928, "Appendix," *IW*, p. 469. Change from "Pickwick Papers (jolly early Dickens) . . . [to] Our Mutual Friend (disillusioned mature Dickens)" reflects the change from "nineteenth-century self-satisfaction to twentieth-century criticism...."
370. 7 Dec 28, "Bernard Shaw Talks about Actors and Acting," Excerpts from address delivered at Royal Academy of Dramatic Arts, London; *New York Times*, 6 Jan 29; West, pp. 187–88. CD, himself a born actor and hence presumably tolerant of the profession, sternly nixed his stage-struck daughter's ambition as non-U.
371. c. 1928–29, "Postscript to Prelude to the 1905 Preface" [to the Shaw-Terry correspondence written for *Neue Deutsche Presse* (Vienna), 24 Dec. 1905, trans. Siegfried Trebitsch]; as "Henry Irving and Ellen Terry," *PPR*, p. 163. Refusal to suppress Terry letters an exception to Shaw's rule: "it does not take much experience of the world to conclude, as Dickens did when he made his famous bonfire at Gadshill, that the safest and kindest thing to do with letters is to burn them. But you could not burn a letter from Ellen any more than you could burn a drawing by Michael Angelo [or Shakespear's sonnets]."
372. 26 June 1929, Preface, *ETL* [1931]; *CP*, p. 781. His nuisance value as a boy in going backstage during operatic performances (A).
373. 26 June 29, Preface, *ETL*; *CP*, p. 784. CD's class prejudice in forbidding Mamie to go onstage [370 supra].
374. 26 June 29, Preface, *ETL*; *CP*, p. 786. Odiousness of stock companies. "The king in Hamlet and Ham Pegotty might have been twins except for the costume, because the heavy man had to play Ham, the juveniles being used up for Copperfield and Steerforth."
375. 31 July 29, to Merle Armitage (Quinn). *Little Dorrit* in many ways CD's greatest book. "I still meet Mr. Sparkler in all directions, and Merdles by the dozens, though they don't unfortunately commit suicide."
376. [1930] *Frank Harris on Bernard Shaw* (London, 1931), pp. 232–33. Quotes Shaw: "Of *Lady Chatterley's Lover* he highly approves—as a document! 'If I had a marriageable daughter,' he said, 'what could I give her to read to prepare her? Dickens? Thackeray? . . . *Lady Chatterley* should be on the shelves of every college for budding girls. They should be forced to read it on pain of being refused a marriage license. *But it is not as readable as 'Ivanhoe' or 'A Tale of Two Cities'* "!!!
377. [1930] "Shaw's Sex Credo," *Frank Harris*, p. 227. Justifies his sitting in the nude for photographer Alvin Langborn Coburn. "Though we have hundreds of photographs of Dickens and Wagner, we see nothing of them except their suits of clothes with their heads sticking out; and what is the use of that?"

378. 1930, *Immaturity* (London, 1931), fn., p. 172. Added fn. to the funeral scene following the hero's stroll to Brompton Cemetery (Bk. 2 ch. 7), explaining that "In 1878 this scene was something more than a description of the macabre side of a young man's fancy." Apart from its being a plea for cremation—at the time a highly controversial subject—"it was a repleading of Dickens's protest against the grotesque mummeries of the old-fashioned funerals" [e.g., *Oliver Twist*, ch. 6; *Great Expectations*, ch. 35].

379. 19 Dec 30, "Shaw Agrees with Lewis," New York *Times* [front page lead article]. Shaw happily endorses Sinclair Lewis's attack on American literature in Lewis's Nobel Prize acceptance address. "Dickens won [Americans] to him forever by merciless projections of typical Americans as windbags, swindlers, and assassins.... I myself have been particularly careful never to say a civil word to the United States.... I have defined the 100 per cent American as 99 per cent an idiot. And they just adore me and will go on adoring me until in a moment of senile sentimentality I say something nice about them, when they will at once begin to suspect me of being only a cheap skate after all..." [363 supra].

380. 15 March 1932, Alexander Woolcott, *The Letters of Alexander Woolcott* (New York, 1944), p. 109, to Laura E. Richards. GBS thinks *Great Expectations* CD's best novel; had read "all except *Bleak House* by the time [he] was twelve." Source of Shaw's famous comment "that a concordance of all his own writings would reveal the Dickens allusions as running four to one against any other writer."

381. 16 April 32, to Mrs. Patrick Campbell, *PCL*, p. 299. Objects to publication of his correspondence with Stella; defends recent publication of the Shaw-Terry exchange [371 supra], alleging the difference in his relations with Stella and Ellen (who "came through with me *virgo intacta*") and Ellen's unique adeptness at self-portraiture. "It was this portrait that broke my resistance to Edy's [Terry's daughter, director and producer Edith Craig] iron determination that it should be published to show the world how silly the Sweet Nell convention was."

382. 1932, *The Rationalization of Russia* (ed. Harry Geduld, Bloomington, Ind., 1964), p. 58. Technical use of the word "revolutionist": "... I am using it in a sense that is modern; and ... do not mean by it a blood-stained man in shirt sleeves and a red cap of liberty ... or a woman sitting before a guillotine and interrupting her knitting occasionally to count the heads of aristocrats.... I mean one who has adopted the study of the history and practice of revolution as a profession."

383. 22 March 1933, Alexander Woolcott, *Letters*, p. 121, to Thornton Wilder. Invites Wilder for a holiday to share their impressions of *Great Expectations*. "Shaw (mistakenly) points to Estella as proof that Dickens *could* paint a real heroine. Estella, he says, is Mrs. Patrick Campbell to the life. Which is the wildest nonsense...."

384. 22 Oct 33, "Private Powers of Life and Death," Preface, *On the Rocks, BH* VI, 583; *CP*, p. 357. All revolutionary movements are attacks on private property. "... the power to exterminate is too grave to be left in any hands but those of a thoroughly Communist government responsible to the whole community. The landlord with his writ of ejectment ... must finally go the way of ... Hannibal Chollop with his bowie knife and pistol" [*Chuzzlewit*, ch. 44].

385. ?late 1933, "To Introduce the Prefaces," Preface to *Complete Prefaces* [1934], pp. vii-viii. The political inefficacy of literature. CD's books viewed as "extraordinarily vivid parables. All the political futility which has forced men of the calibre of Mussolini, Kemal, and Hitler to assume dictatorships might have been saved" had people read *Little Dorrit*. "And Dickens might have been Mussolini's grandfather or my father."

386. 21 March 1935, "Provocations," *G.K.'s Weekly*. The writer's futility as politician; see

foregoing entry. " 'I wonder that you will still be talking: nobody marks you.' Thus one of Shakespear's merry ladies three centuries ago.... In the 19th century Queen Victoria might have said it to Dickens if any sort of contact between their minds had been possible.... We three [Chesterton, Wells, Shaw] roar louder, and over wider circulations, and much more amusingly than Ruskin, Marx, or Henry George. But nobody marks us."

387. 21 March 1935, "Provocations," *G.K.'s Weekly*. "An ex-parliamentary reporter, one Charles Dickens, pointed out three quarters of a century ago that Parliament is not a palladium of British liberty but an unrivalled instrument for finding out, when the people want the Government to do something, how not to do it. The impression produced by Dickens on our governing classes was that of a street boy cocking snooks at an august institution, the greatness of which he, a mere middle class inkslinger, was incapable of understanding. So Parliament went on illustrating the exactitude of Dickens's observation until Belloc... got himself elected to the House of Commons, smelt it, and walked out again."

388. 2 June 35, Preface, *London Music in 1888–89*, p. 15; *SA* I, 190. His saturation with the leading composers and English writers (Handel, Dickens, etc.) as disinfectant against his formal schooling.

389. 27 July 35, "A Letter from Bernard Shaw," *Time and Tide*. Urges CD's younger daughter Kate Perugini not to burn CD's letters to his wife: following Ibsen's demolition of "the sentimental sympathy... with the man of genius... posterity might sympathise much more with the woman who was sacrificed to the genius's uxoriousness to the appalling extent of having to bear ten children in sixteen years than with a grievance which, after all, amounted only to the fact that she was not a female Charles Dickens." (See Walter Dexter, "Mr. Shaw Taken to Task" [for irresponsibly imputing to Kate nasty words against the Dickens Fellowship], *D*, XXXI, 295.)

390. 25 Aug 35, "News and Views of Literary London," *New York Times Book Review*. Shaw quoted as expressing the hope that "the next editor of Dickens will restore the original and honest unhappy ending of *Great Expectations*" [see below, 394–96, 449].

391. 28 Aug 35, "Preface on Bosses," Preface, *The Millionairess* [1936], *BH* VI 860; *CP*, p. 484. Wars naturally encourage employment; all administration of doles with which the million unemployed are bought off recalls "all the infamies of the Poor Law that crushed Oliver Twist."

392. 12 Oct 35, "Notes on the Way," *Time and Tide*. On keeping out of the Italian war with Ethiopia: on the need to remain on terms with Italy on one hand and on the other to assure the Ethiopians of giving them "as fair play as... possible in their hopeless conflict with the march of bourgeois civilization.... [Foreign Secretary] Sir Samuel Hoare is quite sincere in his declaration that he will never desert the Genevan Mr. Micawber [Haile Selassie].... Our real attitude is summed up in Lady Houghton's thrilling 'Damn the League of Nations!' That is almost unladylike; but it is thoroughly sound."

393. 25 July 1936, "This Year's Program," *Malvern Festival Book;* West, p. 242; *SA* II, 5. Regards the range and durability of his characters, not his "philosophy," as his real contribution to drama. (A).

394. [1937] *The Mystery of the Unhappy Ending* (New York, n.d.). Unpaginated booklet which reproduces the correspondence (28 Aug 35 to 24 Dec 36) among George Macy, publisher of the forthcoming *Great Expectations* for Limited Editions, the Edinburgh editor William Maxwell, and GBS's secretary Blanche Patch: on tracking down the original ending of the novel which (as Shaw romanced) he had read

in *All the Year Round,* the prospects of printing the book directly from the Wisbech MS, and other mystifications.

*395. 1937, Preface, *Great Expectations* (Edinburgh, R. & R. Clark for Members of the Limited Edns. Club), pp. v–xxii. Vastly resourceful and pandectic landmark in CD-criticism, not least in its seminal discussion of the 2 endings. *GE* Dickens's "most compactly perfect book . . . built round a single and simple catastrophe. . . ." Candor of Pip's presentation vs. Copperfield's self-pity: "The reappearance of Mr. Dickens in the character of a blacksmith's boy may be regarded as an apology to Mealy Potatoes" [*Copperfield,* ch. 11]. CD's revolutionary view of the bourgeois order as "transitory, mistaken, dishonest, unhappy, pathological" and of the governing classes: "Trollope and Thackeray could see Chesney Wold; but Dickens could see through it." Difference between CD and Marx the difference between an unconscious and a conscious revolutionist. CD's fortunate lack of education ("Better no schooling . . . than the schooling of Rudyard Kipling and Winston Churchill"). The Dickenses "complete [cultural] barbarians"; CD's philistine distrust of metaphysics and his shoddy notions of art: "When Dickens introduced . . . a character whom he intensely disliked he chose an artistic profession for him." CD's conquest of his tendency to manufacture happy endings: "as our minds grow stronger and sterner some of his consolations become unnecessary and even irritating." Original ending of *GE* psychologically far sounder than the second; the second "artistically much more congruous" in its setting. If GBS "ever indulge[d] in the luxury" of rewriting *GE,* he would provide "the perfect ending" by preserving the milieu of the second and the substance of the first. Pip's marriage to Estella ("a curious addition to [CD's] gallery of unamiable women") is surely "the most unhappy ending that could possibly be devised." Pip's abhorrence of Magwitch betrays CD's own unconscious snobbishness. "Save for the last words the story is the most perfect. . . ." And one of the saddest: "saddened by the evil that is done under the sun; but at least [CD] preserved his intellectual innocence sufficiently to escape the dismal pseudo-scientific fatalism . . . descending on the world in his latter days. . . ." Preface ranges over the entire Dickens canon; allusions to some 60 characters. See Humphry House's brilliantly fair corrective, *D* XLIV (1948), 63–70 and 183–86; in *All in Due Time* (London, 1955), pp. 201–20.

396. 1937, "Editor's Postscript," *Great Expectations,* pp. xxiii–xxvi. Reproduces the 2nd "changeling" conclusion of the novel, preceded by a brief note to place it in context and followed by an apostrophe to "*Sentimental readers who still like all their stories to end at the altar* [and] *may prefer this. They have their choice.*"

397. 2 Nov 37, "Religion and the War," BBC broadcast; as "As I See It," *Listener,* 10 Nov; Smith, p. 96. ". . . such a commandment as 'Love one another' . . . is a stupid refusal to accept the facts of human nature. . . . Do you love the rate collector? Do you love Mr. George, and if you do, do you love Mr. Winston Churchill?" (A).

398. 19 Oct 1938, "Bernard Shaw Looks Back: His Schooling—His Teachers—and Those of To-day," *Teacher's World and Schoolmistress.* "Series of replies received from famous people to nine questions designed by *Teacher's World* to elicit their views on schooling. . . ." *Q:* "Do you consider that distasteful and tedious tasks should be part of a child's education?" *A:* "Well, does any child enjoy learning the indispensable multiplication table? But if its utility were explained to a child with a statement that it could never be given more than a penny to spend unless it could give and take change, it would learn more willingly than if it were only Pumblechooked and assaulted if it could not give the correct answer" [*Great Expectations,* esp. ch. 8].

399. 15 Jan 1939, "My Apology for This Book," *SSS,* p. 7; *SA* I, 3. Triviality of "lives"

vs. instructiveness of the texts. So much is known about CD that might apply to lesser mortals "that his biographers have obliterated him for those who do not read his books, and for those who do, spoilt his portrait very painfully."

400. 17 July 39, to Gladys Storey (Quinn). After reading Storey's candidly muck-raking *Dickens and Daughter* (London, 1939), GBS confirms and implements her testimony on the relations among the Dickenses, notably Catherine and Kate Perugini, one of Storey's closest sources. His advice to Kate to preserve CD's letters [526 infra] and his subsequent shock on discovering their general inanity. Ellen Ternan and CD's astute knowledge of women: his shrews vs. his exasperating "idealizations."

401. 29 July 39, "Dickens and Mrs. Perugini," letter to the Editor, *TLS*. Takes issue with review of Storey's *Dickens and Daughter* (*TLS*, 22 July); vindicates Kate Perugini's recollections of Life with Father and testifies to her vigilant memory as a nonagenarian. "The facts of the case may be in bad taste. Facts often are."

402. ?1939, Chappelow, p. 183. Ascribes to CD "a complete disbelief in government *by* the people, and an equally complete hostility to government in any other interest than theirs."

403. 14 Nov 1940, to Anmer Hall (Univ. of Texas Library; Quinn). His contribution on CD to a projected gift book by Hall. On the motives for CD's boozing as distinct from others'; the delicacy of treating the subject in print; and the futility of broadcasting the names of lesser bar hounds to impress the younger generation.

404. Nov–Dec 1940, "Which Side Must Ireland Take in the War?" (BL Add. MS 50698, f. 172). The side of the English: Ireland to insist on military re-occupation by England as protection against German invasion of the islands. Shaw vehemently denounces Hitler's claims to racial supremacy, his ruthless persecution of Polish Catholics, and his assumption of the divine right to global domination. Sam Weller is quoted against Hitler.

405. 8 Jan 1941, to Anmer Hall (Univ. of Texas Library; Quinn). Notifies Hall that he has substituted a scientific lecture for the Dickens piece for Hall's gift book. Ignorance of the young of CD's private life: his separation, the liaison with Ternan, his drinking bouts and killing public readings. Ternan unquestionably Estella's original. Reiterates his conviction that *Drood* is dead stuff. CD's lack of interest in the vital issues of the day; quotes Dean Inge to the effect that CD's sole interest in the Church lay in the pew opener.

406. 22 Jan 1941, to Anmer Hall (Univ. of Texas Library; Quinn). Report by an auditor present at CD's (wholly unconvincing) impersonation of Sam Weller. Shaw is unsurprised: Weller, a figure of fantasy, impossible on the stage. The unique quality of Pickwick in the canon [515 infra]. More general failure of CD's figures in the theatre owing to their static character: significantly, Bohun, who is imitation-Jaggers, is confined to a single scene in Shaw's play. [To similar effects, 334 and 359 supra.]

407. 22 Aug 1942, "To Tokyo on Buttermilk," *Royal Air Force Journal;* in Hector Bolitho, *A Penguin in the Eyrie* (London, 1955). *Aet.* 86, Shaw talks about his longevity, weight (9 stone) and diet. Gluttons like CD and Shakespear died before they were 60; GBS has survived them by some 30 years "and written [his] most famous books and plays during those 30 years.... If I were sent off to bomb, say Tokyo, I should take with me a packet of thinnish slices of brown bread . . . [and] a flask of buttermilk."

408. 11 Sept 42, "That's Not the Party System!" to the Editor of *The Daily Herald*. "Captain Randolph Churchill has found out, as his father found out, and as Charles Dickens found out a hundred years ago [in his days as reporter] that the House of Commons under the Party System is a perfect weapon for the defeat of

Parliamentary government, its only business when anything democratic has to be done being to find out how not to do it."

409. 4 March 1943, "Bernard Shaw as a Biologist," *The Listener* (7th in series of Shaw letters with same caption). More specifically "as a bacteriologist." On Lister's failure to grasp the curative character of bacteria: "That his precautions involved aesthetic reforms and did away with dirty Sairy Gamp, was neither understood nor intended by him, though he has been ignorantly credited with its success."

410. June 1943, "Marx's Theory of Value," to the Editor of *Plebs* (Oxford). Asks Arthur Woodburn to refrain from "galvanizing Marx's stone dead theory of value." Value determined by supply and demand, which defy arithmetic calculation: "by excluding from demand the needs of the people . . . the Supply and Demand men dehumanized economics, and were righteously detested by Marx, by Ruskin, by Dickens and by all friends of mankind."

411. 3 July 43, "Mr. Shaw Responds," *New Statesman and Nation*. Responds to Joad's jeremiad on the vanity of Shaw's dogmatizings which haven't kept "the world [from] going from bad to worse since [he] gave tongue and pen." Shaw agrees "that the England of Pecksniffs and Podsnaps has not become the England of Ruskins and Bernard Shaws" but finds more cause for sorrow in universal suffrage: "Now that the political ignorance of Everywoman has been enfranchised and added to the political ignorance and folly of Everyman, and government is by Anybody chosen by Everybody, both Joad and I may be thankful that we are at the mercy of Winston Churchill rather than of Titus Oates. . . ."

412. ?1943, Chappelow, p. 201. Rips again into Hitler's "anti-Semitic phobia" as pathological. "Whom the Gods would destroy they first make dotty. . . . This chosen Race business is not Socialism but, as my late colleague Charles Dickens expressed it, 'So far from it, on the contrary, quite the reverse' " [Sam Weller supporting Pickwick's claims of innocence in the Westgate plot, ch. 16]. (My error. Almost certainly same entry as 404 supra. Ed.)

413. April 1944, *Fabian Quarterly;* Chappelow, p. 398. Blames the rise of Hitler and Mussolini on the inefficiency of the English "Party System in which, as I said (meaning exactly what Hitler and Mussolini, Dickens and Oswald Mosley said), [to] take 30 years to do a week's work will end in doing 30 years' work in a week" and produce "an extremely unpleasant rush hour—and most likely a very bloody one."

414. Summer 1944, "The Author as Manual Laborer," *The Author;* Tauber, p. 75; Chappelow, pp. 415–16. Shaw's advocacy of a new English alphabet on economic grounds: to save the writer time and effort by adopting simplified spelling. "I wish some person with a mania for arithmetic would count the sounds in Shakespear's plays or Dickens's novels, and then count the letters these unfortunate scribes had to write to make readable manuscripts . . . for the players and printers. I would burn all the commentaries and criticisms that have been wasted on their works for such a cast-up. It would prove that they in their short lives (I lived nearly thirty years longer than either of them) could have written two or three more plays and novels than they had time to get through."

415. Summer 1944, "The Author as Manual Laborer," Tauber, p. 76; Chappelow, p. 416. "The case of Dickens is extraordinary. He began as a parliamentary reporter, and had learnt and mastered Gurney's shorthand. Yet he had to write all his novels in Phoenician longhand because his shorthand was legible to nobody but himself."

416. Summer 1944, "From Bernard Shaw," public letter originally appended to "The Author as Manual Laborer," Tauber, pp. 80–81. Announces his testamentary intentions, including a proposal to support the development of a new English

alphabet. "My particular fad is the saving of labor by establishment of a fit British alphabet containing at least 42 letters...." Cites "The classical instance... of Charles Dickens" to the same effect as in entry preceding.

417. Summer 1944, "From Bernard Shaw," Tauber, p. 81; Chappelow, p. 418. On the futile attempts "of novelists and playwrights to represent the dialects of their characters—of Sam Weller, Caleb Balderstone, Handy Andy, Fluellen and the rest—by grotesque misspellings. My own experience as a playwright in efforts to write modern cockney dialect phonetically with 26 letters has convinced me of its impossibility."

418. 25 Nov 44, "Women in Politics," *The Leader*. Shaw on a sexist crusade; his refusal to co-celebrate Lady Astor's feminist heroics. "When Mrs. Pankhurst and her daughter swept feminism out of the rut of the Parliamentary Liberal road, and made Votes for Women the slogan of a guerilla of militant saboteuses, I was... the speaker at a Suffragist meeting the heroine of which was a rich lady who, being married to a poor man who was legally liable for her surtax, refused to pay, and allowed the Crown to take his body in execution and imprison him for life in the old Pickwickian fashion.... This was being held up by the Suffragettes as an outstanding example of selfsacrificing devotion to The Cause on the lady's part. My comment was that if my wife treated me so I would never speak to her again. I was immediately set down as a bitter anti-Feminist and advocate of the forceful feeding of Suffragette hunger strikers."

419. 1944, "Is Human Nature Incurably Depraved?" *EP*, p. 6. Knowledge of political requirements is no guarantee of their proper execution. "Dickens describes our governing classes as perfect masters of the art of How Not To Do It. But then, thinking themselves very well off as they are, they do not want to do it."

420. 1944, "The British Party System," *EP*, p. 28. "For vivid sketches of what the Party System comes to in practice nowadays, turn to the description of it in... Bleak House, and more thoroughly in... Little Dorrit, both written by Charles Dickens, ex-reporter in the gallery of the House of Commons and on the hustings."

421. 1944, "The British Party System," *EP*, p. 29. Party system to be "ruthlessly discarded in the very fullest agreement with Oliver Cromwell, Charles Dickens, John Ruskin, Thomas Carlyle, Adolf Hitler, Pilsudski, Benito Mussolini, Stalin and everyone else who has tried to govern efficiently and incorruptly.... Stalin and Hitler, the most thoroughgoing disciples of Cromwell and Dickens in this matter, are also the most convinced that government can make no great change until a long propaganda and inculcation of its principles and hopes has persuaded the mass of the people... to follow the flags...."

422. 1944, "Knowing Our Places," *EP*, pp. 49–50. On "the welfare of children as a neglected branch of vital public work"; their proponents by no means consist only of Mrs. Pardiggles. The fitness of mothers to rear their own children: those who can; those who could, given proper guidance; those who are beyond correction [290, 294–95 supra].

423. 1944, "The Proposed Abolition of Classes," *EP*, p. 62. Class differences between parents and children. The misclassed position of John Dickens among "the bevy of celebrities of which his son was the centre" and Kate's admission "that she could imagine nothing more dreadful than the lot of a man of genius in an entirely commonplace household." Children who fail to inherit their father's genius are advised to "change their names and keep the relationship a dead secret, lest they should be dismissed as failures instead of being respected as quite competent mediocrities."

424. 1944, "The State and the Children," *EP*, p. 69. On the need to create schools that

provide "a child world of which [the child] can be a little citizen, with laws ... suited to childish abilities and disabilities." On instruction: "Between Squeers and Montessori there are teachers of many sorts." In the inculcation of religious truths, Aesop, Genesis, and Bunyan are more appropriate than Schopenhauer on Will or Bergson on Creative Evolution.

425. 1944, "Illusions of the Money Market," *EP*, p. 99. Hereditary property rights vs. abrogatory copyright an unfair anomaly. ". . . there is actually an agitation to make copyright perpetual on the ground that it is not fair that a person whose grandfather's father pre-empted a cabbage patch on the site of Chicago should be a millionaire whilst the great-grandchildren of Dickens may be as poor as church mice."

426. 1944, "The Half Educated," *EP*, p. 158. The leading artists, merchant princes, etc. generally found among the sons of the "Half Educated"—those without university degrees. ". . . it is they who run most of the business of the country; and among whose sons are Shakespear and Dickens, Bunyan and Blake, Hogarth and Turner, Purcell and Elgar, and a dynasty of leading actors. . . ."

427. 1944, "The Half Educated," *EP*, p. 159. Pointlessness of university schooling and Old School Ties, "with the ideas and traditions of Sir Leicester Dedlock substituted for those of John Gilpin. Both were worthy and wellmeaning men; but both are out of date. For though commercial John stands against feudal Sir Leicester as Guelf against Ghibelline, his day schools ape the boarding schools of the country gentlemen."

428. 1944, "The Half Educated," *EP*, p. 160. On learning the ancient languages. "I escaped from my classical school just as Homer was threatening. . . . I left school, like Shakespear and Dickens, with little Latin and less Greek. . . . What I did learn at school I should have been better without, as it was only what a convict learns from his fellow prisoners and from fear and suffering. . . ."

429. 1944, "The Half Educated," *EP*, p. 164. The futility of forcefed education again. "Dickens, in Dombey and Son, made us weep over the death of poor little overworked Dombey at his preparatory school [ch. 16]; but it would have done us no harm to think a bit harder about the tragedy of Toots in the same institution, which only made us laugh" [ch. 11 and passim]. Toots's mind "destroyed by a senseless attempt to make him a classical scholar and Latin poet. . . ."

430. 1944, "The Half Educated," *EP*, p. 165. Secondary education, even if voluntary, to be subject to government control. "[Secondary schools] cannot be left to private enterprise: Fagin's private school for pickpockets cannot be tolerated . . ." [*Oliver*, chs. 9–10].

431. 1944, "The Aesthetic Man," *EP*, p. 180. GBS's own education uncontaminated by public school and university: his luck in "having had [his] mind first well stored in [his] nonage" by the great composers and writers, "by Beethoven and Mozart, Shakespear and Dickens and their like, and not by Latin versemongers and cricketers."

432. 1944, "The Aesthetic Man," *EP*, p. 183. GBS learned history not in school, "whereas when I was at home reading Quentin Durward, A Tale of Two Cities, or The Three Musketeers, I was learning it very agreeably." The thought of his being kept from his pleasant reading by his useless attendance in school is still as gall and wormwood to him.

433. 1944, "The Aesthetic Man," *EP*, p. 185. Aesthetic education punished as corrupt: only remedy lies in leisure and money. "A Poor Law which puts food, lodging, and clothing first, and leisure and pocket-money nowhere, is socially half blind. The Frenchman who said he could do without the necessities of life if only he had its

luxuries was wiser than the framers of the statute of Elizabeth or the Gradgrinds of 1832."

434. 1944, "The Medical Man," *EP*, p. 219. Pecuniary pressures an incentive to corruption in all walks of life. "If crime brings promotion to the police officer; if litigation is profitable to the solicitor; if war is the soldier's only avenue to distinction... then, as surely as night follows day, crimes will be 'framed-up'; blackmailing lawsuits will be provoked by Dodsons and Foggs; nations will have to arm to the teeth for fear of one another's warmongers..." [*Pickwick*, ch. 20 and passim].

435. 1944, "The Theocratic Man," *EP*, p. 231. Statesmen who meddle with religion need to act as freethinkers if only to neutralize the indiscriminate overabundance of beliefs: "we, with our characteristic thoughtless inconsistency, have retained Jehovah whilst adopting the Christian trinity, thus establishing a convenient Spenlow & Jorkins combination under which we can forgive our enemies or slaughter them just as it suits us" [*Copperfield*, chs. 23, 35].

436. 1944, "Coercions and Sanctions," *EP*, p. 288. The propensity of governments to "manufacture Awe and Contempt... and [to] abuse this power artificially": the reaction this provokes among individuals. "When the American Revolution claimed the right to carry arms for everybody, it was grossly abused by the sort of American typified by Dickens in Mr Hannibal Chollop, who will finally oblige the American Governments to forbid anyone to carry a pistol..." [*Chuzzlewit*, ch. 44; 384 supra].

437. 1944, "Our Attempts at Anthropometry," *EP*, p. 320. Attraction of commerce is "rare and feeble compared to the attraction of the arts and crafts." "Dickens, in his last complete book, made a character, narrow and mean and greedy and cowardly enough to think of nothing but how to make money for himself, become much richer than the better citizens for whom money making was only an irksome necessity. Commercial ability is often really mere spiderishness" [Fledgeby, *Mutual Friend*, Bk. II, chs. 4–5 and passim].

438. 1944, "Economic Summary," *EP*, p. 349. Though Dickens, like Ruskin and Carlyle, "saw that Capitalism was the robber's road to ruin... [he] would not study its theory. Therefore [he] never understood it, and could not find the political remedy."

439. 1945, Edgar Johnson, *The Heart of Charles Dickens as Revealed in His Letters to Angela Burdett-Coutts* (New York, 1952), p. 22. In conversation with Johnson, Shaw "characterized [CD's letters] as 'roast beef and Yorkshire pudding letters,' explaining that... they were all concerned with things done, places visited... limited to the concrete, sensuous, and immediate, that Dickens had nothing to say about art, philosophy," etc. [400 supra].

440. 6 Dec 45, to J. R. Hayes (chief librarian of the National Library of Ireland), in Dan H. Laurence, "Shaw, Books, and Libraries," *Papers of the Bibliographical Society of America*, LXIX (1975), 473. Shaw's refusal to collect first editions. "I destroy them to suppress their blunders. Other people collect my letters. Keeping [letters] is a mischievous habit. Dickens burned all his at Gadshill very wisely."

441. 14 Aug 1946, "H. G. Wells Was a Man without Malice," *New York Journal-American;* as "The Man I Knew," *New Statesman and Nation*, 17 Aug. Obit. "So, our H.G. is no more." Wells's status ("could anything be more *petit bourgeois*, as Lenin labelled H.G.?") and professional rise as schoolmaster and science graduate; "and presently, like Dickens and Kipling, [he] left all behind and found himself a great popular story teller... with every social circle in the kingdom open to him. Thus he became entirely classless...."

442. 29 Sept 46, "My Way with a Play," *The Observer;* West, p. 268. Rev. of Allardyce

Nicolls's *History of Late Nineteenth-Century Drama: 1850–1900*. Nicolls's confusion of chronology with evolution: his assumption that GBS learned his craft from Pinero, Wilde, "Scribery," et al.; "instead of taking a step forward technically in the order of the calendar, I threw off Paris and went back . . ." (A).

443. 29 Sept 46, "My Way with a Play," West, p. 270. CD's impossible plots: "who cares for or can remember the plots of *Oliver Twist* and *Little Dorrit*" etc. Happy ending of *Great Expectations* as contrived as the happy ending of *Much Ado*.

444. Winter 1946, "Granville Barker: Some Particulars," *Drama* NS 3; *SA* II, 31. Casting about for the part of Marchbanks, Shaw discovered Granville Barker, a person of "wide literary culture, . . . self-willed, restlessly industrious, sober . . . [who] had Shakespear and Dickens at his finger ends."

445. 26 April 1947, "Art Workers and the State," *The New Statesman*. "In [the group of 'burdensome good-for-nothings'] the human stock is not necessarily degenerating: it is in fallow, recapturing the future harvest. It may include brothers and sisters, sons and daughters, of the world's greatest geniuses. . . . Beethoven's nephew was a scapegrace; and none of the kindred of Shakespear or Dickens achieved anything like their eminence. Selection by heredity, the weak point in the feudal system, is thus ruled out under Socialism."

446. 26 April 47, "Art Workers and the State." On the uses and abuses of time for genial work. "Rousseau lived by copying music, Spinoza by grinding lenses, Wagner by conducting (and borrowing), Dickens as clerk. . . . There is . . . no other solution to the problem of original work under Socialism than routine jobs and shorter hours for aspirants." Business training not necessarily harmful to artists: "on the contrary, it saves them from being the feckless nuisances they are, living in an imaginary world and ignorant of the real one. The Harold Skimpole side of Leigh Hunt was an extremely undesirable one."

447. May 1947, "Colossal Labor Saving: An Open Letter from Bernard Shaw," Tauber, p. 130; Chappelow, p. 27. Another ride on his phonetical hobbyhorse [414–417 supra]. Again reflects "on the staggering fact that Dickens . . . had to go through the drudgery of writing all his novels in Johnsonese longhand for a printer. Why could Dickens not have used his shorthand as I used Pitman? Because Pitman . . . corrupted [his] scripts into codes for verbatim reporting. . . ."

448. 5 Dec 47, "Capital Punishment," to the Editor of *The Times;* Chappelow, p. 19. Deterrence to crime, as a substitute for "judicial liquidation," ineffective unless the criminal is detected beyond doubt. Else, the danger of arbitrary punishment. "The police are not impartial. They must do everything in their power to obtain a conviction. As one of Dickens's characters put it, 'Much better hang the wrong fellow than no fellow' " [Dedlock's "debilitated cousin" after the failure to discover Tulkinghorn's murderer, *Bleak House*, ch. 53].

*449. 1947, Revised Introduction to *Great Expectations* (London, "The Novel Library") pp. v–xx. Slightly abridged version of the '37 Preface [395 supra]; omits the mystery-mongering about the search for the original ending—and the original ending itself. Almost certainly written as early as 1936 and intended to supersede the orignal Preface as printed by Limited Editions.

450. 1947, "Sixty Years of Fabianism: A Postscript," Bernard Shaw, Sidney Webb et al., *Fabian Essays in Socialism* [1889] (Jubilee Edn., London, 1948), p. 212. "Webb and myself were left [of the original contributors to *Fabian Essays*]. . . . [Webb's] gifted wife and collaborator Beatrice took up the work begun by Dickens's Oliver Twist and abolished the old Poor Law by imposing a crushing Minority Report on a Royal Commission."

451. 1947, "My Office-Boyhood," *SSS*, p. 30; *SA* I, 68. GBS's experiences of "Circumlocution incivility" as errand boy in Dublin.
452. 1947, ["Bernard Shaw on Temperance"], thus in Chappelow, pp. 17–18. Temperance question is too complex to admit of unambiguous solutions; Shaw concludes "that in literary work only teetotallers can produce the best and sanest of which they are capable." But there is no blinking the fact that geniuses may "draw on their vital capital by dosing themselves with brandy. Ataturk saved Turkish civilization in this way whilst the abstemious Hitler wrecked Germany. . . . Dickens (on his American tour which killed him) lived on fiery stimulants."
453. 1947–48, "Shame and Wounded Snobbery: A Secret Kept for 80 Years," *SSS*, pp. 20, 22. Confesses "to an episode in [his boyhood] . . . so repugnant to [him] that for 80 years" he kept it secret: his being sent to a Roman Catholic school in 1869, losing "caste outside it and [becoming] a boy with whom no Protestant young gentleman would speak or play. . . . It was to me what the blacking warehouse was to Dickens." Instructive experience in that it led him to reject public school education for proletarian children and thus "absorbing them into the service of the capitalist class. . . ."
454. 1947–48, "Shame and Wounded Snobbery," *SSS*, p. 29. Law and Order. Outbursts among schoolboys in headmaster's absence, among privileged passengers and at Fabian Society "spree" "taught me how thin is the veneer of bourgeois civilization, and why I, no more than Shakespear and Dickens, can be persuaded that, without natural leaders and rulers, democratic civilization can be achieved under the pretext of Liberty. . . ."
455. 1948, "Preface," A. R. Wilson, *The Miraculous Birth of Language* (London, 1948); Tauber, p. 125. *Per* Tauber, *summa* of Shaw's ideas on linguistic reform. GBS applauds Wilson's experiment in using an "Initial Teaching" alphabet, teaching students to read along phonemic lines. "In what direction . . . can labor be saved? . . . 1. Discard useless grammar. 2. Spell phonetically. . . . We are all over the shop with our vowels because we cannot spell them with our alphabet. Like Scott, Dickens, Artemus Ward and other writers of dialect, I have made desperate efforts to represent local and class dialects by the twenty-six letters of the Latin alphabet, but found it impossible. . . ."
456. 1948, "Preface," *Miraculous Birth;* Tauber, p. 131. Henry Sweet's attempt "to bedevil [his alphabet] into an instrument for verbatim reporting." Dozens of adequate methods of reporting available: witness the record of Cromwell's debates and St. Joan trial records. "Dickens was a competent verbatim reporter before any of the systems now in use were invented." Needed instead of Sweet's "contractions and guessings": "an alphabet with which the English language [can] be unequivocally spelt at full length, and not a new reporting shorthand."
457. 1948–49, "Am I a Pathological Case?" Preface, *Farfetched Fables*, *BH* VII, 385; *CP*, p. 895. "Is literary genius a disease? . . . Shakespear, Walter Scott, Alexandre Dumas, myself: are we all mental cases?" Free association always recalls literary associations to Shaw: "The word dagger got nothing from me but Macbeth. Highway and stile produced Autolycus, Interpreter the Pilgrim's Progress, blacksmith Joe Gargery. . . . Can I then be given credit for common sanity? . . . If I plead that I am only doing what More and Bunyan, Dickens and Wells did I do not exonerate myself: I convict them."
458. 1948–49, "Divine Providence," Preface, *Farfetched Fables*, *BH* VII, 387; *CP*, p. 896. Mistaken assumption that the Life Force is a respecter of morals. CD's dipsomania on his 2nd American tour.

459. 1948–49, "England's Shamefaced Leadership," Preface, *Farfetched Fables, BH* VII, 426; *CP,* p. 914. Post-war political and economic chaos vs. 19th-century doxologies. "Carlyle called our boasted commercial prosperity shooting Niagara, and dismissed Cobdenist Free Trade as Godforsaken nonsense. The pious Conservative Lord Shaftesbury and the Radical atheist demagogue Bradlaugh were at one in their agitation for Acts in restraint of the prevalent ruthless exploitation of labor. Robert Owen had called for a New Moral world as loudly as any of our present post war Chadbands" [*Bleak House,* chs. 19, 25].

460. 1 May 1949, "George Bernard Shaw on *David Copperfield,*" *D* XLIV, 118. "*David Copperfield,* once Dickens's pet book, was wiped out by *Great Expectations,* much as Dora was wiped out by Flora, and Little Em'ly left as dead as a door-nail."

461. c. July 1949, "Shaw's Marginalia to Bunyan's *Life and Death of Mr. Badman,*" *Shaw Review* IX (1966), 97. Annotates Bunyan's belief in the authenticity of certain brimstone-and-hellfire stories: "The infantile credulity of this from a man of John's mental calibre is astonishing; but in my youth a common form of asseveration was 'Lord strike me dead if I am not speaking the truth.' See Dickens's Great Expectations" [Magwitch, chs. 49–50].

462. c. July 1949, "Marginalia to Bunyan," *Shaw Review,* p. 98. Annotates Bunyan on the choice of bankrupt's creditors either to forgive or exact legal penalty; Shaw conveniently ignores first alternative and underlines second: "Bunyan did not know as much about this as Dickens learnt when his father was a prisoner for [debt] in the Fleet and the Marshalsea. Bunyan makes no protest against the horror of the practice."

463. 6 Nov 49, "More About Morris," *The Observer,* rev. of *William Morris: Prophet of England's New Order* by Lloyd Eric Grey (London, 1949). Morris's enormous impact on his acquaintances; his imperviousness to influence by 19th-century poets; under the spell of Dickens and Dumas, his pet storytellers.

464. 1 Dec 49, "The Problem of Common Language," *The Listener;* Tauber, p. 154; Chappelow, pp. 458–59. "It is Johnsonese that we cannot afford, not a forty-letter alphabet. For more than seventy years I have written books, plays, articles, and private letters, in legible phonetics, and thereby added at least two months every year to my productive lifetime as compared to Shakespear and Dickens. . . ."

465. ?1949, Barbara Smoker, "G.B.S. and the A.B.C.," thus in Chappelow, p. 436. To the same effect as above. Quotes Shaw that "Shakespear and Dickens . . . might have written two or three more plays and novels 'in their short lives' if phonetic notation had been acceptable to their players and printers."

466. 23 Feb 1950, "Old Bachelor Butler," *The Observer;* as "Butler When I Was a Nobody," *Saturday Review of Literature* (New York), 29 April; *SA* I, 146. Butler's hunch about the female authorship of *The Odyssey* quite as plausible as CD's hunch about George Eliot's sex.

467. 6 May 50, "The Play of Ideas," *New Statesman;* West, p. 292; *SA* II, 153. "Theatre technique begins with the circus clown and ringmaster and the Greek tribune, which is a glorified development of the pitch from which the poet of the market place declaims his verses, and, like Dickens's Sloppy or a modern playwright reading his play to the players, reads all the parts in different voices" [*Mutual Friend,* Bk. I, ch. 16; 356 supra].

468. 1950, "Shaw and the Alphabet," *New Statesman,* 26 Jan 57; Barbara Smoker quoting from a letter written by Shaw "only a few weeks before his death to Russell Scott, who was still trying to interest Shaw in the phonetic script *Sprechspur*"; cited in Tauber, p. 157. Shaw to Scott: "Never waste time writing to very old men. I am 94, finished, I can do no more. You must carry on from where I left off" (A).

469. n.d. Blanche Patch, *Thirty Years with G.B.S.* (London, 1951), p. 221. Quotes Shaw on the difficulty of convincing the world that Shelley and he, as vegetarians, "surpassed Shakespear and Keats and Dickens and the rest of the carnivorous authors."

IV. Addenda: 1885 to 1913.

470. 25 Aug 1885, "Folk Lore, English and Scotch," rev. of "Twixt Ben Nevis and Glencoe" by the Rev. Alexander Stewart (Edinburgh, 1885), *PMG*. "The banished Duke in As You Like It, who found sermons in stones, has probably often been envied . . . by ecclesiasts at a loss for the morrow's discourse. He also found books in the running brooks, but on this point . . . he is equalled by [Stewart], who finds articles in streams, storms, rats, mice, birds, and fishes. . . . For example, in discoursing on rats, he opines that 'the scene in Hamlet would lose much of its grim humour . . . if it were not for the rat behind the arras.' This almost reminds one of Mr. Wopsle's dresser, who maintained that the secret of all great actors of Hamlet was that they never permitted their tights to be seen in profile" [*Great Expectations*, ch. 31].

471. 17 Sept 85, "Physical Expressions," rev. of book by Francis Warner, M.D., *PMG*. Mildly sardonic but generally favorable comment on Warner's solemn scientific earnestness. "Hitherto writing a novel has been, like spelling Mr. Weller's name, a matter of taste and fancy. The heroine has turned bright red or deathly pale quite arbitrarily. . . . But the criticism of the future will diagnose all such symptoms and judge the work accordingly. . . . The actor will be even worse off. He will be expected to determine Hamlet's diathesis from his acts and speeches" [*Pickwick*, "I puts it down a 'Vee,' " ch. 34].

472. 9 Oct 85, "Andromeda; or, A Castle in the Air," rev. of "Andromeda" by George Fleming (pseud.), 2 vols., *PMG*. On women writers who assume masculine pseudonyms, which is "neither a sensible nor a sincere [practice]." Fleming past mistress at building fictitious castles in the air. Holiday romance about idlers "unproductively consuming their wealth while travelling" abroad. Fleming "sees [these tourists] in the light of their own dreams, and has no suspicion of that relation of theirs to the work-a-day world in view of which Dickens, in 'Little Dorrit,' made the British abroad appear so deplorably futile and disreputable. . . . Indeed, [Fleming's characters] should be very good company if they were not so low-spirited in consequence of having nothing to do but fall in love."

473. 21 Oct 85, "History from a Genteel Point of View," rev. of "The Journal of Mary Frampton from 1779 to 1864," ed. by her niece Harriot Georgiana Murdy, *PMG*. Capital reading for idolators of English royalty, who will brave all weathers "in loyal fulfillment of their mission to stare at Majesty in uniform." Even George IV gets off lightly: "He took some trouble to procure for his daughter a trustworthy governess . . . who seems to have been a sort of aristocratic Mrs. Gummidge. . . . One cannot help suspecting that the poor young Princess would have been content with a less respectable and more cheerful preceptress." On Frampton's style, which is "generally free from the correctness of the professional writer. Thus she says of Lady Jersey:—'Amongst other freaks she was a very fine lady, but in general respected my aunt.' "

474. 5 Dec 85, "A Strange Voyage," rev. of novel of same title by W. Clark Russell, 3 vols., *PMG*. Russell's "nautical novels are refreshingly briny and breezy results of the discovery of the picturesque." Russell "a literary Turner" in his atmospheric

effects and the superiority of his landscapes to his figures. His obsession for detail: "Like Mr. Pecksniff's articled pupils, who were condemned to draw Salisbury Cathedral from every possible point of view, Mr. Clark Russell presents his ship in all weathers, at all hours, and from all quarters of the horizon" [*Chuzzlewit*, ch. 2].

475. 6 Jan 1886, "The Truth About Shakespeare," rev. of "Shakespeare's Sonnets," Facsimile in Photo-lithography of the first Quarto. Introduction by Thomas Tyler (London, 1885), *PMG*. Almost unstinted praise for Tyler's success in "changing all [the romantic obscurity about Shakespeare] to broad daylight" and avoiding the "national pretense that the black spots in human nature are white...." Cites Bret Harte's spoof on genteel English novels; comments: "There spoke the typical English lady, carrying out Mrs. General's great precept of never appearing conscious of anything that is not perfectly proper, placid, and pleasant" [*Dorrit*, Bk. II, ch. 5]. Relevance to Shakespeare's sonnets: as "the autobiography of the greatest of Englishmen" sonnets are peculiarly prone to conventional conspiracy to "exhibit great men, not as they were, but as ideal figures in which the Village Blacksmith and Mr. Pecksniff are blended in proportions determined by the degree of sophistication suggested by the [subject's] social circumstances...."

476. 3 March 86, "John Hullah," rev. of "Life of John Hullah, LLD," by his Wife, *PMG*. Begins with brief survey of 19th-century music: "All this prolific period... fell within Hullah's experience"; but instead of exploring this vein, Mrs. H. prefers to dwell on commonplaces which "like Rogue Riderhood's imprisonment, 'might have happened to any man' " [*Mutual Friend*, Bk. I, ch. 12]. Hullah's own fragmentary memoir touches on his collaboration with CD's youthful *Village Coquettes* (1836); his opinion of CD that " 'He had, like the majority of literary English of that day, no critical knowledge of music....' " "Pleasant as [Mrs. Hullah's] touch is, we feel that a little more of Hullah in his intercourse with Mark Pattison, F. D. Maurice, Dickens, and others, and... a little less of him in his packings and unpackings and Channel crossings, would have given us a deeper insight into the man."

477. 21 April 86, "In the Picture-Galleries: The Royal Institute," *World*. The "painters of the British school display hardly enough invention, per thousand, to furnish a single shilling dreadful. If the sentimentalities that are meant to be tragic, and the good-natured imbecilities that are offered as humorous, were as ill painted as they are ill thought out, a painter to-day would be deservedly less esteemed than a circus athlete.... Mr. C. Green sends some pictures from Dickens, and they are by no means bad; but they are tame, and lack the native perception of the extravagant aspects of everyday-life without which Captain Cuttle and the Weller family cannot be fully revealed."

478. 30 April 86, "Two Insidious Volumes" [subsequently issued as "Mr. Barlow Again"], rev. of "A Sporting Quixote" by S. Laing, 2 vols., *PMG*. Idiotically disquisitory novel, with ill-instructed observations on music, art, economics. Laing assumes that what isn't good enough for a volume of essays "is good enough for a novel—a most pernicious extension of the principle that 'ce qui est trop sot d'être dit, on le chante.' " An "omniscient [schoolmaster] Barlow is hard enough to bear, but a fallible Barlow is beyond all endurance." Laing's resolute cheerfulness "if the book be widely circulated, will induce a pessimistic reaction. The Cheeryble twins in 'Nicholas Nickleby' are not more insufferable than [Laing's Quixote]. Even Dickens found it necessary to atone for Cheeryble by giving us Mr. Bounderby, who may be regarded as the dual Cheeryble found out and shown up, as Flora Finching was the exposure of Dora Spenlow." Laing's bromidic perception that an awkward person may be superior to his Thersites: "did

he not know that we already have Tom Pinch and Dobbin to console us for our guilty consciousness of a share in their deficiencies?...."

479. 5 May 86, "In the Picture-Galleries: The Academy and the Grosvenor," *World*. "Mr. Whistler's Notes, Harmonies, and Nocturnes are arranged in brown and gold, beneath a brown and gold velarium, in charge of a brown and gold porter. It may be said of Mr. Whistler, as of Mr. Sparkler's ideal mistress, that he has no nonsense about him [*Dorrit*, II, 14]. He has the public about him; and he not only humours their nonsense but keeps it in countenance by a dash of nonsensical eccentricity...."

480. 12 May 86, "In the Picture-Galleries: The Academy and the Grosvenor," *World*. "Mr. Spencer Stanhope's 'Why seek ye the living among the dead?' might have been produced by 'the profeel machine' alluded to by Samuel Weller [ch. 33]. Three persons, with exactly the same profile and exactly the same love lorn air—as of Mrs. Gummidge thinking of the old one—thrust forward their chins at an angle, also in profile, but facing the opposite way, and in comparatively high spirits" [*Copperfield*, ch. 3 and passim].

481. 19 May 86, "In the Picture-Galleries. Water-Colour and Other Art Shows," *World*. "Ernest Hart's astonishing Japanese collection" at the Society of Arts. Native ideas of Japanese art based on "sixpenny umbrellas ... and paper fans" jolted by the swords, lacquer boxes, etc., "each of which is a ... miracle of such craftsmanship as seems impossible even under the most favourable feudal conditions." GBS himself amazed: "Not that either [exhibitor] would have practiced *hari-kari* on me if I had expressed a doubt; but that my senses could not refuse the evidence of swords which ... looked—to quote Mr. Smallweed—'awful sharp and gleaming...'" [*Bleak House*, ch. 26].

482. 11 June 86, "Mr. Laurence Oliphant's New Novel," rev. of *Masollam: A Problem of the Period*, 3 vols., *PMG*. On the Art of Lying. "... the introduction of quack theosophy into works of art raises the whole question of the morality of fiction." Quackery vs. legitimate literary lies: "... what is the business of a novelist if not to describe events that never happened and to repeat conversations that never took place? Dickens ... not only did both, but actually held up one of his fictitious characters to reprobation and ridicule for following his example. If his reproach to Mrs. Gamp that there was 'no sich person' as Mrs. Harris be a valid one, does it not equally condemn himself, seeing that as a matter of fact, there was no such a person as Mrs. Gamp? A distinction cannot be made between the two cases on any other ground than that Mrs. Gamp was true as a type if not as an individual ... whereas Mrs. Harris with her morbidly sympathetic temperament ... and her heroine worship of the monthly nurse, was non-representative, impossible ... and in effect a piece of false evidence brought forward by the most interested party to support an inaccurate theory of Mrs. Gamp's moral character." Query then: Is Oliphant "in the position of Dickens towards Mrs. Gamp, or in that of Mrs. Gamp towards Mrs. Harris [?]" [Betsey Prig to Mrs. Gamp, *Chuzzlewit*, ch. 49].

483. 20 Aug 86, "A Brace of Novels," rev. of "In a Silver Sea" by B. L. Farjeon, 3 vols. and "Alicia Tennant" by Frances Mary Peard, 2 vols., *PMG*. Re. "Alicia Tennant": though of female authorship, book "enforces the masculine moral that the ... hardest duty to perform [is] ... to oneself." Alicia to marry a Mr. Lynne but attracted to a Major Saunderson, "'a tall, soldierly looking man, with a keen eye and a closely fitting nose.'... No such subtlety as the attraction of a closely fitting nose is needed to explain the preference, for Mr. Lynne is a ... person stuffed with unassimilated knowledge, chiefly about the ancient Etruscans. Alicia does not

like the match, but . . . she lumps it, as the nursery locution runs, much as Captain Bunsby lumped his nuptials with Mrs. MacStinger" [*Dombey*, ch. 60].

484. 2 Sept 86, "Mr. Norris's Friend Jim," rev. of W. E. Norris's "My Friend Jim," *PMG*. Laudatory. On the proximity of author to narrator. "Lady Bracknell has not a gleam of virtue nor a stroke of ill-luck throughout. It is true that she loses both her little boy and her husband; but does without the one very cheerfully and replaces the other to considerable advantage. . . . The boy's deathbed is capitally described. Jefferies . . . would not weep so very copiously over it as over the death of Paul Dombey [ch. 16]; but many who protest against the pathos of 'Dombey and Son' as egotistical, unphilosophic and suburban, will spare a tear for little Lord Sunning without feeling compromised." Norris's "quiet realism" and authenticity of presentation.

485. 20 Oct 86 [untitled notice], *World*. "Mr. Jan Van Beers is in the field again at the Salon Parisien, with corpses, nightmares, skeletons, peepholes, dark closets, and other devices for making British flesh creep. . . . As you advance, . . . your funeral knell tolls, and a green light flashes on your face. . . . When this palls, you stumble about in the dark in search of excessively inconvenient peepholes, through which you can obtain precarious glimpses of decapitated persons, 'steepled in their goar,' like Mr. Squeers [Fanny Squeers to Ralph Nickleby, ch. 15]. . . . it pays better to be a first-rate charlatan than a second-rate Academician."

486. 24 Nov 86, "A Science of Ghosts," rev. of "Phantasm of the Living" by Edmund Gurney, Frederic W. H. Myers, and Frank Podmore. 2 vols., *PMG*. "This formidable array of ghost stories . . . reminds one of those several manuscript confessions upon which Mr. Wemmick set particular value as being, to use his own words, 'every one of 'em lies, sir' [*Great Expectations*, ch. 25]. It is useless to mince matters in dealing with ghost stories—the existence of a liar is more probable than the existence of a ghost."

487. 6 Jan 1887, "A Life of Madame Blavatsky," rev. of "Incidents in the Life of Mme Blavatsky," ed. A. P. Sinnett, *PMG*. "Only such faith as [Sinnett's] could achieve a reverent and sincere account of a lady to whose 'first command and look there came rushing to her through the air her tobacco pouch, her box of matches, her pocket handkerchief or anything she asked'—. . . who, above all, is under the spiritual guidance of a guru. (This is not the place to explain what a guru is; but it may interest theosophists to know that as long ago as 1850 there was published in the thirteenth chapter of David Copperfield a description of a marine store dealer at Chatham whose usual mode of address was, 'Oh, my eyes and limbs! oh, my lungs and liver! oh, goroo, goroo!' and we are told that 'he was well known in the neighbourhood, and enjoyed the reputation of having sold himself to the devil.')"

488. 11 Jan 87, "Something Like a History of Music," rev. of "A History of Music" by J. F. Rowbotham, 3 vols., *PMG*. "Mr. Rowbotham's style is one that challenges special attention. [In vol. 2], which is entirely devoted to Greek music, he . . . not only begins all his sentences with 'And,' as Edgar Poe did in his more affectedly written tales, but actually ventures on such constructions as 'a voluntary omission for the purpose of producing a pleasing effect on the ear, which how it did so we cannot now judge.' This sort of English is pardonable in a Greek or in Mrs. Gamp, but not in an historian whose native tongue is English."

489. 30 March 87, "A New Novel by Bertha Thomas," rev. of "Elizabeth's Fortune," 3 vols., *PMG*. "Edmund Sparkler's ideal woman, 'well educated and with no nonsense about her,' has not yet been realized among lady novelists. They have gained the education . . . but they have not shaken off the nonsense. Perfect novel-writing requires nerve." Nevertheless, high praise for Thomas's sharp character definitions and general tact—"all these are manna in the desert of fiction."

490. 13 April 87, "Picture Shows," *World*. Exhibit by Society of Lady Artists, Egyptian Hall. "Mrs. Perugini opposes a mild Millais to a crude Frank Holl by Miss Katherine Bywater (for most of these ladies imitate some favoured gentleman). . . . Mrs. H. G. Moberly's . . . conception of Little Nell as a rather dark, determined girl, and of Nell's grandfather as something like Mrs. Ruskin in a heroic mood, is certainly not Dickensian."

491. 20 April 87, "In the Picture Galleries," *World*. Nothing new to be said about the excellent collection mounted by the Royal Society of Painters in Water-Colours. But "Mr. C. Gregory harps on the ups and downs of San Remo, as Mr. Pecksniff's pupils harped on Salisbury Cathedral" [474, supra].

492. 27 April 87, "In the Picture Galleries," *World*. The Royal Institute and "the levelling effect of water-colour. . . . Mr. Charles Green's 'Fanny Dorrit' is not like her: Mr. Sparkler would never have accepted such a person as his ideal well-educated woman, with no nonsense about her. . . . [Mr. F. Goodall's] 'Andromeda' . . . undeniably 'a fine figure of a woman,' lies . . . on a sea-bound rock and is so pleased with herself . . . that she does not worry about the monster, and indeed seems to know all about Perseus beforehand" [479, 489, supra].

493. 11 May 87, "The Grosvenor Gallery," *World*. ". . . may I say, whilst in a plaintive strain, that I doubt whether Mrs. Stillman shows any real appreciation of a strong man like Dante by repeatedly painting him as a limp, sprawling, moping, mediaeval Mrs. Gummidge?"

494. 25 June 87, "Poet's Corner," ominbus rev. of 8 vols. of verse, including " 'A Trilogy of the Life to Come' and Other Poems" by Robert Brown, Jun. "Mr. Robert Brown is a learned man and an inveterate rhymester . . . but he is only a poet insofar as all men, like Silas Wegg, drop into poetry occasionally [*Mutual Friend*, Bk. I, ch. 5 and passim]. When he 'sat beside the margin of the gently sweeping deep ere yet the brightest star of heaven had passed the western steep,' he moralizes thus:—'Q.—What is Eternity? A.—Myself. Q.—What am I? A.—Progress.' " etc., etc.

495. 6 July 87 [untitled notice], *World*. ". . . clever and pretty drawings offered at very modest prices at Messrs. Cassell's exhibition, Memorial Hall." "Mr. Fred Barnard's studies from Thackeray are by no means so happy as his Dickens pictures."

496. 15 July 87, "A Runaway from Civilization," rev. of "Episodes in a Life of Adventure; or, Moss from a Rolling Stone" by Laurence Oliphant, *PMG*. Contemptuous dismissal of Oliphant's traffic in spiritualism, sham politics, etc. "Mr. Laurence Oliphant is a many-sided man. To be precise, he is four-sided, as a square man ought to be; and one of his complaints is that he could find nothing but round holes in English society, wherefore he dwells in the East, and holds communion with spirits. That is one of his sides. . . . Fourthly, he is a novelist, in extenuation of which he may plead, like the wife beater in the Wellerist fable, that, after all, it is an amiable weakness" [ch. 23].

497. 12 Oct 87, "Some Books About Music," rev. of 3 histories of music, including "The Great Composers" by George T. Ferris, ed. Mrs. William Sharp, *PMG*. Apart from "orthographic peculiarities," "inaccuracies of spelling" and "inaccuracies of statement," only stale opinions. "Some of [Ferris's] enthusiasm's are not unwelcome as echoes of a bygone time. . . . If the Camelot Classics are intended to 'strike a chord,' as Mr. Guppy said, in the breast of the old fogey, then no doubt Mr. Ferris was well chosen for the musical part [of the Camelot series]. Young students . . . recommended to seek fresher councils" [*Bleak House*, ch. 20 and passim].

498. 19 Oct 87 [notice signed "Atlas"], *World*. Harry Furniss's drawings at the Gainsborough Gallery. Furniss no match for Leech or DuMaurier, who know how to get

"abundant fun out of society without forgetting the artistic impulse ... or overstepping the line between ridicule and insult which divides the satirist from the street-boy." "Seriousness of intention and width of sympathy ... [make] a great humourist. Pickwick is a very funny book; but it is not Pickwick that we think of when we make large claims for the author of Little Dorrit and Great Expectations. Mr. Furniss must be satisfied for the present with the compliment implied in illustrating his case by that of Dickens."

*499. [7 Nov 87] "The Best Books for Children" (BL Add. MS 50693, ff. 248–51). Charming, detailed account of his childhood reading; his reading of Shakespeare while he still took Shakespeare to be a book, not a man; his discovery of Tale of Two Cities and Great Expectations in old issues of All the Year Round and his surprise at discovering the source of Pip's wealth. On naive vs. trained reading: his critical powers in childhood already fully developed; his favorite activity as an adult is to allege reasons for the literary opinions he formed as a child. Concludes that while second-rate novels will do for adults, children require first-rate stuff. Shaw subjoins two rosters listing the 9 most highly recommended novels respectively for children and for older boys; CD the only author to get two entries (with Two Cities and Great Expectations in the children's category).

500. 23 Nov 87, "Old Stories in New Novels," rev. of "Like and Unlike" by the Author of "Lady Audley's Secret," "Old Blazer's Hero" by D. Christie Murray, and "The Fiddler of Lugau" by the Author of "The Atelier du Lys." PMG. On the popular craving for lack of novelty in fiction and the arts, fostered already in the nursery. "... one thing that will not succeed [in reading to children] ... is what critics call originality." Once a child hears a story it likes, "it only desires to hear that story over and over again.... When it grows up, its culture may be wide and its taste exalted, yet when it wants to be amused you find it reading its Shakespeare and Dickens for the hundredth time; ... or listening to the 'Messiah,' or 'Don Giovanni,' or Beethoven in C minor, as if these were the latest fashions in music."

501. 30 Nov 87, "In the Picture Galleries: The Royal Institute and the British Artists," World. Mostly Whistler. While Whistler has decisively routed the opposition, he hasn't taken in Shaw, whose "delight in seeing a picture with something to breathe in does not ... reconcile [him] to the occasional prevalence of a ghastly lilac-coloured fog, worse, almost, than the good north light of the studio.... In much the same spirit as that in which Joseph Gargery met the supersubtleties of Mr. Jaggers, I ask Mr. Whistler if so be as he can draw a girl reading, to up and draw her; if not, to let her alone and give us more red notes" [Great Expectations, ch. 18].

502. 27 Dec 87, "Some Small Poetry of 1887," omnibus review of 22 vols. of verse, PMG. "England is famous among nations for her poetry. Here are twenty-two volumes of it. Heigho! First, seven Jubilee poets, knowing nothing, or thereabouts, of the history of the reign, the geography of the Empire, and the personal characteristics of our Royal family, yet loyally ready, like Mr. Wemmick's witnesses, to 'swear, in a general way, to anything' courtly on these subjects" [Great Expectations, ch. 20].

503. 14 Jan 1888, "Realism in Fiction," delivered 18 Jan at meeting of The Blackheath Essay and Debating Society (MS Univ. of Texas Library; Quinn). Realism as the goal of fiction; the general shiftiness of the operative term when applied to different 19th-century novelists. Dickens's approach to a kind of supra-realism in his later novels; yet even Dickens at his best falls short of the (hypothetical and unattainable) realistic novel as Shaw conceives it.

504. 21 March 88 [untitled notice], World. "The French Gallery harbours ... a couple

of capital Seilers, with Voltaire in a rage in one, and Benjamin Franklin, strongly suggestive of Mr. Casby, in the other...."

505. 18 May 88, "A New Novel with a Heroine," rev. of "The Romance of the Canoness" [*Der Roman der Stiftsdame*] by Paul Heyse, trans. J. M. Percival (New York, 1888), *PMG*. Difficulty of creating a woman in fiction who is neither a Rowena nor a Jezebel; Heyse's success in "depict[ing] a noble woman.... [Heyse] a realist in the true sense, whole skies above the naturalists who offer you a photograph of Polly Jones.... Heyse, in the person of [his] student, drops one criticism in English noveldom. 'Thackeray ... was my special favourite, whilst Dickens seemed to me a sentimental mannerist, striving for effect, with no correct ideas of women.' The reproach is hardly as just to the Dickens of 'Little Dorrit' as to the Dickens of 'Bleak House'; but the truth is that the heroines of even our best novelists are by no means the master-creations of English literature. No English novelist seemed able to conceive such women as George Sand drew for us." Ibsen's influence on Heyse; the friendship between the two; the absence "in Heyse's pages [of] any malign touch of the competitive spirit" against Ibsen.

506. 23 July 88, "Two Unimpressive Pamphlets," rev. of "Death—and Afterwards" by Edwin Arnold and "Preface to a new edition of 'A Romance of Two Worlds' " by Marie Corelli, *PMG*. "The zest with which [Arnold] decorates trivial subjects and vulgar prejudices by magnificent platitudes and impetuous alliterations is as extraordinary as his power of saying, with perfect and sincere gravity, things that make an ordinary man lie down on the hearthrug and scream himself breathless with merriment. One single grain of susceptibility to the ridiculous would spoil him for ever, as irremediably as it would have spoiled Mr. Pecksniff. Not that [Arnold] is here liked on the moral side to the Salisbury architect; but ... [their] resemblance in descriptive genius ought to ... make the *Daily Telegraph* very popular with the Pecksniffian section of the Island. For example, who but Seth Pecksniff or Sir Edwin Arnold could have described a young woman in the Health Exhibition, looking at a showcase containing the ingredient of human flesh and bone as 'the bright maiden who contemplated with unconvinced smiles those alleged materials of her being'?"

507. c. July 1888, To Covent Garden Manager, *CL* I, 192. Complains of the prescribed apparel, acting and "obsolete and ridiculous" scenery at Covent Garden under Augustus Harris's management. "I cannot stand sky borders, tragedy queens in black dresses, old men made up like Father Christmas, heroes in blue satin tunics ... and all the other things that I have read about in Crummles, and seen the relics of in provincial theatres in my boyhood."

508. 13 March 1889 [untitled notice], *World*. Pokes fun at resolution prefaced to catalogue by The Royal Society of Painter-Etchers " 'in partial acknowledgment of [his] invaluable services' " to feature prominently the etchings of its president, Seymour Haden. "As Mr. Merdle's representative of the Bar would have said, this is 'cheering to know, cheering to know' [*Dorrit*, Bk. II, ch. 12].... Mr. Axel Haig's gloomy interiors remind one here and there of the effects obtained years ago by Hablot Browne in his illustrations to *Little Dorrit*."

509. 20 March 89. "In the Picture Galleries: The Royal Institute," *World*. "At the Royal Institute, the first thing you do after paying a shilling for admission is to pay another for a catalogue.... As to criticizing the pictures, ... that is out of the question.... Still, as there is always a certain piquancy in disparagement ... it may please Mr. Charles Green's friends to hear that his inveterate rusticity makes him impossible as an illustrator of Dickens. The young man from the country, whom

he labelled Dick Swiveller, was bad enough; but what is to be said of the bucolic Mantalini and the flagrant parish clerk effectually masquerading as a broker's man in 'What's the demd total?' It is a pity that the only capable artist-devotee of Dickens, who is neither mannered nor vulgar, should be pleased at such a demnition discount by the ineradicable villager in him. [*Nickleby*, ch. 10 and passim]. Be it also observed that Kate Nickleby was the last person in the world to put her elbow on the mantelpiece of the show-room and strike an attitude."

510. 20 March 89, "In the Picture Galleries: French Gallery," *World*. "At the French Gallery there is a prodigious 'Descent from the Cross,' ... the most striking characteristic of which is its extreme cheerfulness. The subject is treated much as Mark Tapley might have made a point of honour of treating it, if he had had occasion to come out strong in an altar-piece."

511. 24 April 89, "In the Picture Galleries: The New English Art Club—Monet at the Goupil Gallery," *World*. Winthrop Sargent's "overpowering" cleverness. "In 'St. Martin's Summer,' and especially in 'A Morning Walk,' which out-Monets Monet ... Mr. Sargent shows how to do it as conclusively as Mr. Wilson Steer in his 'Head of a Young Girl' shows how not to do it."

*512. 1889, "From Dickens to Ibsen" (BL Add. MS 50693, ff. 201–22). Shaw's fullest treatment of CD before 1900. Abandoned long before Shaw gets on to Ibsen and, for that matter, to any of the novels after *Bleak House*. The more revealing for the seriousness which Shaw here accords CD's earlier books—those he subsequently disavowed in favor of late Dickens; notably detailed and sympathetic comments on *Chuzzlewit*, *Dombey*, *Copperfield*, *Bleak House*. Initial distinction between CD's struggle for social equality among men and Ibsen's for individual liberty for women. CD's failure to understand his mother's social position: conspicuous omission from his books of the "maternal superstition": all his fictional mothers are failed mothers. His snobbish refusal to understand the working class and futile descriptions of mawkish and eccentric domestics; his ignorance of scientific and historical processes. Exposure of middle-class shamming originates in the centrally important presentation of Pecksniff; after Pecksniff, CD the story teller abdicates to CD the social militant. Splendid brief analysis of *Dombey*, whose title character typifies the tragedy of middle-class life; Paul's death trivial compared with the attack on institutionalized marriage. Similarly, *Copperfield*, despite some notable power failures, a book fraught with pain and self-doubt; e.g., the remarkably ambivalent picture of Dora. *Bleak House* reflects a decisive rupture from early novels in dispensing with stagey physical violence; the quality of its "villains" (Smallweed, Vholes) categorically different from the stage villains of the Squeers variety. For all its allusiveness (to some 60 characters), extraordinarily compact fragment. On Pecksniff, ff. 210–14; *Dombey*, 215–17, *Copperfield*, 217–19, *Bleak House*, 219–22.

513. 6 Sept 1890, "Sir Arthur Sullivan," *The Scots Observer; MCr*, p. 191 [unsigned]. On the iniquity to composers by Grove's *Dictionary*, which gives 9 columns to Sterndale Bennett and one column to Offenbach. "Grove ... owes it to society not to mention that La Grande Duchesse ... places its composer heavens high above the superfine academicians who won rest and self-complacency ... by doing for Mendelssohn what Pasteur has done for the hydrophobia virus, and who by example and precept urged his pupils never to strive after effect. This counsel, worthy of the best form of Mrs. General, was not only, as Wagner remarked, 'all very well, but rather negative': it was also a rebuke to Offenbach, who was always striving after effect, as every artist ... must unceasingly strive. ... The reader is now in a position to understand the tragedy of Sir Arthur Sullivan. He was a Mendelssohn scholar ... and now he has five columns in Grove and is a knight."

514. 23 Dec 1891, "Brahms, Beethoven, and The Barber of Bagdad," *World; MCr*, p. 204. Student performance of Goldmark's violin concerto at the Royal Academy of Music by one Philip Cathie: "Every generation produces its infant Raphaels and infant Rosciuses [Barkis about David Copperfield, ch. 10] . . . who can perform all the childish feats of Mozart. . . . Mr. Philip Cathie must . . . take it to heart that having made a fiddler of himself, everything now depends on his success in making a man of himself."

*515. 14 April 1892, "The Pickwick Pantomime," rev. of *Pickwick Papers*, Macmillan edn., ed. Charles Dickens Jr. By far Shaw's most exhaustive and fairest reading of CD's first novel. Idle to deny *Pickwick* the status of a classic. Readers who are taken in by the revoltingly "insistent facetiousness . . . and the melodramatic vulgarity of the tragic episodes" ("an adulteration . . . of Swift and Fielding") blinded to the genuine social critique: we fail to appreciate the opening chapter not "because it is barefaced and overdone" but because its reportorial veracity is lost on us. Unrivalled popularity of *Pickwick* rests on its being CD's one book "which can be read without an occasional uncomfortable suspicion that the author was in downright earnest. . . . His view of politics in it is often that of a rowdy undergraduate; and . . . his view of humanity . . . sometimes that of a street arab." If our affection for Pickwick himself mustn't blind us to the sordid social realities, the book is essentially a harlequinade and "as a harlequinade, [it] is incomparable. . . . Molière might have written a Pickwick had he been let run wild from all artistic tradition and provided with a British middle-class audience." The "horribly and squalidly funny" treatment of the elderly shrews; the failure of CD's "columbines" hardly matters. Comparison with later Dickens: no figure in *Pickwick* is funnier than Sparkler in *Dorrit;* yet Sparkler's public appointment [Bk. II, ch. 12] is both "more farcical and more deeply observed" than Slumkey's return at Eatanswill [*Pickwick*, ch. 13]: "Sparkler's sinecure, however sardonically laughable . . . leaves the reader much more uneasy than the death of the Chancery prisoner in the Fleet" [ch. 44] and the transactions of the Finches in *Great Expectations* are more ludicrous and convincing than the scientific hocus-pocus in *Pickwick:* "They form part of [the] tragedy . . . of the miserable emptiness and shiftlessness of the life which society offers to such young men; and you laugh with the wrong side of your mouth." " 'Little Dorrit' and 'Great Expectations' are immeasurably the greatest works of their kind" produced in 19th-century England. Allusions to some 25 *Pickwick* persons.

516. 29 Nov 92, "The Playwright on His First Play," interview drafted by Shaw on *Widowers' Houses, Star; BH* I, 128. Actors' favorite role that of Lickcheese, the slum rent collector: GBS looks forward to interviewer's opinion of James Welch's interpretation, after Welch's role as the Artful Dodger at the Olympic.

517. 27 June 1893, "Playwright Cut Playwright," *Star.* Interview re. George Moore's published play *The Strike at Arlingford.* "The weak point of the play to me is the assumption throughout it all that Socialism is to middle-class man exactly what keeping a turnpike was to old Mr. Weller in 'Pickwick'—the last resource of a soured and desperate wretch [ch. 22]. John Reid, jilted by Lady Ann, takes to Socialism as being just a degree more suicidal than taking to drink."

518. July 1894, "A Dramatic Realist to His Critics," *The New Review; BH* I, 485. On dramatic illusion. "Put a thing on the stage for [the drama critics] as it is in real life, and instead of receiving it with the blank wonder of plain ignorance, they reject it with scorn as an imposture. Offer them Mr. Crummles's real pumps and tubs, and they will denounce both as spurious on the ground that the tubs have no handles, and the pump no bung-hole" [*Nickleby*, ch. 23].

519. 1894, "Socialism and Superior Brains," *Essays in Fabian Socialism* (London, Const-

able, 1931; 1961 edn.), p. 261. On author-economist W. H. Mallock's proposition "that exceptional personal ability is the main factor in the production of wealth...." "... since Labor [per Mallock] gets enough ... to keep it half alive or so, it must get more than its due.... And the excess is a clear tribute levied upon Ability for the benefit of Labor. I take it that this is an inexpugnable proposition. Far from repudiating it ... I embrace it in the spirit in which Mrs Gamp asked Mrs Prig, 'Who deniges of it, Betsey?' [*Chuzzlewit*, ch. 49]. What on earth use would Ability be to us if it did not lighten our toil and increase our gain?"

520. 25 July 1896, "Bassetto at Bayreuth," *Star; MCr*, p. 235. "Radically bad" stage management of the Festspielhaus under Cosima Wagner's stewardship. "I call this amateurish, but from the Bayreuth point of view it is even worse ... it is heretical, being the most foolish characteristic of Italian opera acting.... Probably it is not possible at present to convince a German *prima donna* that Mrs Leo Hunter was not thoroughly right and ladylike in wearing a modish gown along with her helmet when she impersonated Minerva [*Pickwick*, ch. 15]. I do not for one moment dare to suggest that the Rhine maidens should take a hint from our 'living pictures,' and dress like Rhine maidens. The world is not decent enough for that yet. But is it necessary for the three ladies to ... swim about in muslin *fichus* and teagowns?"

521. 1 Jan 1898, to Mrs. Richard Mansfield, Henderson, p. 450. On the first production of *Devil's Disciple,* in which Mansfield created the role of Dick Dudgeon. "I quite understand that the last scene is so arranged that nobody watches Judith, and that the spectacle of Richard Dudgeon making Sidney Carton faces keeps the theatre palpitatingly indifferent to everything else. And that's just what I object to: ... they ought to long for a delay instead of that silly eagerness to see whether the hanging will really come off...."

522. 16 Aug 1901, "Spelling Reform v. Phonetic Spelling: a Plea for Speech Nationalization," to the Editor of *The Morning Leader;* Tauber, p. 14. Early treatment of the subject which was to obsess Shaw during the '30s and '40s. Reply to Archer's "Spelling Reform or Phonetic Spelling" in *The Morning Leader,* 10 Aug; contra Archer's insistence on conventional as against phonetic spelling. "The fact is, you must either let our spelling alone or else reform it phonetically." Conventional spelling "obscures the history of the language.... Shakespear's English is a dead language.... Early nineteenth century English is equally obsolete to young men. No journalist under forty could write anything like one of the 'Sketches by Boz.' "

523. 16 Aug 01, "Spelling Reform," Tauber, p. 14. On the changes in vernacular speech. "Our conventional spelling has not hindered any of these changes: they would have occurred at the same rate if the English language had been spelt all the time on the Weller principle, 'according to the taste and fancy of the speller' [ch. 34; 471 supra]. All that the conventional spelling has done is to conceal the one change that a phonetic spelling might have checked: namely, the changes in pronunciation, including the waves of debasement that produced the half-rural cockney of Sam Weller and the modern metropolitan cockney of Drinkwater [in *Captain Brassbound*]...."

524. ?Feb. 1903, "Feuiletton fuer die Zeit," *Die Zeit*. Introduces his plays in Trebitsch's German translation. "Those critics who, like Dr. Kellner, are experts in English literature, will discover that the character of the Teufelskerl's mother [Mrs. Dudgeon in *Devil's Disciple*] is one of my numerous plagiarisms, being stolen straight out of Charles Dickens's 'Little Dorrit,' just as the barrister in 'You Never Can Tell' is stolen straight out of the same author's 'Great Expectations.' I am a great admirer of Dickens; and I hope to steal many more characters from him before I die."

525. 23 Feb 03, to dramatic agent and critic Reginald Golding Bright, *AYC*, p. 97. Opening of *Devil's Disciple [Ein Teufelskerl]* in Vienna on 25 Feb and row in Berlin over *Arms and the Man [Helden]* between the Social Democratic "Freie Volksbuehne" and the "Deutsches Theater" under Paul Lindau's management. "The Social Democrats say that they cannot be prevented from giving a 'private' performance of a play by a world-renowned Socialist. Lindau threatens legal proceedings. The author and the translator (Siegfried Trebitsch) play Spenlow and Jorkins, Shaw declaring that he prefers a Socialist audience because his plays are intended for exceptionally intelligent people, but that Herr Trebitsch (Mr. Jorkins) must be consulted in the matter; and Trebitsch regretting that his contract with Herr Lindau makes it impossible for him to comply."

*526. 2 June 03, to Kate Perugini (Shaw Collection, Cornell Univ. Libraries). Urges her to write her father's biography so long as she lets the skeletons out of the closet: family prejudice itself may be productive of a truth which is hidden from the objective eye. As a pure story-teller, CD unequal to the low level of popular journalism: e.g., the abysmal interpolated stories in *Pickwick;* his lack of inventiveness such that he should have emulated Shakespeare in pilfering plots. Required the stimulus of socially hinged characters and institutions; but, like Shakespeare, hampered by contemporary philosophy and religion. Yet this very deficiency may have kept him from codifying his materials artificially, thus coming between him and his sheen powers of observation: the description of Chancery from a Fabian viewpoint would have killed its effectiveness. All first-rate writers are Dickensians; all second-raters, Thackerayans. The unexcelled greatness of *Little Dorrit;* its characters vindicated by their complete authenticity. Dorrit's death one of the triumphs of Literature.

527. 3 July 03, "The Fiscal Policy of the Empire," *Daily Mail*. On Joseph Chamberlain's proposed tax reforms. "Mr. Chamberlain . . . protests that he never dreamt of taxing food; that . . . raw material and the food of the people will ever be sacred to him; declares, like Mrs. Micawber, that he will never desert Mr. Balfour; in short, climbs down as far as he dares . . . to the strains of 'For he's a jolly good fellow.'"

528. 11 Feb 1905, "The Dying Tongue of Great Elizabeth," *The Saturday Review;* West, p. 98; Wilson, p. 142. Beerbohm Tree's Production of *Much Ado*. ". . . Mr. Tree is the first [manager] within my experience for whom Shakespear does not exist at all." Tree's "inconsiderate tomfooleries" and distractions: "you should not, like Crummles's comic countryman, catch flies when another actor is trying to hold the audience [*Nickleby*, ch. 30] . . ." Tree's mind "completely free from all preoccupation with Shakespear."

529. 7 Oct 95, "Does Modern Education Ennoble?" *Great Thoughts*. "Obviously no. . . . It is an open fact that the line which divides stupid, ignorant, and prejudiced people from sagacious, well-informed, and open-minded people does not coincide at any point with the line which divides the educated from the uneducated. Dr. Johnson and Gladstone were classically educated men of great natural force. John Bunyan and Charles Dickens were virtually uneducated men of great natural force. Dr. Johnson and Gladstone were conspicuous among the most absurdly ignorant . . . prejudiced . . . society-blind . . . and yet undisciplined men who have ever risen to commanding eminence. Bunyan and Dickens were equally conspicuous for great knowledge of men and things, great penetration in exposing social prejudices . . . and cheerful co-operation combined with vigorous freedom and initiative in social activity. Could anything but the education of a gentleman have produced the endless volumes of unashamed tittle-tattle on which Thackeray wasted his genius?"

530. c. Dec. 1905, "Interview with GBS" (BL Add. MS 50964, f. 130). Largely on his

activities as music critic; GBS on Richard Strauss. Gist of interview: relation of his musical criticism, dramatic activities, and literary know-how. Cites Shakespeare, Bunyan, Dickens among his literary masters when his readers are forever digging up German and Scandinavian sources for his ideology. " 'Please go away, or I shall take another two columns about this.' And the Editor did."

531. 29 June 1907, "Mr. Bernard Shaw's Lecture on 'The New Theology,' " to the Editor of *The Academy*. Takes issue with narrow practice of polytheism as advocated by Lady Grove. "Sir Isaac Newton's confession of ignorance and inexperience seems to her to mark a lower grade of character and intelligence than the assurance of Mr. Stiggins, who knows everything and can move mountains with his faith [*Pickwick*, ch. 27 and passim]. I know this high-class deity very well.... I find his portrait in the best bedroom [of my holiday lodgings]. It is the portrait of a perfect gentleman ... with nice hair, a nice beard, nice draperies ... and an expression which combines the tone of the best Society with the fascination of Wilson Barnett as Hamlet. The ladies who worship him are themselves worshipped by innumerable poor Joblings in shabby lodgings who pin up the Galaxy Gallery of British Beauties on their walls" [*Bleak House*, ch. 20].

532. 10 Dec 1910, rev. of Frank Harris, *Shakespeare and His Love*, *The Nation;* Wilson, p. 199. "Coming to the play itself, the first thing one looks for in it is Shakespeare; and that is just what one does not find. You get 'the melancholy Dane' of Kemble and Mr. Wopsle; but the melancholy Dane was not even Hamlet, much less Shakespeare."

533. 1911, "The Post-Ibsen Renascence of the Drama," Wisenthal, p. 248. Originally intended as preface to a new edition of *The Quintessence*. Habit in the early '80s of referring all natively popular ideas to the influence of Ibsen and the Germans "an illiterate one"—there is "as much English leaven in the lump of modern thought as German and Scandinavian.... Not that the English drama was morally imbecile." Leading playwrights (Grundy, Pinero, Jones, Gilbert) occasionally ruthless critics of society and marriage morality; thus, "Jones, in his efforts to focus the limelight on contemporary social questions, was as much in earnest as Dickens himself."

534. 17 July 1912, "The Idea of God. Mr. G. Bernard Shaw's Surrejoinder to Mr. Campbell," *The Christian Commonwealth;* as "God Must Be Non-Sectarian and International" in Smith, p. 57. Shaw's vindication of his dissent from Reginald John Campbell, enormously popular Congregationalist pastor of City Temple from 1902 to 1915, whose views were often and mistakenly identified with Shaw's in *The Christian Commonwealth*, unofficial organ of City Temple. Where Campbell understands life necessarily in terms of Christianity, "my congregation is as wide as the English language...." How to answer "worshippers of all stripes" who object to Beethoven's harmony as dull and Dickens as unreadable? "... they are none the less entitled to their sensations because I am saturated with Dickens and Beethoven"; hence if he were to work with them, he mustn't make "[his] views hinge on an adoration of Beethoven and Dickens. But for the purpose of a Beethoven Society or a Dickens Fellowship I might safely disregard them, and do very good work by appealing to the love of Beethoven and Dickens. Just so can Mr Campbell do good work by appealing to the love of Jesus felt by [his] congregation.... But this very thing that helps him so powerfully would be fatal to me.... Finally ... my mind is so constituted that if I could conceive a god as deliberately creating something less than himself, I should class him as a cad.... *My* god must continually strive to surpass himself."

535. 19 Aug 12, to Mrs. Patrick Campbell, *PCL*, p. 41. Has advised Granville Barker "to bring *Fanny* to a violent end" because of its chronic box-office failure; wants to get

on with the production of *Pygmalion*. "As the gentleman in *Bleak House* says, il fo manger" [Jobling to Guppy and Smallweed, *Bleak House*, ch. 20].

536. 4 Jan 1913, to Mrs. Patrick Campbell, *PCL*, p. 71. Her performances in Pinero's *Notorious Mrs. Ebbsmith* and John Davidson's *For the Crown* in the '90s. "Nothing that you could do was wrong: everything was a glory. And you, wretch, dare reproach me for this because I did not say 'Mrs. Campbell's . . . readings of the text were original and profound.' That was what you wanted, Mrs. Crummles. And I rolled Pinero in the dust beneath your feet. . . ."

537. 2 April 13, to Mrs. Patrick Campbell, *PCL*, p. 105. Writing from Dublin: "Oh if it were not for this new paper . . . and these serious political schemes in which so much of my work lies . . . I would fly with you and play Higgins to your Liza in little fit-ups in obscure places as Mr. and Mrs. Vincent Crummles, and stay with you in public houses, and raise up a family of Infant Phenomena. But our destiny is higher."

538. n.d. pre-1900. Long fragment on Marx (BL Add. MS 50699, ff. 260–61). The literary bourgeois hampered by his limited intercourse with classes and professions other than his own. Dickens's shock on discovering the lives of the working classes in writing *Hard Times;* its permanent supersession of CD's earlier works.

Cecil Lewis

GEORGE BERNARD SHAW. A PEN STUDY

[*Cecil Lewis's long career has encompassed theatre, films, broadcasting and journalism. An early flier, he wrote of his R.A.F. experiences during the Great War in a memoir,* Sagittarius Rising *(1936), which Shaw praised in one of his rare late reviews. The 1926 interview with Lewis, a look at Shaw at seventy which Shaw so blue-pencilled that it never saw the light of day, has remained unknown until now. The manuscript is published now with the permission of the Humanities Research Center at the University of Texas at Austin, where it is archived; the Estate of Bernard Shaw (see copyright line, p. iv); and Cecil Lewis (see copyright line, p. iv). Shaw's many interlinear corrections and additions are published separately as notes, with lines crossed out indicating his recommended excisions, and lines and words added representing his augmentations or emendations. Lewis's manuscript is published as it was before Shaw took his pen to it, with punctuation left in English style.*]

About eleven o'clock every morning a white launch would be seen, patiently chugging its way over the pale waters of the lake from Stresa and carrying a solitary figure who sat bolt upright in one corner. Nearer came the visitor until the white beard, the panama, and the long burberry proclaimed him George Bernard Shaw.

At fifty yards it was our habit to exchange the Fascist salute—for when you are in Italy you must do as the Italians do—and G.B.S. would finish this off with a friendly, jaunty turn of the wrist. When the launch was safe ashore, he would spring ashore with all the agility of a young man.

Bathing was the order of the day. We would strip under the trees and board the launch, which backed deep into deep water. Then G.B.S. would lead off with a dive, clean and straight, the envy of my less-than-thirty summers. He would come up, wide-eyed and blowing,[1] as if he were seeing the world for the first time and had a great deal he wanted to say about it. Then, with all the leisurely dignity of some ancient marine monster, he would turn on his back and swim away[2] resolutely using his arms like a paddle steamer and making a great deal of splash without much progression! After a little he would lie out and float. "The great thing about[3] floating," he would say, "is[4] to keep your head back."[5] When I had tried and sunk ignominiously into the depths, we would swim off together while I fired questions at him, such as "What is Kantian biology?" There would be no answer. Then after a few gargantuan strokes: "Read Kant." would float up into the blue.

It was after the swim was over, as we sat having sun baths, that the story telling would begin. And such story telling! For what a fermenting world it was in the days when G.B.S. was young! Revolution in thought had never been more rife: revolution in deed was to follow. Nietzsche, Marx, Tolstoy, Ibsen, Wagner, all engaged in turning established standards inside out and showing us how dirty the linings were! Then Shaw himself, ranging like an eagle over the thought, condition and tradition of our time, assimilating his forerunners at a glance, and stooping with the claw of epigram and paradox while the transfixed world wriggled and giggled by turns, unsure whether they were being pricked by a dangerous madman or tricked by an irresponsible jester!

It is common to associate genius with insanity; but those who find anything irresponsible or unbalanced about the Shavian doctrine cannot be familiar with his work. He is in truth ruthlessly sane and consistent. His reputation having been gained (to use his own words) "by my persistent struggle to force the public to reconsider its morals." To this struggle he brings every weapon that sanity can command—humour, human understanding, knowledge and logic, together with the most convincing lucidity of thought and speech.

"Better see sanely on a pound a week than squint on a million" he says and in his effort to convince he dives down through the wrappings of prejudice, hypocrisy, and falsehood with which civilization is overlaid and comes up with an epigram that the world laughs at as a paradox and winks at as a truth.

Storytelling is a great art. It depends so much on gesture, pause, and accent. You may imagine that Shaw, with fifty years of public speaking behind him, does not fail to get his points home. In retailing some of them, nothing, alas!, will convey the noble manner of throwing back the head, the reminiscent chuckle lost in the beard, the spice of Irish accent, the excited—almost nervous—gestures of the arms and the incomparable vigour and good humour with which the most slashing epigram or criticism would be portrayed.

G.B.S. has described himself as a man "up to the neck in the life of his times" and morning after morning he would tell of it. Perhaps it would be Bradlaugh's manner of public speaking, or Rodin sighing, as he cut off the Shavian nose with a piece of string while working on his bust in clay; perhaps Mrs Pat at the rehearsals of *Pygmalion* or[6] Anatole

France embracing[7] him on the platform at the famous meeting of the Fabian Society in the great Frenchman's honour; perhaps it would be Sidney Webb confounding the German Post Office officials by knowing more about their regulations then they did themselves, or[8] meeting Einstein at a London reception. So amusing this last, that it must be recorded in detail. Einstein, the greatest Jew since Jesus—as Haldane describes him—speaks no English. G.B.S., presented to him, mustered all his German in an effort to ask when he was returning to Germany. "Lundi" replied the scientist shortly. He evidently prefers French, thought Shaw, so he tried again in that language, inquiring when the famous mathematician intended to deliver his next lecture.[9] "Dienstag" he replied. "After that" said Shaw, "I gave it up, threw my wife into his arms, and left."[10]

It is, I imagine, only within the last decade that Great Britain—which adds to her many qualities that of resolutely refusing to recognize her great[11] men[12]—has deigned to acknowledge Shaw's existence. Perhaps this is not surprising in a people which allows Shakespeare to die in obscurity and is still too apathetic and ignorant to demand a state building in which his plays might be regularly performed; perhaps it is not surprising in a people which outlaws Byron, persecutes Shelley and falls foul of Keats! The wonder is we think as much of Shaw as we do.

It is true that[13] the news that he is regarded as a classic by every other civilized country in the world has been gradually filtering through to us. In view of that we have gone to the length of supporting one persistent pioneer touring company and even the West End Theatre finds room for him once a year. People dub him a socialist (without knowing the meaning of the word) and give him the go by. This is a pity, because whether you happen to be a Shavian or not, there is no doubt that his pieces for the theatre—all moral issues aside—are superb pieces of theatre craft. Like the Newly Born in the last part of *Methusalah*, Shaw breaks his shell and leaps onto the theatre[14] a fullgrown playwright, with all the tricks of the practised dramatist at his finger's ends—an unerring technique, a flair for character and stage situation, which made his first play *Widowers' Houses* a sensation some forty years ago.

Since then many have followed and we can trace the development of their genius in the growing bulk of those uniform green volumes. We can see their writer turning from the denial of all accepted standards to the heights of spirituality and tolerance on which he stands today. We see the realization that Humanity changes its morals almost as often as it changes its shirt; that the burning question of today is the accepted order tomorrow. Not on these grounds would we wager on Shaw's immortality; but Caesar before the Sphinx, the death of Louis Dubedat and the speeches of Lilith will live in the world's memory when the moral aspect of the plays containing them is of no more interest than the topical allusions in Shakespeare.

Besides, has not the septuagenarian drawn the cloak of prophecy about his shoulders? A different prophecy from others ancient or modern. Jules Verne may foresee the submarine, Wells may predict broadcasting,[15] Kipling the electric hedge—these men foresee what men may *do*. Shaw conceives what mankind may *be*. *Back to Methuselah* is the most prophetic visualization of human destiny that has ever been uttered.

"Why are you so generous with your plays, including three or more in one volume?" I asked Shaw one day.

"Books ought to be sold by weight." he answered.

"But one poem by Browning is worth a hundred other volumes of poetry." I protested.

"That kind of value cannot be measured in terms of money." he replied. "I keep my type small and my volumes are packed with matter. Anyone buying a volume of mine has plenty to read and the volume can be passed round the household. It lasts quite a long time."

This is a typical example of Shavian reasoning, which appearing at first sight invalid, turns out to be sound. Here is another: At a trench mortar demonstration during the war, the shells bursting made huge craters in the earth.[16] To the officer in charge Shaw said: "Very interesting. Now have you, by any chance, another sort of shell that will fill up the craters again?" No doubt the officer wrote him down a fool; but the fact remains that the problem of filling up the holes—in the larger sense of the word—is still *the* problem of the world today.[17]

Are there plays yet to be written? Plays that have been started and never finished? There is at least one and I am not likely to forget the morning when G.B.S., naked to the waist, with his panama on the back of his head, outlined the plot to me under a hot Italian sun.

"When Chesterton was a young man, before he had written any work for the theatre, I said to him one day, Look here: why don't you write a play? He said he couldn't think of a plot and I told him I would supply him with a plot.[18] Of course, he didn't need one really, because shortly afterwards he wrote *Magic* which is a very fine play.

You remember the scene at the end of Goethe's *Faust* when the Devil is sitting alone? Well, the play starts there. St Augustine comes by. 'Good afternoon' he says to the Devil.

'I don't think I know you.' says the Devil.

'Not know *me!*' says the other. 'I am St. Augustine.'

'I don't recall the name.'

'But you must remember me.' says the Saint. 'I converted England to Christianity.'

Then the Devil lets out a long guffaw of very ribald laughter. St Augustine is naturally affronted.

'What are you laughing at?' he asks. After a pause to collect himself the Devil explains that [19] he is laughing at the idea of England's[20] being Christian. St Augustine is extremely shocked and annoyed. He insists vehemently on the success of his conversion. But the Devil begins to give him very cogent reasons, in the Shavian manner (see the Preface to *Androcles and the Lion*) that England is no more Christian than Timbuctoo.[21] His arguments begin to upset the Saint who says he must drop down to earth and see about it.[22]

Accordingly he comes down and lands in front of the Houses of Parliament,[23] where he invites the constable on duty to take him in to see the Prime Minister.

'Any appointment?' inquires the constable.

'No.' says the Saint.

'Can't see the Prime Minister without an appointment.' says the constable officially.

'Appointment!' says Augustine, 'Appointment indeed! I need no appointment. Don't you know who I am?[']

'Can't say as[24] I do' replies the policeman.

'Really!' the Holy Man expostulates, 'Really! No-one seems to know me! I converted your country to Christianity.'

'Did you really!' says the imperturbable constable, 'Fancy that now!'

'I am a Saint.' the holy man goes on.

'Go on!' says the constable, 'What's a Saint anyway?'

'A Saint' says St Augustine, controlling himself with an effort, 'is a man that can perform miracles—a superior being.'

'Well', says the policeman, opening his pocket book and glancing through it, 'there's nothing about Saints or Miracles in my regerlations, so you'd best move on.'

'I tell you I am a Saint.' Augustine goes on, somewhat angrily, and then more graciously,[25] he adds, 'Let me perform a miracle for you.'

'If you're a conjurer' says the policeman, 'I can do a bit of sleight of hand myself. Go on; but no monkey tricks, mind.'

'What would you like me to do?' asks St Augustine.

'Dunno' says the constable, scratching his ear and then, brightening, he laughs, 'You turn my truncheon into a cucumber. That'd be a proper miracle, that would.'

'Pull it out.' says St Augustine. The constable pulls it out and, of course, it is a cucumber. Whereupon he becomes enormously impressed and respectful and takes St Augustine straight in to the Prime Minister. And there, (said G.B.S.) the real play begins."[26]

And how is the old patriarch, I can hear someone say, after these seventy years of life pressed down and overflowing with every kind of mental crusade and venturesome, vicarious activity? As you may imagine, as full of life as ever, interested in everything and everybody, alert in body and mind, full of that kind of humour which is not the veneer of the moment but springs from the habit of an intensely original mind, benignant in regard, courteous in manner, Olympian in aspect and great of heart.

One day, I said to him, the church will canonize you Saint Bernard Shaw.

Probably, he rejoined; they've canonized worse.

Cecil Lewis
26.12.26

Notes

1. Do I really blow? [encircled in left margin]
2. supine
3. ~~great thing about~~: only thing that prevents you from
4. your reluctance
5. ~~keep your head back~~: let your ears go under water
6. ~~Mrs Pat at the rehearsals of Pygmalion or~~: No. The secrets of rehearsal are as sacred as those of the confessional. [encircled in right margin]
7. ~~embracing~~: kissing
8. Shaw
9. The questions should be transposed. [encircled in left margin]
10. ~~left~~: bolted
11. ~~great~~
12. of genius
13. ~~that~~
14. ~~theatre~~: stage
15. ~~broadcasting~~: tanks and atomic bombs
16. and incidentally spoilt a cultivated field. [in left margin]
17. ~~"Very interesting. Now have you, by any chance, another sort of shell that will fill up the craters again?" No doubt the officer wrote him down a fool; but the fact remains that the problem of filling up the holes—in the larger sense of the word—is still the problem of the world today.~~: "That is easy; but can you smooth it out again for the farmer when you are done with it?" The officer thought a moment, and then replied confidently that he could. Shaw, who has always maintained that the proper use of artillery is to replace the plough in agriculture and to demolish slums, was delighted. [in left margin and bottom of page]
18. ~~a plot~~: one
19. ~~that~~
20. England~~'s~~

21. ~~St. Augustine is extremely shocked and annoyed. He insists vehemently on the success of his conversion. But the Devil begins to give him very cogent reasons, in the Shavian manner (see the Preface to Androcles and the Lion) that England is no more Christian than Timbuctoo.~~

22. His arguments [so: in left margin] ~~begin to~~ upset[s] the Saint ~~who says he~~ [that he] ~~must~~ drop[s] down to earth [to] ~~and~~ see about it[,] [, landing in Westminster Hall,]

23. ~~Accordingly he come down and lands in front of the Houses of Parliament,~~

24. ~~as~~

25. ~~,~~

26. [As a second thought, Shaw crossed out the whole of the Chesterton episode, and wrote the following note in the left margin:] I'm sorry; but this must come out. First, it gives away a plot. Second, I have no right to intrude as I did on Chesterton, and then give away what passed.

27. [Handwritten note by Shaw at the end of the article:] When I struck at the Augustine story I put the thing by until I had time to suggest something else. But I am working violently at my book and never had time. So you must fill it up as best you can. It's all frightful nonsense, & will not suit the ferocity of your microphone style—that is, if you talk as you did at poor Huxley. We shall be down here—Hydro-Hotel, Torquay, Devon—until the 23rd. I must be in London on the 27th. G.B.S. 12/1/27

Christopher Hollis

MR. SHAW'S *ST. JOAN*

[*(Maurice) Christopher Hollis (1902–77) was a prolific author and journalist who wrote on a wide range of subjects from history and religion to economics and politics. The Son of an Anglican bishop, he converted to Roman Catholicism at the age of twenty-two. As a young man he was an active member of the Oxford Union Debating Society, assistant master of an English college, and graduate student in economics at Notre Dame University, Indiana. After six years in the RAF during World War II, he served as a Conservative member of Parliament from 1945–55. Hollis's background in debate, religion, history, journalism, economics, and politics, combined with his conversion, made him a fit figure to cross swords with Shaw. His books on Saint Ignatius (1931) and Thomas More (1934), plus later works on converts Newman (1967) and Chesterton (1970) reveal his immersion in the issues of sainthood and Catholicism. While many of his writings were published in England and America, this essay, written early in his career, has never appeared in the United States. It was first published as an article in* The Dublin Review *of April, 1928, then revised and enlarged in 1933 as a pamphlet for the Catholic Truth Society, London. Here a committed Catholic engages central assertions of* Saint Joan, *whose London production had coincided with his conversion.*]

On the 28th of December, 1923—or so I read—Mr. Shaw's *St. Joan* was first played at the Garrick Theatre in New York. On the 20th of March, 1924, it appeared on the London stage in the New Theatre in St. Martin's Lane. Its appearance was greeted with that howl with which it has become a tradition of English dramatic criticism to greet Mr. Shaw's plays. Men asked whether the great revolutionary had turned Fascist. Freethinkers whispered Browning's *Lost Leader* to one another in undertones. Broad-minded Mayfair purred, and some Catholics even went so far as to use language dangerously laudatory of the apologetics with which Mr. Shaw had been good enough to provide the Church. Even Mr. Chesterton, if I remember rightly, enthusiastically exclaimed that the Inquisitor was the hero of the play.

To-day all these press notices are ancient history. They have perished. Yet Mr. Shaw we have always with us. And *St. Joan* we shall have with us at least for a considerable time to come. Mr. Shaw is one of the few living writers of importance. And not many things can be more necessary than an attempt to examine his attitude towards the Church, as he has revealed it both in *St. Joan* and elsewhere.

Mr. Chesterton wrote in the early years of the century a characteristically readable book upon Mr. Shaw. Yet since that book was written, Mr. Chesterton has become a Catholic and Mr. Shaw has written *St. Joan*. They have changed, and with them the times. And, in these changed times, there is plenty of room for a reconsideration of this question.

In such a task two obvious dangers must be avoided. On the one hand a merely vulgar intolerance would clearly stultify everything. If we are unable to write about Mr. Shaw in terms other than those of silly jeers at his inferiority because he does not happen to be a Catholic, it would be much better not to write about him at all. The Church, it may be true, as the greatest of living Spanish artists has said, has not yet found an enemy worthy of her steel. But that does not mean that every individual Catholic penny-a-liner must walk with difficulty through a Protestant world and sigh in vain for his intellectual equal.

Yet, on the other hand, it is necessary to recognize the nature of the Church, and that the Church by her nature cannot be defended from outside. The Catholic position is reasonable. The man to whom the reason of Catholicism is apparent either becomes a Catholic or is in bad faith. A non-Catholic who defends the Catholic position must, then, if he is a man of intellectual honesty, be defending it for a partial, if not for an absolutely wrong reason.

The recent history of France, if nothing else, shows the necessity for such a warning. M. Charles Maurras is one of the ablest of living controversialists, a man who, though himself unable to accept Catholicism, has yet been taught by an intensely vivid sense of history the enormous services of the Church to civilization. In the ordinary way the Church would have said to him, "Thank you very much. That you are not a Catholic is clear enough. We can take no responsibility for what you say. Yet, nevertheless, that you can see so much good in the Church is well for us and well for you." Unfortunately the stupidity of a number of French Catholics who accepted M. Maurras as an authoritative teacher upon their Catholic political duties has forced the hierarchy of the Church to take more direct action.

It would, I am well aware, be a great exaggeration to pretend that Mr. Shaw has gained a position of authority over any set of English Catholics at all comparable to that which M. Maurras held over some

French Catholics before the condemnation of the *Action Française.* Yet everyone must have come across notices and articles in which it has been assumed that Mr. Shaw, in *St. Joan,* has said everything that there is to be said for the Inquisition, and assumed with a readiness that makes impartial examination of his apologetics very necessary.

Now Mr. Shaw has one great advantage over most modern writers who dictate to us their views upon society. It is an advantage so large as to put him at one bound in the front rank of such writers and to make certain that anything which he writes will always be worth reading and worth criticizing. He is not a progressive.

This negative virtue of a lack of faith in the dogma of progress it is difficult to overestimate. It is a virtue which at once transforms a man from an irrational animal into one that at least starts with a fair chance of being rational.

As long as a mind is dominated by the old Macaulayesque formula, by which everything that is going on in 1920 is inevitably better than everything that was going on in 1820, Mrs. Pankhurst necessarily a better poet than Sappho, and the United States a nobler country than England, because it started later, there is clearly an end of all thought and of all argument. For there is an end of standards. It is to Mr. Shaw's credit that he is one of the few men who has made a real attempt to set Free Thought free. He fell into a world in which the fashionable and daring thing was to challenge accepted belief after accepted belief. The man (or woman) who challenged six accepted beliefs was voted more brilliant and more progressive than the man who only challenged five. It was Mr. Shaw who spoiled that very silly game at the time that he wrote *Cæsar and Cleopatra.* "If it is challenging dogmas that you want," he argued, "then I will challenge your dogma of progress. I see no evidence for it at all." From that moment he who had before been merely a progressive, taking on every question the revolutionary side for the extraordinarily stupid reason that it was the revolutionary side, became instead a thinker. The advance was immeasurable.

Yet this advantage, which he gives with the one hand, Mr. Shaw takes away with the other. Because he repudiates progress, we can reason with him. But no sooner has he repudiated progress than he must needs go on to repudiate reason.

Into the details of the metaphysics of the Bergsonian school, to which Mr. Shaw belongs, this is not the place to enter. Let it suffice that it is the faith of these men that Will is the grand creative force in the Universe, and that Reason is but a faculty evolved by Man comparatively late in his progress in order to be a practical adviser upon means for attaining his superrational ends. Such irrationalism has its difficulty. We have, after all, only our reason with which to challenge the instrument. And the position is certainly one quite irreconcilable with any possible Catholic metaphysics.

Yet the Bergsonians and, prominent among them, Mr. Shaw, at least frankly proclaim the insufficiency of their reason. They do not think—but then they do not pretend to. Yet such a proclamation, greatly as it may increase our admiration for Mr. Shaw's honesty, cannot but be a handicap to him when he sets out on a criticism of the claims of the Church. For a refutation of Bible Christianity, such as he undertook in the preface to *Androcles and the Lion,* the disability may be hardly felt. For Bible Christianity is even less rational than he. But Reason can only be answered by Reason. The Elan Vital, whatever its virtues, cannot criticize.

A wise man should, then, before he has picked up the book or taken his seat in the theatre, realize that a play by Mr. Shaw upon St. Joan will be bound to suffer from certain disadvantages. He will expect to find in that play many virtues which, if I were writing as a dramatic critic, I should spend more space in praising—and he will not be disappointed. He will find there wit and sympathy—and that is much. He will find, what is far more, a passion for impartiality—a desire to defend everything as well as it can be defended. There is no other writer in England to-day who, holding the opinions which Mr. Shaw holds and able to command the fees which he is able to command, would take the trouble that he will take in order to be fair to the Church. He is not content as many men would be, merely to "vamp up" a bit of Andrew Lang. That is enormously to his credit. Yet it would be fatal to forget that a criticism of the Church by Mr. Shaw is a criticism of a rational institution by an irrational man, an attempt to explain Catholicism in terms of Creative Evolution. Where such criticism is attack it will probably be futile. Where it is defence, it will be doubly dangerous, for it will be a false defence—a defence of the Church for the wrong reasons, a defence of the Church for something which she is not, a defence of something else which he will then label the Church. We must be on our guard.

We find, then, in an examination of Mr. Shaw's *St. Joan,* that it contains historical misrepresentations of three kinds. The first kind is small and need not detain us. Writing not as an historian but as a dramatist, Mr. Shaw has, of course, as must all dramatists, altered and concentrated the facts of history so as to give them more dramatic power. Thus, as he himself says in his Preface, the two characters of Dunois and the Duc d'Alençon are knocked into one, thereby saving the theatre manager a salary and a suit of armour. Rightly, too, St. Joan's trial, recantation, and burning are all concentrated into a single scene. Doubtless there are other instances. It would be waste of time to search them out.

The other two kinds of historical misrepresentation are more worthy of notice. They are misrepresentations not only of the incidents but of the spirit of the story of St. Joan, and misrepresentations of the institutions which he criticizes.

Let us consider the first of these two kinds and let us begin with small things. In ascribing to him the invention of the word "Protestant" Mr. Shaw pays a large tribute to the Earl of Warwick's mastery of a phrase. That would matter very little if only he made the Earl of Warwick, when he invented the phrase, use it with the right meaning. He does not do so. He imagines, like the Irish nurse in Mr. Wells's *Meanwhile,* that "Protestants protest against Roman Catholics." Historically, at least, they do not. Catholics, if anybody, protest against Catholics, Protestants protest against the toleration of Catholics. It is with such a meaning that the word emerged, a century after the death of St. Joan, from the failure of the Diet of Worms, summoned to regulate the religious troubles of Germany in 1524.

Yet we do not want to sink into antiquarian pedantry. Let us rather consider the main purpose of Mr. Shaw's play.

The main purpose is to present a dramatic clash between the mediæval and the modern world. If that clash is to be dramatic, both worlds must be shown at their best. St. Joan's judges must be made to say everything that there is to be said for the mediæval world; St. Joan to say everything that there is to be said for the modern. Such a formula demands a large violence to history. How conscious Mr. Shaw is of the violence which he is doing, it is not always easy to see.

"St. Joan was condemned," says Mr. Shaw, "after a very careful and conscientious trial." And again, "Joan got a far fairer trial from the Church and the Inquisition than any prisoner of her type and in her situation gets nowadays in any official secular court; and the decision was strictly according to law." In the play itself the Inquisitor is allowed to boast that "we have proceeded in perfect order." And Cauchon is throughout made to appear, in contrast with the political Earl of Warwick, as the impartial servant of God, determined only that the justice of God shall not be mocked. The "corrupt job" of the Rehabilitation of 1456 is, from Preface to Epilogue, held up in contrast with the impartiality of the Trial.

It is true that Mr. Shaw seems himself to have some doubt of the virtues of the real Cauchon and the real Lemaître. "Although there is," he writes, "as far as I have been able to discover, nothing against Cauchon that convicts him of bad faith or exceptional severity in his judicial relations with Joan . . . yet there is hardly more warrant for classing him as a great Catholic Churchman, completely proof against the passions roused by the temporal situation. Neither does the Inquisitor Lemaître, in such scanty accounts of him as are now recoverable, appear quite so able a master of his duties and of the case before him as I have given him credit for being."

One does not wish to be captious. Yet, in strict language, St. Joan was not tried "before the Church" at all. The Church, as Mr. Shaw elsewhere admits, was uncompromised by the decision.

Again, that "Cauchon was threatened and insulted by the English for being too considerate to Joan" is true, and Mr. Shaw does very well to bring it out, though he might also have brought out that Cauchon answered the threats by the not too judicial repartee that "We will have her yet." Mr. Shaw is right, too, to protest against the naïve methods of Andrew Lang, who pounces with such delight upon every question of the Inquisitor and shouts out that it was "a trap." Yet Mr. Shaw's reading does not seem to have brought him across a most important piece of evidence, which goes far to destroy all eulogies upon the Trial. At least he alludes to it neither in the play nor the Preface. The evidence is that of the refusal of St. Joan's appeals to the Pope and the Council of Basle and the attempt to suppress record of those appeals.

The evidence for this is, I think, conclusive. Andrew Lang has collected it. St. Joan was condemned, according to the official account of her Trial, because of her refusal to submit to the judgement of the Church authorities the question of the truth of her visions. If such anarchy were to be allowed, the Inquisitor said, "men and women will arise everywhere, pretending to have divine and angelic revelations and sowing lies and errors in imitation of this woman."

What is the story?

During the preparatory inquiry on March 17th St. Joan had been asked whether she thought that her voices would desert her if she married.

"I know not," she answered, "and leave it to my Lord."

"Would you answer plainly to the Pope?" they asked.

"I summon you," she replied, "to take me to him, and I will answer all that it will be my duty to answer."

Again. On March 27th began the Trial proper. Of that Trial there is a French minute, and of the minute a Latin translation. In the Latin translation St. Joan is made to say: "I well believe that our Holy Father, the Pope of Rome, and the bishops and other churchmen are for the guardianship of the Christian faith and the punishment of heretics, but as for me and my facts"—so Andrew Lang. The Latin is *factis*. "Things which have happened to me," "experiences" would be perhaps clearer—"but as for me and my facts, I will only submit to the Church of Heaven, to God, Our Lady, and the Saints in Paradise. I firmly believe that I have not erred in faith, nor would I err."

The Latin record here ends. The French contains two words more, "et requiert" "and summon."

"Requiert" was the word which she had used ten days previously in her appeal to the Pope. Is it not probable that she had here repeated that appeal and that Cauchon had ordered record of it to be suppressed?

If Mr. Shaw's admiration for Cauchon will not allow him to believe this, then he has to explain away the two other stories of St. Joan's appeal to the Council of Basle. Among the doctors who, on April 10th, were to approve of the Twelve Articles against St. Joan, of which the twelfth said that "she refuses to submit her conduct and revelations to the Church," was a Dominican, Isambart de la Pierre. Isambart de la Pierre had been present during the Trial as one of St. Joan's assessors, and, at the time of her Rehabilitation, he deposed that he had one day advised her to submit to the General Council at Basle.

" 'What is the General Council?' she had asked.

" 'It is the Congregation of the Universal Church and of Christendom and therein are as many of your party as of the English.'

" 'Oh!' she cried, 'since there are some of our side in that place, I am right willing to submit to the Council of Basle.'

" 'Hold your tongue in the devil's name!' cried Cauchon, and commanded the notary not to record this appeal. Jeanne said that they wrote what was against her, not what was in her favour."

It might be objected, of course, that de la Pierre at the Rehabilitation was anxious only to save his skin and to throw all the odium on to the dead Cauchon. There would be much plausibility in such an objection. Yet, if a liar, de la Pierre was not a very competent one. Even on his own story he cuts no very noble figure. For the more certain that he knew of St. Joan's appeal, the larger was his baseness in approving afterwards of the Twelve Articles.

Yet de la Pierre's story is not uncorroborated. Manchon, the clerk, also tells that de la Pierre, Ladvenu (St. Joan's friend in Mr. Shaw's play), and La Fontaine advised her to appeal to the Council of Basle, and that the next day she did so. Cauchon, discovering who had been her advisers, was furious. La Fontaine had to flee, and de la Pierre and Ladvenu were in great danger of death.

It is true that Manchon does not go on to tell of the falsified record—for an obvious reason, since he himself was secretary of the Trial.

It seems probable, then, on the whole, that Andrew Lang is right—that the expurgation contained record of a second appeal to the Council of Basle, a record which was suppressed. Yet the point is not vital.

One appeal is enough for our argument. If you prefer it, reject as impossibly corrupt all evidence given at the Rehabilitation—the whole story of de la Pierre, the whole story of Manchon. It still remains certain both that the official record of the Trial was tampered with and that even the tampered record contained evidence of an appeal to the Pope, made on March 17th. It is as certain that, just before her abjuration, St. Joan said: "I have told you, Doctors, that all my deeds and words should be sent to Rome to our Holy Father, the Pope, to whom, and to God first, I appeal." "The Pope is too far," they had replied.

It is clear, then, that St. Joan was a better Catholic than her accusers. She recognized, where they refused to recognize, the authority of the Pope. Yet it is by no means as certain as Mr. Shaw seems to think that, even had she refused to accept the Pope's judgement, she would have been a heretic. She would have been guilty, doubtless, of a certain disobedience and lack of respect for authority. That is a very different thing.

Mr. Shaw, in his Preface, rightly reminds his readers that Papal Infallibility is not unconditioned. It is conditioned by its own nature. The Pope is infallible when he speaks "*ex cathedra* on matters of faith and morals and to the whole world." He speaks then with the voice of God. But it is not only through His Popes that God speaks. He also gives to certain chosen people direct mystical experience. Nor has the Church any right *a priori* to deny the validity of a direct Divine message which any person claims to have received. Because a claim is made it is not, it is true, necessarily valid. "By their fruits ye shall know them." If, as a result of revelation which pretends to be Divine, a person ascribes to God a purpose different in any way from that which the Church teaches Him to possess, then the Church has the right to condemn that pretended revelation. If the revelation is not itself heretical, the Church claims no right to deny that it is from God. Of the fact that the voices spoke to her St. Joan alone could know. Her distinction between questions of faith and questions of fact was perfectly valid and much better theology than any that was opposed to her.

However corrupt may have been the judges at the Rehabilitation, however true it may be that the Rehabilitation was only a "political job" whose object was to justify Charles VII, yet those judges were at least able enough to realize the strength of St. Joan's argument. "In the case of a fact," they said—as I have already explained, I should prefer to translate the Latin by "experience"—"in the case of a fact which only the percipient knows for certain, no mortal has the right to make him disavow what he knows beyond possibility of doubt. . . . To deny a fact which we know to be certain beyond doubt, though others do not know it, is to lie and is forbidden by Divine law; it is to go against our conscience." Again, "If Jeanne received revelations from God, it was not reasonable to bid her abjure them, especially as the Church does not judge concerning hidden things. She had a perfect right to refuse to abjure ... she followed the special law of inspiration which exempted her from the common law.... Even if it be doubted whether her inspiration came from good or evil spirits, as this is a hidden thing, known of God only, the Church does not judge."

If these arguments be sound, it becomes clear that Mr. Shaw's suggested parallel between the Trial of St. Joan and that of Galileo falls utterly to the ground. It is true, as he insists, that the infallibility of the Church could no more be compromised by the one decision than by the other. Yet when he goes on to suggest that for that reason the Church "might do worse" than canonize Galileo, he has let phrase-making and sentimentality run away with him. Canonization is not a reward for an extra good first-class in Science. For it there are required qualities a little more positive than that of not being justly burnable. It is clear that there is no parallel between the two cases. St. Joan spoke as a mystic, vindicating a claim to personal revelation. Galileo, at the best, spoke as a scientist, vindicating a claim to free investigation.

Mr. Shaw has seen in the Trial of St. Joan a dramatic conflict between Catholicism and Protestantism. It will not do. The fable was old when Andrew Lang wrote, and Andrew Lang has destroyed it. "St. Joan," writes Mr. Shaw, "was, in fact, one of the first Protestant martyrs." He praises the "magnificently Catholic gesture" of "the canonization of a Protestant saint by the Church of Rome." This is journalese, and we must fear the journalist, even when he brings us compliments.

God speaks to man in two ways. He speaks through the regular mechanism of the Church which He has founded. He speaks directly to chosen individuals. It suits the symmetry of Mr. Shaw's mind to call the one way the Catholic way and the other the Protestant. This is false. Both ways are Catholic ways. Does Mr. Shaw really imagine that St. Joan was either the first or the last Catholic to possess channels by which to learn the Will of God other than that of the regular dogmatic pronouncements of the Church? May one not remind him of his own brilliant *mot* in *John Bull's Other Island*, "Whatever the blessed St. Peter was crucified for, it was not for being a Protestant"? His formula is one which would make a Protestant of St. Francis, of St. Teresa, even—to reduce it to utter absurdity—of St. Ignatius Loyola himself; it would, in fact, make the virtue of sanctity an exclusively Protestant virtue.

This brings us on to the third class of Mr. Shaw's mis-statements. Mr. Shaw rightly enough reminds us several times that it is impossible to write of St. Joan without understanding the Church of the Middle Ages. It is important to realize how far Mr. Shaw has failed and how far succeeded in his task. He must be praised for conscientiousness. He is one of the few popular writers who realize clearly that the united Europe before the Renaissance and the divided Europe after the Reformation were two different sorts of society and that it is childish to judge one by the standards of the other. Such a realization at once raises his work above the merely red-nosed comedy of Mark Twain. Yet at the same time one must be careful when one agrees with the dictum that Mr. Shaw's study of St. Joan has shown him how much he has in common with the Church. It is not really true. He has not discovered that he is, to some extent, a Catholic. He has merely discovered that, five hundred years ago, the Church was, to some extent, by anticipation Shavian. There is in him no readiness to submit the Will. There is no demand to use the Reason. Without these two things there can be no Catholicism.

The truth of this can be shown from his attitude to the supernatural. He believes in the supernatural no more than did Hume or Matthew Arnold or Huxley. He differs from them only because time has made him a little more of a sceptic. He is willing to admit that the laws of nature are a bit queerer than people in the last century had taken in. Where they said that "miracles do not happen," he says that miracles do sometimes happen but that they are not miracles. Neither they nor he dream of saying that miracles are miracles. Such a confession would be, to quote a phrase from *Back to Methuselah,* a confession of faith in "a disorderly God."

Let us take instances. St. Joan, according to Mr. Shaw, heard voices, but that was only because of a "vividly dramatic" imagination, and such imagination, he is careful to explain, is "not a whit more miraculous" than the most normal and prosaic of calculations. She was "a Galtonic visualizer." One might have hoped that Mr. Shaw would have risen superior to this extraordinary formula by which a miracle ceases to be a miracle if only you can call it after a Don. What on earth have you explained by merely stroking your beard and remarking wisely, "Ah, Galtonic visualization, I perceive"?

Mr. Shaw "cannot believe" that "three ocularly visible well-dressed persons" came to visit St. Joan. If he cannot, he cannot. But what does Galtonic visualization explain? The Galtonic theory of visualization records the observed fact that, when people either expect or greatly desire a certain sensation, they are apt to have the illusion that they have received that sensation. A familiar illustration is that of the audience at a concert. If a violinist passes his bow across the face of his instrument at the conclusion of his piece, most people, say the supporters of this theory, imagine that they have heard one more note than has, in fact, been played.

I am willing enough to believe this. But unless Mr. Shaw can show that St. Joan expected a vision from St. Catherine before St. Catherine appeared to her, it clearly is no explanation of her voices. Anatole France has attempted to show that she did expect some such thing—and a very poor attempt it is. Mr. Shaw has not made the attempt. Without it the scientific phrase is merely a piece of pedant's bluff.

How, then, are the voices to be explained? "There are forces at work which use individuals for purposes . . ." "There is an appetite for evolution." "There is a superpersonal need."

Such language comes perilously near to the dreadful metaphors of Mr. Wells, when he speaks of life "using" him. For whose purposes? What is an appetite for evolution? For whose evolution? For the evolution of what into what? What is a superpersonal need? Who is the superperson who needs? Happiness is the end of Man, and the longing of a St. Francis for the Beatific Vision is a need no more superpersonal than the desire of a drunkard for a public-house. Happiness is the end of Man, and a happiness which is vaguely floating about, although nobody in particular is happy, is unworthy nonsense.

As irritating is Mr. Shaw's hesitating accusation that the Church was in St. Joan's time deeply corrupted "by primitive Calibanism (in Browning's sense), or the propitiation of a dreaded deity by suffering and sacrifice." Caliban thought that a powerful God spent His time in giving pain to others. The Christian believes that an all-powerful God in humility consented to suffer pain Himself. Mr. Shaw has, if he wishes, the right to think such a notion nonsense. He has not the right to slip past an argument with a phrase—an irritating little habit of his. One does not wish to be either irreverent or unfair. But his complaint really is not against Caliban, but against Christ. It is that Christianity has never quite recovered from the accident of being founded by Jesus Christ—a misfortune which prevented the Church of the fifteenth century from understanding more than the tag-ends of the philosophy of Samuel Butler.

It is hardly necessary to say that to the Catholic mind this is a putting of the cart before the horse. To such a mind it is not the Church which has to be judged by Samuel Butler, but Samuel who has to be judged by the Church. Nor is it mere bigotry which says such a thing. For all these modern speculations—the psychology of the modern world, its psycho-analysis, its Galtonic visualization, its Creative Evolution—are, so far as they are true, nothing but thefts of some little corner or other of mediæval scholasticism, whence comes all our thinking. Psycho-analysis is simply confession without absolution. Visualization is effects without causes. Creative Evolution is freedom without reason. It is absurd to seek to judge the whole by the part.

Yet, so long as Mr. Shaw keeps his opinions to his Preface, we have perhaps no great cause of complaint against him. It is different when he puts them into the mouths of his fifteenth-century characters. Of this fault there are many instances. There is his treatment of St. Joan's miracles. These "miracles" were, in his opinion, but curious coincidences. The hens began to lay eggs as soon as Robert de Baudricourt agreed to conduct St. Joan to the Dauphin. The wind changed as soon as she appeared to Dunois. It is well enough, but one has only to turn to the conscientious record of Free-thinking Quicherat in order to see that the miracles of St. Joan are by no means all such as can be thus easily laughed away. Take, for instance, the story of the child of Lagny. St. Joan herself believed that the child was dead, that by the prayers of herself and others it was for a little time brought back again to life and was thus able to be baptized and to be buried in holy ground.

The objections of the *advocatus diaboli* to such a story it is easy to guess. Such scepticism it is very right to respect, for it is rare to meet with anything so respectable as scepticism. My complaint against Mr. Shaw is not that he treats this story as a sceptic would treat it. Anatole France treated it as a sceptic would treat it, but Mr. Shaw does not treat it at all. He merely leaves it out, telling us instead about eggs and the wind. Such a method, in one who is professing to make alive the fifteenth century, is as bad as any method can be. For it at once gives us a wholly false picture of all those people in the fifteenth century who believed that St. Joan could work miracles. Such people may have been wrong, but at least they were not idiots. What they believed, they believed on very solid evidence and not, as Mr. Shaw would have it, on the hearsay of a couple of silly nursery-tales.

So obsessed is his mind with the idea that only very simple people can believe in miracles that, when he has to present any character of intelligence, he is at pains to show that that person believed in miracles only in the Shavian and not in the Catholic sense.

"They come from your imagination," he makes Robert de Baudricourt say of St. Joan's voices.

"Of course," says St. Joan. "That is how the messages of God come to us."

Now if the voices were the product of imagination, they did not exist objectively, whether St. Joan listened to them or not. It is certain that St. Joan, rightly or wrongly, believed that they did exist objectively.

Again Mr. Shaw puts into the mouth of the Archbishop of Rheims a characteristically Shavian defence of miracles.

"A miracle, my friend," he is made to say, "is an event which creates faith. That is the purpose and nature of miracles. They may seem very wonderful to the people who witness them and very simple to those who perform them. That does not matter: if they confirm or create faith, they are true miracles." "An event which creates faith does not deceive; therefore it is not a fraud, but a miracle." "To do that, the Church must do as you do: nourish faith by poetry."

I have no objection at all to Mr. Shaw depicting an Archbishop as a blackguard. More likely than not he is right. Many an Archbishop has been perfectly capable of staging a fraudulent miracle. My only objection is to that particular defence of the fraud. Such a defence, such a desire to have the advantages of a miracle without suffering the inconveniences of a God, reeks of the Rationalist Press. It is of the twentieth century. It would have been as impossible in the fifteenth as would a motor-bicycle and side-car.

Of all these anachronisms the most offensive comes in the Epilogue, where the English priest, de Stogumber, who had been before St. Joan's burning a violent persecutor but had by it been shocked into kindness, is made to say, "It was not Our Lord that redeemed me, but a young woman I saw actually burned to death."

The Christian theory of the Redemption is that Man, born in sin, was brought back into a possibility of companionship with God by God's death upon the Cross. If such a theory is nonsense, if it is, as Mr. Shaw would say, Calibanism, then it is nonsense, and he ought to leave it alone. But if it is meaningless to say that Man could be redeemed by the sacrifice on Calvary, it is far more meaningless to say that he could be redeemed by the sacrifice at Rouen. That a callous person may be shocked into kindness by seeing the sufferings of a noble saint, nobly borne, is perfectly true, but has nothing on earth to do with redemption. And why Mr. Shaw should jeer at us if we use the language of Redemption in context in which it has a meaning and then himself use it in context in which it is vulgarest rhetoric, it is hard to see. If we are muddle-headed fools, cannot he let us alone and describe his own superior emotions in his own superior language, instead of rejecting our metaphysics and then stealing our metaphors?

We have further quarrels with Mr. Shaw's history—quarrels which it would take too long to substantiate. He has, I think, mis-stated the relations between the Church and feudalism. It is true that in the feudal period the Church's organization became partly feudalized. The relation of bishop to Pope, or of priest to bishop, took upon it certain of the marks of the relation of a tenant to his lord. This was the accident, not the essence, of ecclesiastical organization. The ecclesiastical organization existed before feudalism and survived after it. In one main province of Catholic Europe, Spain, feudalism never truly established itself at all.

Again, Mr. Shaw harps throughout upon the familiar joke that the

English are natural heretics. There is no evidence that this is true of pre-Reformation England. The English were vigorous, indeed, in their resistance to papal financial exactions, which is a wholly different affair. Doctrinally the English was the most obedient of all the provinces of Europe. The Albigensian heresy, for instance, got no footing there at all. Nor can the accidents of sixteenth-century despotism justify Mr. Shaw in drawing any general parallel between the development of royal power against feudal authority and the development of Protestant criticism against ecclesiastical authority.

Yet these are all but minor points which lead up to the general complaint against the defence of the Inquisition which Mr. Shaw puts into the mouth of the Inquisitor. That defence is not a defence of the Inquisition at all. It is a very brilliant and lucid defence of the Fascist State. There is in it no hint of supernatural religion nor of "a kingdom that is not of this world." The Inquisitor's appeal is to "the accumulated wisdom of the Church." "What will the world be like when the Church's accumulated wisdom and knowledge and experience, its council of learned, venerable, pious men, are thrust into the kennel by every ignorant labourer or dairymaid?" "The new heresy," he says again, "sets up the private judgement of the single erring mortal against the considered wisdom and experience of the Church." In such arguments there is force. But they are not, in the last resort, the Church's argument for her infallibility. She claims infallibility because her voice is the voice of God. If that claim is false, her conduct is unjustifiable. And if he cannot but believe it false, then all Mr. Shaw's attempts to justify her conduct, brilliant, able, honest though he is, must necessarily end in failure.

It would be wearisome to continue, though it would be very possible to do so. In conclusion, let me rather insist again on the thesis of this essay. It is not an attack on Mr. Shaw. I have always read Mr. Shaw with pleasure. And I shall always continue to do so. Mr. Shaw has never claimed to be a Catholic, and with him Catholics have no cause of quarrel. All that this essay professes to do is to point out that Mr. Shaw's attitude to the Church, though the attitude of a man who is anxious to understand, is also the attitude of a man who has failed to understand, and to warn Catholics of the error of allowing Mr. Shaw to defend them.

Yet in spite of its failures, his *St. Joan* has, to my mind, one triumphant superiority, at least, over any other modern work about her—the Epilogue, in which it is shown that the age which canonized St. Joan would be as little ready to receive her as was the age which burnt her. Critics and theatre-goers condemned the Epilogue as inartistic and undignified, an unworthy anti-climax. By their abuse they meant, if they did not merely mean that it had made them miss their last train home, that they wished to be allowed to go away with a comfortable feeling inside them that they were ever so much better than those rough people of the fifteenth century, and would never have dreamed of behaving in such a brutal fashion to a poor girl. By this Epilogue Mr. Shaw has forbidden the modern world such a luxury. This sturdy refusal to flatter is a great quality. It is, perhaps, the quality which may bring Mr. Shaw most nearly to an understanding of that mediæval mind after which he gropes so unfamiliarly.

Susan Rusinko

RATTIGAN VERSUS SHAW: THE "DRAMA OF IDEAS" DEBATE

Six months before his death in 1950, Shaw, at the age of ninety-four, fired one of his parting salvos in his contribution to a theatre debate initiated by Terence Rattigan in the March 4, 1950, issue of the *New Statesman and Nation*. Every week thereafter, concluding with Rattigan's letter on May 13 of that year, writer after writer joined the debate. First to respond to Rattigan's attack on the Shavian play of ideas was James Bridie, who was followed, among others, by Benn Levy, Peter Ustinov, Sean O'Casey, Ted Willis, Christopher Fry, and, finally, Shaw himself.

Rattigan began his letter with his oft-reiterated statement about his belief that plays should be about people and not about things. As the essence of drama, character and narrative should not be dominated by sociological commitment and ideological propaganda. Response to the attack was swift and mostly harsh. It was obvious almost from the start that the debate ultimately would prove nothing, nor would it even become a forum for the expression of new ideas.

The backdrop for the debate was a milieu of staleness and even malaise about the state of the English stage. Fry and Eliot had been seen by some as dramatists who would revitalize the realistic and naturalistic drama of the time with their poetic language. Rattigan agreed. "The revolution in the contemporary theatre begun a few years ago by T. S. Eliot and Christopher Fry, and maintained and developed by such dramatists as James Forsyth, Ronald Duncan, Peter Ustinov and the late and much-missed James Bridie, is, I sincerely believe, a movement to be whole-heartedly welcomed, for it has rescued the theatre from the thraldom of middle-class vernacular in which it has been held, with rare intervals, since Tom Robertson, and has given it once more, a voice."[1] Vitality, nevertheless, seemed not to come from this direction.

At one point, a playwrights' company, like the American model, was talked about by Bridie, Levy, Priestley, Rattigan and others. Peter Ustinov writes about two meetings held in Priestley's flat to discuss the forming of such an organization "in emulation of celebrated American producing organization run by the playwrights themselves: Elmer Rice, Maxwell Anderson, Sidney Howard, Robert E. Sherwood, and Marc Connelly."[2] Yet the dramatic scene did not change radically but evolved into what has been called the twilight period, dominated by the so-called establishment dramatists, Rattigan and Coward.

Indeed, Rattigan's commercial success had earned for him the title of a "one-man theatrical establishment" by the general press. Record-breaking successes of the pre-World War II *French Without Tears* and his critically successful *The Winslow Boy* and *The Browning Version* in the immediate post-war period brought him wide acclaim in England, on the continent and in America. However, between these successes and those of his uncompromisingly realistic plays of the early 1950s, *The Deep Blue Sea* and *Separate Tables*, Rattigan keenly felt the critical failure of *Adventure Story* (1949), his first history play, about Alexander the Great. Rattigan later explained *Adventure Story* as "an attempt to express, in terms of dramatic narrative, my view of the character of Alexander, and though, as my critics said at the time, it lacked the language of the poet and the perception of the philosopher, those deficiencies were both conscious and allowed for, and the attempt, I believe, was not entirely vain."[3] Criticized for its construction by some, for its language by others, and for its lack of ideas by still others, the play, which remained Rattigan's favorite for a long time, seemed to have catalyzed his long-standing hurt at not being taken seriously.

His frustration had expressed itself in his many interviews, articles and prefaces. Indeed, as early as the thirties when his first professionally produced play, *French Without Tears,* journeyed across the Atlantic, he defended his style and subject matter in the American press. Implicitness of language and action, naturalistic language, well-crafted style, the primacy of people, the importance of narrative over ideas—all these summed up in his purpose: to move to laughter and to tears—formed the basis for a lifelong defensiveness about his dramas. Now, the time had come to proclaim the end of the fifty-year domination of the stage by the Ibsenite-Shavian theatre of ideas.

Taking on the nonagenarian in that bastion of Shavian liberalism, the *New Statesman and Nation*, Rattigan, then thirty-nine and himself active in liberal ideas and causes, only exposed his own vulnerability to venerable minds and wits among his contemporaries, not the least of whom was Shaw himself.

Rattigan began his letter with a reference to Shaw's 1895 article in the *Saturday Review* in which Shaw "began his battle . . . on behalf of the 'New' theatre, the Ibsenite theatre, the 'theatre as a factory of thought, a prompter of conscience, and an elucidator of social conduct.' "[4] If a play didn't conform to the pattern Shaw had laid down, then it just wasn't a good play, Rattigan observed. In support of his accusation, he quoted some of Shaw's comments on Shakespeare: *Othello* as pure melodrama without a "touch of character that goes below the skin"[5] and the bogus characterization of Enobarbus in *Antony and Cleopatra*. And, finally, he quoted Shaw's famous statement: "With the single exception of Homer there is no eminent writer, not even Sir Walter Scott, who I can despise so entirely as I despise Shakespeare when I measure my mind against his."[6] The Rattigan-versus-Shaw-versus-Shakespeare controversy, thus, was on. In fact, it seized the journalistic imagination of the time, spreading to a variety of journals and newspapers. In their biography of Rattigan, Michael Darlow and Gillian Hodson quote one of the most devastating replies, by Robert Muller in *Theatre News Letter* of March 25, 1950.

> Who are these Playwrights of Ideas that make Mr. Rattigan foam at the mouth, these spoilers of the drama who splutter ideas only because they cannot create character? Mr. R. mentions Shaw and Ibsen in his lines, and between them we read the name of every other writer for the theatre who possessed that dangerous thing—a social conscience. It is all very transparent. Mr. Rattigan condemns the writer of ideas whose ideas are not identical to his own. He does not condemn Mr. Noel Coward's adventure into ideas, *This Happy Breed*, because it drew no bothersome conclusions. Only the Shavian penslavers who dare to plumb the lower depths and come up with an idea are the ones that rouse his fury and get his goat. . . . Equate character with Right thinking and Idea with Subversive thinking, and you begin to appreciate what Mr. Rattigan is trying to say.[7]

The first response in the *New Statesman* was by James Bridie, who called attention to two mistakes Rattigan had made: to get angry with Shaw and as "one of our best dramatists" to turn critic. Siding with Shaw, Bridie wrote that "it is difficult to believe that he [Rattigan] has ever read or seen a play by Shaw."[8] He further listed ways in which Rattigan was indebted to Shaw and concluded with a warning to his friend Rattigan to "think twice before challenging the Master on his own undisputed field. We are on the point of removing into the era of Christopher Fry, and it would be a pity if we were utterly lost in transit."[9]

Then Benn Levy, in an on-target, level-headed commentary the next week, pointed out the rootlessness of the controversy. The difficulty, he stated, lay in Rattigan's not making distinctions among "the ideological play, the play with an idea, and the next moment the play of ideas."[10] So, he concluded, "the battle of 'schools' is a sham battle."[11]

Admitting to leaning more toward Rattigan than toward Bridie, Peter Ustinov then joined the debate to register his personal quarrel with all. He supported Shaw's right to attack Shakespeare, Rattigan's to attack Shaw, Bridie's to attack Rattigan, and his own to "attack the lot of them."[12]

It was now time for the big guns. Sean O'Casey argued that "we'd have to get ideas out of life before we could remove them from the drama."[13] Predictably, he called attention to the social content of the great English poets from Chaucer and Langland to Auden and Eliot. And he looked "forward to the day with confidence when British workers will carry in their hip pockets a volume of Keats's poems or a Shakespeare play beside the packets of lunch attached to their belts."[14]

Admitting to ducking "under the ropes" to side with the protagonists of the theatre of ideas, Ted Willis described "the spectacle of Bridie and Rattigan taking the ring against each other armed with nothing more lethal than cream puffs."[15] But he disagreed with Bridie's view of Fry as the beginning of a new era of drama; rather, he contended, prophetically, Fry is the end of an old one. And taking up O'Casey's insistence on the poet's responsibility to his society as a writer, Willis maintained that "perhaps the theatre will reach out to new forms to match new ideas."[16] Unlike Rattigan, he envied the social dramatists in America during the thirties, "when a whole new band . . . arose to give social direction to the realism their theatre had achieved a decade before."[17]

Avoiding specifics and reacting obliquely to Willis' charge regarding himself as the end of an era, Christopher Fry next joined the fray, taking issue with the practice of literary labelling and with Willis' calling trivial "whatever is alien to our own corner of thought."[8] "We should be glad of whatever tends, with some difficulty, towards creation; be ready to find truth in any aspect, and to plunge on through the darkness carrying the world, if possible, to full fig."[19]

Finally, calling attention to Rattigan's vulnerability as a reasoner, Shaw proceeded to discourse on the "irrational genius" of Rattigan, who, no doubt, "does not like my plays because they are not exactly like his own."[20] He then lectured Rattigan on the differences in the mental capacity of one playwright and another and on the mysterious origins of the theatre in circus clowns, street poets, and Hyde Park soapbox speakers. The lecture included a short history of the theatre from the Middle Ages, the Elizabethan era, the Italian opera to "Barry Sullivan . . . and Chaliapin."[21] He concluded: "I am writing all this to show that without knowing [the theatre] . . . historically and studying critically the survivals of it that are still in practice . . . no playwright can be fully qualified nor any theatre critic know what he is pontificating about."[22]

In the final word of the debate, Rattigan's letter expressed relief at the editor's decision "to close this controversy—if by that term you can dignify the weekly belabouring of a cheeky fourth former by some of the biggest and brainiest boys in the school."[23] He went on to "confess himself quite unrepentant and still cheeky enough to ask why, if what he said was, as so many of the illustrious contributors to this series have either stated or implied, so nonsensical as hardly to merit a reply, it should in fact have merited not merely one, but six."[24] Furthermore, although a certain part of his anatomy may have been red from the whacking given him, the color in part was due to his pride that the whacking should have been administered by such distinguished canes. Indeed, his whole anatomy was "quivering with the shock and delight of having been considered worthy of the high honour of a birching from the head boy himself, who, with characteristic and Olympian generosity, dealt far more leniently with the cheeky fourth former than with the school prefects who had been bullying him. And so encouraged thus in my cheek, I shall wish my opponents well of their theatre that is—to quote one of them—'one third arena, one third temple, one third music hall.' Personally I shall just stick to the theatre."[25]

Throughout the two months, some acrimony and much reiteration of well-known positions characterized the debate. Variously labeled as sham and cream-puff, it benefited Rattigan very little, indeed, as he would later only carry his grievance to the prefaces of Volumes II and III of his *Collected Plays* in the person of Aunt Edna of Kensington, the middle-class, middle-brow average theatregoer, who through the centuries had sustained the theatre and eventually adapted even to the most experimental innovations.

Disappointed by the mixed receptions of *Variation on a Theme* (1959) and *Man and Boy* (1963), even though *Ross* (1960) was favorably reviewed, Rattigan spent the years from 1963–1970 away from the stage, devoting his time to radio, film and television writing.

In a preface in 1964, Rattigan dramatized a fictional trial with himself as defendant and Aunt Edna (his fictional character created in an earlier preface) as plaintiff. In the course of the trial, the defendant recalls "the compliment paid me of being pummelled on successive weeks by Benn Levy, James Bridie, Peter Ustinov, Sean O'Casey, Ted Willis, Christopher Fry and finally Bernard Shaw."[26] Lectured on those occasions by O'Casey and Shaw on the history of the theatre, Rattigan in his latest round of the controversy extended that historical sense in the person of Aunt Edna, "who is a majority audience for which true theatre exists."[27] "Since Euripides she has always risen to meet any new theatrical situation. Look how she embraced the Elizabethan dramatists at their bawdiest and bloodiest, most morose and most obscure. Then we know how she fumed and fretted when the Puritans closed the theatres and how gladly she rushed to those candle-lit sexual frolics known as Restoration Drama which she now justifies because of its style and wit, but which she went to then, and I suspect does now, for no more impelling reason than to get herself some good, dirty, elegant belly-laughs."[28] Although the present era has seen dramas labelled "'French Window-School,' 'Kitchen Sink School,' 'Fry-Eliot School,' 'Brechtian Epic School,' 'Chekhovian School,' even 'Coward-Rattigan School,'... the theatre remains the theatre."[29] In any period, Rattigan continues, Aunt Edna's demands on the theatre are two-fold: "first that it excite her to laugh or to cry or to wonder what is going to happen next; and, second, that she can suspend her disbelief willingly and without effort."[30] "She is bored by propaganda, enraged at being 'alienated,' loathes placards coming down and telling her what is going to happen next, hates a lot of philosophical talk...."[31] "Her greatest joy is still and always will be for a good strong meaty plot told by good strong meaty characters."[32]

Rattigan's vindication of his reputation as a dramatist of the theatre of entertainment through the fictional Aunt Edna was his way of retorting to some critics, one of whom, Kenneth Tynan, called him the Formosa of the British theatre.[33] His long-standing sense of injury, however, was counter-productive, as his dealing with it publicly only called attention to his popular image as the fashionable, well-made playwright of the West End. Even in his more mellowed years, he carried the scars of his wounds.

Ironically, the controversy did, albeit unwittingly, underscore the end of the Ibsenite-Shavian era, but, perhaps, not as Rattigan had intended. For six years later, the advent of Jimmy Porter in John Osborne's *Look Back in Anger* clearly marked that end. Yet, even this event had its built-in irony, as Ibsenite-Shavian social criticism is the very basis for the frustration vented by Jimmy Porter on the Royal Court stage on opening night. However, it was not the social criticism that caused the upheaval, but the total honesty, the animal magnetism (the English equivalent of Stanley Kowalski's impact on the American stage), and the uninhibited freedom to express raw emotions. The long-awaited stage revolution arrived and with it the first and second waves of the new dramatists. Rattigan attended the opening night performance, acknowledging afterwards the force of the drama and its impact on his own career. Henceforth, he said, assessments of future plays would be made with the attitude, "Look how unlike Terence Rattigan I'm being."[34]

Ironies multiply as one notes Rattigan's own concern in his dramas with the damage to people caused by the British national characteristic of emotional repression. *Look Back in Anger,* although dealing with lower middle-class problems, appeared after Rattigan's *The Browning Version, The Deep Blue Sea, Separate Tables*—plays which dealt with the same theme. Certainly Freddie Page in *The Deep Blue Sea* and John Malcolm in *Separate Tables* are precursors of Jimmy Porter, as Hester Collyer is of Alison Porter. The subject received its most explicit dramatization in Rattigan's last three stage plays: *A Bequest to the Nation, In Praise of Love* and *Cause Célèbre.*

But the overall irony of the debate is that Shaw, Wilde, Rattigan and Osborne can be seen as contiguous dramatists in the mainstream of twentieth-century English stage history. Echoes of Shaw and Wilde may be found in many of Rattigan's farces, particularly in *French Without Tears* and *While the Sun Shines.* Furthermore, Rattigan's *Ross*, in its psychological exploration of the Arabian adventure of T. E. Lawrence, complements Shaw's characterization of Lawrence as adventurer in *Too True To Be Good.*

As predicted by Benn Levy early in the epistolary controversy, the debate was rootless; no real issues emerged. Indeed, Rattigan's comments about the state of the theatre in his time are more effectively explored and debated in his farce about a theatrical touring company (*Harlequinade,* 1948) and the battle of the books in his penultimate stage play (*In Praise of Love,* 1973) than in the *New Statesman* correspondence. With little substantive argument to respond to in Rattigan's initial letter, even Fry, O'Casey and Shaw replied without their usual poetry or wit. Rather, as Rattigan has aptly put it, one hears the tones of prefects and headmaster punishing a recalcitrant schoolboy.

To the end Shaw had remained his intractably lecturing self. Rattigan nursed his wound until his death in 1977, even though age had tempered somewhat his pique with the critics. The battle of the theatres in 1950, indeed a sham battle, curiously did mark an important mid-century point in English stage history, becoming a small part of a centuries-old English tradition of debate about the old and the new. But the real confirmation of the passing of an era came with Shaw's death six months later.

Notes

1. Terence Rattigan, *Collected Plays* (London: Hamish Hamilton, 1953), vol. I, p. xix.
2. Peter Ustinov, *Dear Me* (Boston: Little Brown, 1977), p. 338.
3. Rattigan, *Collected Plays,* II, p. xviii.

4. Terence Rattigan, "Concerning the Play of Ideas," *New Statesman and Nation*, March 4, 1950, p. 241. Subsequent reference to other letters in the *New Statesman* are noted by writer, date and page number.

5. Ibid.

6. Ibid.

7. Michael Darlow and Gillian Hodson, *Terence Rattigan: The Man and His Work* (London: Hamish Hamilton, 1977), pp. 184–185.

8. James Bridie, March 11, 1950. p. 471.

9. Ibid., p. 472.

10. Benn Levy, March 25, 1950, p. 301.

11. Ibid.

12. Peter Ustinov, April 1, 1950. p. 367.

13. Sean O'Casey, April 8, 1950. p. 397.

14. Ibid., p. 398.

15. Ted Willis, April 15, 1950. p. 426.

16. Ibid., p. 427.

17. Ibid.

18. Christopher Fry, April 22, 1950. p. 458.

19. Ibid.

20. George Bernard Shaw, May 6, 1950. Reprinted in *Shaw on Theatre*, ed. E. J. West (New York: Hill and Wang, 1958), pp. 289–294.

21. Ibid.

22. Ibid.

23. Terence Rattigan, May 13, 1950. p. 545.

24. Ibid., p. 546.

25. Ibid.

26. Rattigan, *Collected Plays*, III (1964), pp. viii–ix.

27. Ibid., III, p. xxv.

28. Ibid., II, p. xiii.

29. Ibid., III, p. xx.

30. Ibid., III, p. xxvii.

31. Ibid.

32. Ibid.

33. Darlow and Hodson, p. 234.

34. John Barber, *Daily Telegraph*, December 1, 1977.

THE STATE AND FUTURE OF SHAW RESEARCH: THE MLA CONFERENCE TRANSCRIPT

[*At the December 1980 meeting, Shavians gathered to discuss, on the 30th anniversary of Bernard Shaw's death in 1950, the state of research on Shaw and the directions in which research was needed. Panelists were Dan H. Laurence, Margot Peters, Daniel Leary and Charles Berst. Chairman was Stanley Weintraub. Opening by discussing bibliographical matters, Laurence itemized publications in the pipeline or about to appear, these unmentioned here because the time-lag until this transcript was to appear would have made most of the references moot. Laurence also discussed his bibliography of Shaw, and how it was intended to make information accessible, from primary works to the locations of manuscripts. His listing is thus not repeated here. Some of his references, however, overlapped references in the other presentations and will appear in their turn below.*

In order by author, the transcripts which follow present Margot Peters on biographical research, Daniel Leary on textual studies and Charles Berst on Criticism. It is hoped that such up-dates can occur, as in the past, every five years to keep those studying Shaw current on what is happening and what might further be accomplished.]

Biography

With Shaw's death in 1950, Shaw biography reached an obvious watershed. Up to that point, Shaw had controlled in one way or another virtually every biographical word written about him. Although he once declared that every biography was nine-tenths the biographer, that fraction was a luxury he did not allow his own commentators. Perhaps no other author has exercised such self-conscious control over his own personality: the prefaces to the novels, the prefaces to the plays, the self-interviews, the hundreds of self-interpreting letters, the constant revision of letters and personal essays during his lifetime. Finally, like Little Dorrit who told Arthur Clennam, "I have written a great deal about myself; but I must write a little more still," Shaw published *Sixteen Self Sketches* in 1949 with the chapter "Biographers' Blunders Corrected." Similarly, there were few pieces written about him during his lifetime that he did not retouch or approve: Ada Shaw Tyrrell's brief memoir of "Sonny" Shaw, McNulty's reminiscences, the Shaw-Farr-Yeats letters, the Shaw-Terry letters, Frank Harris's biography, Stephen Winsten's biography, G. M. Shaw's family memoir, Hesketh Pearson's life and, of course, Archibald Henderson's three authorized volumes. Naïvely happy to let Shaw fashion his own myth, Hesketh Pearson announced in *George Bernard Shaw: His Life and Personality* (1942): ". . . I was greatly helped in the writing of this book by Bernard Shaw, who not only gave me a deal of what he called 'unique private history,' but corrected and checked all the facts, supplied many passages . . . [and] authenticated or rejected the anecdotes that had been told of him by other people." In more than one sense, Shaw was a self-made man. When Mrs. Patrick Campbell announced she was going to publish his letters, he went through the roof; partly because of their contents, more, I believe, because the thought of anything being published without his blue pencil terrified him. He did finally select and edit the letters, but did not get to explain away the relationship in a preface—one of his few defeats. Shaw biography has thus suffered from the same malady as Shaw criticism: Shaw seems to have accounted for everything better than anyone else, making further interpretations superfluous.

Of course it is invaluable to have the eyewitness accounts of biographers writing during Shaw's lifetime, just as it is invaluable to have Shaw's version of his life. But biography written while the subject is alive to read it can never approach the kind of objectivity we expect from the craft. As D. H. Lawrence observed, "I am what I am, not merely what I think I am," and, we must add, "Or what I say I am." Shaw biography has for the most part dealt with what Shaw thought and said he was: it has been in this sense autobiography, a perspective fortified by such genuine autobiographical records as Stanley Weintraub's *Shaw: An Autobiography* (1969–1970) and volumes one and two of the *Collected Letters* edited by Dan H. Laurence (1965, 1972). And on the whole it has not been well-balanced biography: even Hesketh Pearson's lively and perceptive life lacks the coherence and tension of a work of art. Shaw himself pronounced upon Henderson's enormous labors: "As biography," said Shaw, "NO." One problem, besides Shaw's iron control, has been the biographer's own intrusiveness into the work. It was immensely gratifying, as Molly Tompkins once said, to know the Great Man and bray about it; and most of Shaw's biographers have been only too delighted to appear as Boswells to their own Dr. Johnson. Frank Harris's biography of Shaw is mainly about Frank Harris. Stephen Winsten, St. John Ervine and Archibald Henderson are omnipresent in theirs, and even Hesketh Pearson cannot resist appearing at every turn to remind us that he disapproves of most of Shaw's opinions. Then there is the question of past biographers' commitment to Shaw. The essential element of good biography is the biographer's identification and sympathy with his subject: whether Shaw's biographers have written from sympathy—or a desire to cash in on Shaw's fame. In short, until 1950 Shaw biography had as its chief merit the biographer's first-hand record of Shaw's behavior and conversation; it had as its chief defects Shaw's inhibiting presence, and the biographer's difficulty in handling his own relationship with Shaw, resulting in most cases in his inability to grasp the whole of his subject objectively and present Shaw's life from a coherent point of view.

After 1950, biographies of Shaw took a somewhat different tone. There is a marked difference between Stephen Winsten's *Days with Bernard Shaw* (1949) and his *Jesting Apostle* (1955), for example. Winsten had always seen the positive and negative in Shaw's character; in 1955 he fell upon the negative with vigor. Similarly, writing a postscript to his biography in 1963, Hesketh Pearson could now say, "His humour, seldom of a rich nature, had become inhuman"—an observation he would have thought twice about printing during Shaw's lifetime. Blanche Patch (admittedly, however, a narrow and provincial person) contributed *Thirty Years with G.B.S.* in 1951, and she did not like her former employer very well: "He never said thank you for anything," she complained. H. G. Farmer defended Shaw's sister Lucy in 1959; Janet Dunbar championed Charlotte Shaw in 1963: both Shaw the brother and Shaw the husband suffered. Gradually the negative side of Shaw emerged in the letters, memoirs, and diaries of his contemporaries. H. M. Hyndman had not liked Shaw, nor had Gordon Craig, nor had Beatrice Webb. And there were other dissenters.

I began my group biography *Bernard Shaw and the Actresses* (1980) believing, like Barbara Bellow Watson, that Shaw was a firm feminist and friend to women. The more I read the words of the women who had known him, however, the more doubtful I became. True, he had his partisans: Ellen Terry, Lillah McCarthy, Ellen O'Malley, and Gertrude Kingston, for example, genuinely liked him, though there is ambivalence in Terry. Three hundred and seventy-three letters from Jenny Patterson to Shaw in the British Library, however, testify to her temper and vulgarity, but more to his callousness. Three volumes of letters to Shaw from the novelist Elinor Huddart reveal that while she was delighted with his epistolary camaraderie, she also found him mentally bloodthirsty and appallingly conceited. Alice Lockett's letters tell the same story. Elizabeth Robins, the Ibsen actress, detested him for much of their acquaintance. May Morris had severe reservations. Beatrice Webb was critical, if not hostile. Florence Farr attacked him in a novel and in reviews. Lena Ashwell, who created Lina Szczepanowska in *Misalliance*, did not have a kind word to say about G.B.S., although she was a close friend of Mrs. Shaw. Dame Ethel Smythe could not understand his failure to support the suffrage movement. Virginia Woolf found his harangues unbearable. Mrs. Campbell found him as cruel and untrustworthy as she found him kind and supportive. Rebecca West wrote to tell me that she had not liked Shaw, though she had liked Charlotte very much. Listening to the voices of the women who had known him, I found it impossible to retain my original view of Shaw as woman's champion, even though I could account for some of the negative reaction—Elizabeth Robins: feminist resentment of his gallantries; Beatrice Webb: jealousy; Virginia Woolf: snobbery. I could no longer trust the man. Could I trust the works? I returned to them, and found I could not. The same ambiguous attitudes toward women Shaw displayed personally are present in his art, where, although ambiguity might be expected, it has often been overlooked.

Actually none of the revisionism since 1950 is really damaging to Shaw's personality or his work, though it may be damaging to Shaw's version of both. It reveals him as a man of infinite contradictions and complexities, a far richer view, providing biographers and critics a wider interpretive range than was thought possible. And that will be the principal task of future biographers: interpreting the records. A start has been made by Daniel Dervin in his *Bernard Shaw: A Psychological Study* (1975). While not everyone may agree with Freudian analysis, we can agree that it is one handle by which to take a hold of this Protean Shaw and come to terms with him. My handle was a feminist perspective. In my biography I have interpreted Shaw's contradictory attitude toward woman as stemming from a simultaneous fascination with and repugnance towards sex, and thus necessarily towards women; and have attempted to trace the growth and permutations of that dualism in his life and work. Michael Holroyd is currently writing an authorized life of Shaw, due in 1985 in several volumes. According to Holroyd, his biography will stress the emotional life of the private Shaw and, as theme, the fading of the private man in the growth of the public G.B.S. Holroyd believes that Shaw's first twenty years were acutely unhappy. Rejected by his mother—an experience that inspired a lifelong fear of women and of rejection—Shaw had to be reborn as a child of his own writing, only then finding his personal equilibrium. Holroyd would agree, I believe, that although there is a great deal of unused material about Shaw, the real challenge to the biographer is interpreting the evidence to create a coherent view of the man and his work.

Not that new evidence is not revealing. The sheer amount of unpublished Charrington material at the Humanities Research Center, for example, convinced me that apart from Harley Granville Barker, Janet Achurch and her husband Charles Charrington were the most important of Shaw's theatrical relationships. Previously unpublished letters from Jenny Patterson reveal that their physical liaison endured for years, despite Shaw's denials. The Elinor Huddart letters are extremely interesting in that they show the young Shaw wrestling with ideas about women and marriage that would become central to his work. The Gordon Craig correspondence, some of which I used in my biography, gives a deeply hostile view of the Shaw-Terry relationship. I found enough missing parts and whole letters from Terry to Shaw to warrant a new edition of that correspondence. At Ayot St. Lawrence I pulled open a drawer to find dozens of Charlotte Shaw's diaries; their contents reveal how far apart hers and Shaw's lives grew. Affectionate letters from George Carr Shaw to Lucinda in 1857—he calls her "my Honey," "my own Bessie," "my darling one"—indicate that the couple were close and writing almost every other day during her absence one year after Shaw's birth—an unexplored aspect of that relationship. Numerous unpublished letters from petitioners to Shaw in the British Library confirm and expand our understanding of Shaw's financial generosity with friends, relatives, strangers.

In the face of Michael Holroyd's forthcoming authorized biography, more biography of Shaw may seem superfluous. But no biography is ever definitive. There remains room for a Marxist life, perhaps; or for more group biographies like Stanley Weintraub's *Private Shaw and Public Shaw: A Dual Portrait of Lawrence of Arabia and G.B.S* (1963), or my own biography, since Shaw's relationships were multiple and well-documented. Although there is a biography, *The Fabians*, by Norman and Jeanne MacKenzie (1977), there is still much to be said about Shaw and the Webbs, more than enough for a separate biographical account, Or there are the Court years with Vedrenne, Barker, and Lillah McCarthy. There is room for more biographical criticism, even though biographical criticism is currently unfashionable. Nor does there seem to be unreasonable restriction on Shaw materials to deter biographers. With the exception of several letters that Dan Laurence wished to reserve for the third volume, I had no difficulty obtaining permission to use unpublished Shaw material; the Shaw Estate was very co-operative. In summary, then: much has been said biographically about Shaw with his permission; much remains to be said without it. It may even be proved that, after all, he was his own best interpreter.

Margot Peters

Textual Studies

Five years ago at the 1975 MLA Conference of Scholars on Shaw, Louis Crompton cited as a major textual need the publication of a set of manuscripts of Shaw's plays, most of them the British Library's Shavian holdings. Nothing yet has been done about the shorthand drafts there of *Widowers' Houses, Misalliance, Back to Methusaleh, The Millionairess,* and *The Simpleton of the Unexpected Isles.* However, all the longhand drafts archived in the British Museum are being published by the Garland Press in a twelve volume series: *Bernard Shaw, Early Texts: Play Manuscripts in Facsimilie.* In chronological order the plays are *Widowers' Houses,* edited by Jerald Bringle; *The Philanderer,* edited by Julius Novick; *Mrs Warren's Profession,* edited by Margot Peters; *Arms and the Man,* edited by Norma Jenckes; both *Candida* and *How He Lied to Her Husband,* edited by J. Percy Smith; *You Never Can Tall,* which I edited; *The Devil's Disciple,* edited by Robert F. Whitman; *The Man of Destiny* and *Caesar and Cleopatra,* both edited by J. L. Wisenthal; *Captain Brassbound's Conversion,* edited by Rodelle Weintraub; *Major Barbara,* edited by Bernard Dukore; and *The Doctor's Dilemma,* edited by Margery M. Morgan. The last play in the series, *Heartbreak House,* edited by Stanley Weintraub and Anne Wright, differs from the other texts in that it is not a longhand draft but the recently discovered, heavily revised typescript of which the shorthand draft is lost or destroyed.

Other manuscripts and drafts have been found in the last five years. The shorthand draft of *Widowers' Houses,* transliterated by Barbara Smoker, is reproduced in the Garland edition. There is a manuscript for *John Bull's Other Island* at the Humanities Research Center of the University of Texas which at this time is not available for publication. *Pygmalion,* also at the HRC, has been transliterated for a dissertation on the play. And then there are lengthy extracts from the *Saint Joan* manuscript, which will appear in a book being written by Brian Tyson.

In his over-all introduction to the Garland series, the General Editor of the project, Dan H. Laurence, sketches in the busy life Shaw was living in the years during which the early plays were written and then goes on to describe the long, narrow reporters' notebooks which Shaw presumably pulled from his coat pockets whenever inspiration moved him on trains, buses or park benches: "Meticulously he would date the start of the new scene or act and, when traveling, indicate where the composition had been undertaken. The play's dialogue would be composed first, with comparatively little correction or revision; cuts would come later, often during rehearsal. Stage directions would be inserted last of all, in preparation for the typist or printer. All through the creative period, however, the notebooks would serve as catch-alls for memoranda and bursts of inspiration: . . . drawings of music; research notes; lists of props; lecture outlines for platform speakers; draft correspondence; addresses of newly-met acquaintances; colloquialisms or phrases to be worked into the speeches of characters." Laurence concludes the paragraph with the assurance that, in the Garland texts, whenever Shaw shifts to his idiosyncratic Pitman shorthand, transcriptions are given.

By the way, I did bring to this meeting photocopies of *You Never Can Tell*—the facsimile copies from the British Museum—in case anyone not acquainted with the notebooks would like to see what we were working from. When I started working from that, I was amazed. I had seen some of the notebooks years before while working at the British Library, but since they could not be quoted from, I had read through them quickly merely to gain an idea of Shaw's methods of composition. Now, working closely with them, I was chagrined at the truth of Laurence's observation that Shaw wrote dialogue "with comparatively little correction or revision." Those dates at the beginnings of the acts indicated how rapidly the inspiration was flowing. It was taking me much longer to piece together Shaw's deletions and comment on them than it had taken for him to write the play. However, deciphering those deletions proved worthwhile. For example, in an article on *You Never Can Tell* in the Shaw issue of *Modern Drama* in 1971, Stanley Weintraub concluded from "internal and circumstantial evidence" that Sarah Grand's novel *The Heavenly Twins* had influenced Shaw's *You Never Can Tell*. I discovered on the title page of the first notebook that Shaw had considered and then rejected the title "The Terrestrial Twins." This confirms, it seems to me, Weintraub's case.

I think that documentation of that sort will occur quite frequently because of the availability of these early texts, but what intrigues me about them is that they should stimulate new, exciting Shaw criticism. I, for one, because of cuts and additions in the manuscript I was working on, became aware of how carefully Shaw used on-stage laughter to cue and occasionally disturb his audience. I noted too that many of the changes were prompted by sound rather than sense. Shaw's musical and poetic ear was constantly at work at these moments of revision and these texts prove it over and over again. I note in their introductions—to limit my comments to the scholars on this panel—that Margot Peters observes that "Comparison of Shaw's original and published texts [of *Mrs Warren's Profession*] reveals how far he was initially inclined to melodrama himself. The incest theme, for example, prominent in the first, is clipped to suggestion in the latter." And in their introduction, Stanley Weintraub and Anne Wright cite the 1917 typescript of *Heartbreak House* as "of very great critical interest "since it permits us to see how Shaw gradually clarified themes and resolved the dramatic action."

My interest in texts, then, is the interest of a critic who can use them. I find very much to my liking J. L. Wisenthal's recent *Shaw and Ibsen: Bernard Shaw's "The Quintessence of Ibsenism" and Related Writings*. It is a scholarly text in that it gives us *The Quintessence* of 1891, together with the variant readings of 1913 and 1922. He also includes "Fragments of a Fabian Lecture" which are discards from *The Quintessence* as well as published items helpful in casting light on the Shaw-Ibsen relationship. (All of this material was noted as being in existence and not published at the time of the 1975 meeting.) In his introductory essay Wisenthal uses these variant texts, manuscript materials, and fugitive pieces to reveal the changing attitudes Shaw had toward Ibsen. Wisenthal's book has been authoritatively evaluated by Frederick P. W. McDowell in *The Shaw Review* (September 1980) and deemed "an essential volume for the library of every Shavian."

I agree with that judgment but I also sympathize with McDowell's uneasiness that Wisenthal does not quite see how deep, how intense the relationship between Shaw and Ibsen is, and how it accounts in part for our own use of oxymoron in writing about Shaw: heart-broken rebirth; bitter comedy; genial cruelty. I think that Shaw, who both in personal accounts and in the plays themselves toys with the idea of multiple fathers, experienced his share of anxiety over his literary fathers and could both reject and accept their influence simultaneously. Such a hidden and complex battle can *only* be traced if all—or, at least, a substantial amount—of the evidence is available, and I find myself again in agreement with McDowell when he suggests in his carefully thought-out review-article the need for a companion volume, a collection of Shaw's journalistic commentary on Ibsen not included in Wisenthal's *Shaw and Ibsen*.

I would apply that suggestion to Shaw's other literary fathers. For example, Edwin Wilson in his *Shaw and Shakespeare* collected a good amount of the published material but gave no idea of the life-death struggle going on. A companion volume of manuscript material and fugitive pieces analyzed—no, it would be better to say meditated on—by a scholar-critic saturated in both dramatists would do much to give us an idea of the workings of Shaw's mind as he both used his influence and devised tactics to avoid that influence. Perhaps my own readings of Shaw may be too much influenced by Harold Bloom at present and I may eventually become anxious about that influence, but what I have said about Shaw and Ibsen, Shaw and Shakespeare, I would also say about Shaw and Shelley, Shaw and Dickens, Shaw and . . . , but go back to the transcript of the 1975 MLA Conference. Frederick McDowell is not with us tonight since he is in Europe, but I find I can't resist his fraternal influence. He said at the time, "It seems to me . . . that one prime desideratum for Shaw scholarship in the next twenty-five years will be the detailed study of Shaw's relationship to those who were formative upon him, so that a more precise impression can emerge as to the exact contours and configurations of his mind."

At the 1975 meeting, Louis Crompton also noted that there were a number of film scripts not yet in print. The six complete and partial scripts are now available in Bernard Dukore's *The Collected Screen Plays of Bernard Shaw*. This seems to me to be a major textual offering. In his masterful introduction—some 170 pages—Dukore traces the history of Shaw and the cinema as well as analyzing the merits and flaws of the Shaw films that were actually made. I have not yet had an opportunity to look closely at the film sequences Shaw added in the film scripts of such plays as *Arms and the Man* and *Pygmalion*, but I assume from my knowledge of the 1945 Penguin version of the film *Major Barbara* they will further reveal how willing Shaw was to break from stage tradition and explore new territory. I know that Shaw's interest in the camera dates way back, but I am suggesting here that films, even in the beginning, were more than a novelty to Shaw—that they offered an opportunity to break from his dramatic fathers. Dukore informs us that as early as 1908 Shaw told Arthur Wing Pinero that if the gramophone could be successfully synchronized with motion pictures a fresh career might open for both of them!

Daniel Leary

Criticism

The 1975 MLA Conference of Scholars on Shaw ended with the observation that although Shaw scholarship was apparently coming of age, there remained projects for virtually hundreds of articles, dissertations, and books. The transcription of that conference in the May 1976 *Shaw Review*, plus Stanley Weintraub's survey of Shaw studies published in *Anglo-Irish Literature: A Review of Research* (New York: MLA, 1976), provide an informed account of the state of Shaw criticism through 1975 and clearly suggest future priorities. Given the excellence of those reviews, my job here is relatively easy: first of all I refer you to them. I shall recapitulate them only briefly, cite major works of the past five years and a few currently in progress which are relevant to criticism, and then elaborate on several areas which in my opinion deserve special critical attention in the immediate future.

There is a certain consensus that at long last Shaw's dramatic genius has received its due. From 1969 through 1974, a brief time indeed in Shavian terms, substantial studies of his plays were published by Louis Crompton, Charles Carpenter, Marjorie Morgan, Maurice Valency, Bernard Dukore, J. L. Wisenthal, and myself. In toto this critical abundance was unprecedented for its combination of concentration, sophistication, and scope. The 1975 conference moved from this base. Charles Carpenter presented statistics to prove that despite all the recent critical work on Shavian drama most of the plays have received far less academic attention than plays by Joyce, Yeats, and Eliot. Louis Crompton observed that valuable Shaw manuscripts and uncollected essays remain to be edited. Stanley Weintraub stressed the need for studies of Shaw's influence on a host of modern playwrights; and Frederick McDowell, citing Shaw's list of kindred spirits in the preface of *Man and Superman*, proposed that a priority for the future was the exploration of Shaw's mind, the influences upon it, and his influence on others. To Shaw's acknowledgement of Bunyan, Blake, Hogarth, Turner, Goethe, Shelley, Schopenhauer, Wagner, Ibsen, Morris, Tolstoy, and Nietzsche, McDowell added Swift, Butler, Molière, Ruskin, Marx, Mill, Carlyle, Bergson, Voltaire, Chekhov, Strindberg, Plato, Hegel, Darwin, Wilde, Beerbohm, and Wells. Further, McDowell observed the need for a variorum edition of Shaw's works and for separate volumes of letters between Shaw and his literary or theater associates, plus volume-length studies of individual plays. Picking up this thread in his review of Shaw scholarship for the MLA, Weintraub emphasized the value of close studies of the play manuscripts and the practical convenience of critical anthologies focused from particular perspectives.

In the past five years Shaw scholars appear to have harkened to many of these suggestions, or to related ideas of their own. No more works devoted specifically to Shaw's plays have come forth, although Shavians are looking forward to a critical study by Frederick McDowell. Rather, three fine books on his intellectual development and a large survey which includes that development have been published. Using *The Quintessence of Ibsenism* and *The Perfect Wagnerite* as touchstones, Alfred Turco's *Shaw's Moral Vision: The Self and Salvation* (1976) finds in Shaw an evolution from pragmatism to heroic idealism and, finally, a frustration and disillusionment. Robert Whitman's *Shaw and the Play of Ideas* (1977) complements Turco's work. Whitman proposes that Shaw's movement from Marx to Fabianism and through Schopenhauer, Samuel Butler, and Ibsen, was informed by his perception of Hegel, a perception he gained from reading the now-neglected English socialist and philosopher Ernest Belfort Bax. Recently, as Professor Leary has noted, J. L. Wisenthal has shed yet more light on Shaw's relation to Ibsen in an edition of the *Quintessence* (1979) which includes Shavian revisions and related writings plus a long critical introduction. And extraordinarily ambitious in its biographical, philosophical, and critical scope is Jean-Claude Amalric's *Bernard Shaw, du réformateur victorien au prophète édouardien* (1977), which provides and extensive bibliography.

Shaw's political life and views have also seen more light. Lloyd Hubenka's edition of *Practical Politics: Twentieth-Century Views on Politics and Economics* (1976) collects Shavian political and economic lectures from 1905 to 1933. This volume has been complemented by substantial discussions of Shaw in Norman and Jeanne MacKenzie's *The Fabians* (1977), Stanley Pierson's *British Socialists, The Journey from Fantasy to Politics* (1979), and Stephen Ingle's *Socialist Thought in Imaginative Literature* (1979). Lighter in weight is Gordon Bergquist's *The Pen and the Sword: War and Peace in the Prose and Plays of Bernard Shaw* (1977). And most recently Bernard Dukore combines economics, politics, and comparative literature in *Money and Politics in Ibsen, Shaw and Brecht* (1980).

The idea of publishing critical anthologies which adopt a specialized perspective appears to be gaining ground. Stanley Weintraub, who made the suggestion in 1975 and who, like Shaw, often precedes expectation, collected essays for a volume on *Saint Joan* in 1973. Subsequently Rodelle Weintraub edited *Fabian Feminist* in 1977. This latter springs from articles published in a *Shaw Review* issue on "Shaw and Woman" in 1974. Such special issues of the *Review* have had the character of small anthologies. Since 1975 they have featured "Shaw Around the World" (January 1977), "Shaw and Dickens" (September 1977), and "Shaw and Myth" (May 1978). Carrying forward this tradition is the first annual volume of the *Review* under its new title, *Shaw: The Annual of Bernard Shaw Studies* (1981), which deals with "Shaw and Religion." It will contain eleven pieces plus a large bibliography on its subject by Charles Carpenter and the usual reviews and checklist. Related to this one-topic approach is William Searle's *The Saint & the Skeptics: Joan of Arc in the Work of Mark Twain, Anatole France, and Bernard Shaw* (1976). The section on Shaw's Joan is the best in the book. More general in coverage are T. F. Evans's *Shaw: The Critical Heritage* (1976), and a collection of critical essays edited by Michael Holroyd, *The Genius of Shaw* (1979). The Evans anthology is especially valuable as it reprints contemporary responses to Shavian drama from 1892 to 1951.

Forthcoming publications by Dan Laurence and Stanley Weintraub promise to be of great utility to Shavian critics. Around the corner are Laurence's massive Shaw bibliography and his edition of Volume III of the *Collected Letters* which will cover the years from 1911 through 1925. More immediately in press are the *Early Texts: Play Manuscripts in Facsimile,* for which Laurence is general editor. In his 1976 review of Shaw research, Weintraub observed that Louis Crompton's and Bernard Dukore's use of the *Major Barbara* manuscripts demonstrates the value of closely studying such materials. Now there will be a good number at critics' fingertips. Also useful for Shavian critics and scholars will be a transcription of Shaw's diaries from 1885–1897, a project started years ago by Stanley Rypins and soon to be completed by Weintraub. References to these diaries by J. Percy Smith in *The Unrepentant Pilgrim: A Study of the Development of Bernard Shaw* (1965), and Robert Whitman in *Shaw and the Play of Ideas* attest to their biographical and critical potential.

In sum, present Shaw scholarship is taking fruitful new directions relevant to Shaw criticism. Shaw's ideas and indebtedness are receiving more critical attention. Critical anthologies are increasing in number. Source materials essential to the critic are in the offing.

What areas, then, deserve greater attention? One cannot help but observe that the progress so far is just a good beginning. Many areas of need cited in our last conference remain. While scholars have perceptively related Shaw to Ibsen, Wagner, and Hegel, the list of his sources and kindred spirits reaches far beyond these, and very little has been written about his influence on numerous twentieth-century playwrights and novelists. There is no close critical examination of his music and drama criticism. Many of his plays have received scant critical attention. Challenging avenues abound; there are still more questions than answers. For example, in his listing of "writers whose peculiar sense of the world I recognize as more or less akin to my own," Shaw sets "four apart and above all the English classics": Bunyan, Blake, Hogarth, and Turner. Is there any significance in this combination? Why do three happen to be artists? Bunyan's and Blake's relation to Shaw is now receiving attention, but scarcely enough. In the forthcoming "Religion" volume of *Shaw* two essays explore Shaw's metaphysics in a remarkably revealing Blakean manner. But there has been little analysis of his unusual ranking of Hogarth and Turner. Later Shaw commented that "Bergson is the established philosopher of my sect." No detailed study of this has yet come forth. Further, Shaw's poetic qualities remain intriguing. T. S. Eliot wrote that "the poet in Shaw was stillborn," while Pirandello wrote of "the most secret depths of poetry that exist in Shaw." Why the disparity? What are the poetics of Shaw?

Out of the multitude of possibilities for future critical work I should like to emphasize two which particularly appeal to me. Stanley Weintraub and Frederick McDowell and others have mentioned them in the past; my desire, therefore, is to serve as a selective advocate.

First, it seems to me that critical books and anthologies on single plays and topics remain a worthy priority: they are valuable not only to the scholar but also for the fact that they can help forward an intelligent appreciation of Shaw beyond the academy. In the MLA publication *Profession 78* [1978], William Schaefer, in retiring as Executive Director of the MLA and Editor of *PMLA*, viewed the English profession in a singularly blunt essay entitled "Still Crazy after All These Years." His major point was that the profession is so tied up in its own narrow professionalism that it has failed to communicate its humanistic point of view to society at large. One of his most telling examples was the publish-or-perish syndrome which has been at least partly responsible for a proliferation of academic journals which almost no one reads—from 1,000, containing 13,000 entries in 1960, to 3,000, containing more than 45,000 entries in 1976. He commented: "we have been led to absurd specialization, forcing us to write articles of less and less interest to fewer and fewer of our colleagues." Although we may not necessarily agree that this is true in Shaw studies, I believe we all recognize that good articles on Shaw in a wide assortment of academic journals have almost disappeared onto a few dusty library shelves while weaker ones in the popular press disseminate platitudes. Shavians may be diligent in ferreting out the best, but non-Shavians are likely to have trouble locating them, or unlikely even to try. Given this fact, anthologizing according to specific plays and topics has special virtues: it can be critically selective, giving exposure to the best work, and it can provide the specialist and non-specialist alike with a handy, reasonably complete reference on a Shaw play or subject. Books by good critics on individual plays would serve a similar function. Articles or chapters dealing with specific plays must necessarily be narrowly focused or cursory, while book-length studies can allow for the fuller, deeper analyses the major plays deserve. So far there are only several of these.

My second point relates to this first one: there is a need for books on the staging of Shaw's plays—on the plays as living theater.* E. J. West's

---

*The 1983 volume of *Shaw*, edited by Daniel Leary, is subtitled "Shaw's Plays in Performance." It will begin to address the point made here.—Ed.

edition of *Shaw on Theatre* (1958), Bernard Dukore in *Bernard Shaw, Director* (1971), Vincent Wall in *Bernard Shaw: Pygmalion to Many Players* (1973), Sidney Albert in his articles on "Shaw's Advice to the Players of *Major Barbara*," and several volumes of Shavian correspondence to individuals connected with the theater have made a notable start in this direction, but much remains to be done. Most of the critical work on the plays has been from a literary perspective which often neglects the fact that they achieve distinctive aesthetic and didactic qualities *in performance*. For Shaw's opinion on this matter we may recall his refusal to allow his plays to be incorporated into textbooks for classroom study. He repeatedly supervised their casting and staging, carefully distinguishing between aesthetics on the page and in the theater. For example: "A play by a great poet, in which every speech is a literary masterpiece, may fail hopelessly on the stage because the splendid speeches are merely strung together without provoking one another, whereas a trumpery farce may win an uproarious success by its retortive backchat"; and further: "Contrast—continual contrast—is essential to my dialogue: if the performers take their tone and speed from one another, all glibly picking up their cues and rattling on in the same way, the scene will be unintelligible."

Besides being intrinsically Shavian and sound from an aesthetic point of view, a focus on the plays as living theater answers in part to William Schaefer's objections to the isolationism, elitism, and compartmentalization of our profession. It not only moves consideration of the plays off the printed page but has the potential of influencing the ways in which Shavian drama is presented to the public. Shaw felt that *"The most desirable director of a play is the author."* Since G.B.S. is no longer physically around, critics and scholars may bring about a reasonable alternative by searching for and conveying as nearly as possible his theatrical intentions.

I'm sure we have all witnessed performances of the plays which have violated these intentions. In the last dozen years Los Angeles has seen major productions of five, any one of which would have benefited greatly from a director responsive to Shaw's sense of theater in general, and to his specific ideas about performing the play at hand. In Los Angeles' monstrous Ahmanson Theatre *Captain Brassbound's Conversion, Saint Joan,* and *The Devil's Disciple* sagged around a star-casting system: Greer Garson could not carry the first nor Rex Harrison the last, and in *Saint Joan* Sarah Miles herself sagged: instead of charging onto the scene with the energy of a Sybil Thorndike she habitually wandered onto the stage as if to say, "Gee whiz, is this really me, here and now?" In all three productions Shavian balance, dynamics, and vocal variety were flawed or lacking. Sometimes key speeches were cut. Missing from the Epilogue of *Saint Joan* was Cauchon's lament: "Must then a Christ perish in torment in every age to save those that have no imagination?" Sometimes the sets and props obscured or perverted Shaw's intention. In Scene III of *Saint Joan* a large tree limb hung in front of the pennon whose fluttering change of direction is so central to the action; but little matter, since the pennon itself wafted limply and aimlessly. In a production of *Major Barbara* the great cannon of Act III faced the audience, not Perivale St. Andrews, and there were no mutilated dummy soldiers on stage, not even one for Undershaft to kick. In a production of *Pygmalion,* actor Robert Stephens apparently overlooked the fact that he was supposed to be a professor of phonetics who preaches "the divine gift of articulate speech": he swallowed not only syllables but whole phrases and sputtered unintelligibly at strategic moments.

Shavians should not be fatalistic about such things. The theatrical values of Shavian drama are too important to be violated in this manner. Although the theater world is not noted for modesty and research, there are some directors and actors who would appreciate knowing Shaw's intentions for producing his plays as well as the aesthetics and ideas which underly their action. On a trip to the Shaw shelves of the UCLA Research Library in 1977 two visiting Shavians and I encountered a pleasant but harried man seated on the floor with books scattered about. Hearing us talk about the collection, he introduced himself: his name was Jeffrey Hayden. He was soon to direct a production of *Candida* in the Schubert Theater, Boston, which was to star his wife, Eva Marie Saint. Could we lead him to materials on the play?

We offered impromptu recommendations, and in this case both the director and the leading actress were sufficiently serious to pursue the matter further, attending my classroom lectures on the play and consulting with me about it in the following weeks. But such conscientiousness should not have to rely on chance encounters in a library. While Shaw's ghost need not roam the stage like Hamlet's father, the full range of his intentions regarding his plays should be at hand at least as a starting point for both scholar and director. This range includes not only his meaning, special emphases, and literary aesthetics, but, fully as much, his canny perceptions on such matters as producing, directing, acting, costuming, lighting, props, and sets. By making these readily available and by explicating them clearly both in general and according to specific plays, critics can promote a more Shavian presentation of Shaw. Here is one way academics may move beyond dusty library shelves, classrooms, and conferences (thirty years after) into a worldly theater.

Charles Berst

REVIEWS

Bernard Shaw: Film-maker

Bernard Shaw. The Collected Screenplays of Bernard Shaw. Edited with an introduction by Bernard F. Dukore. Athens: University of Georgia Press, 1980. 487pp. Illustrated. $35.00

There were the makings of a great screenwriter in G.B.S., but he was born too soon. With his gift for dialogue, cinema was not ready for him until he was nearly eighty. Only the sound-film could have utilized his abilities, as he put it in the preface to *Saint Joan*, to represent characters "as saying . . . the things they actually would have said if they had known what they were really doing." Even so, he saw the possibilities early, becoming a good amateur photographer in the 1890s, and telling playwright A. W. Pinero in 1908 that if the gramophone could be successfully synchronized with motion pictures, fresh careers might open for both of them.

Shaw attended his first movie rehearsal in 1913, and in 1915 announced that his just-published short play *Great Catherine* "ought to do excellently on the movies. It is a scenario almost as it stands." He had already predicted that cinema, with its appeal to the illiterate as well as literate, would "produce effects that all the cheap books in the world could never produce," and would "form the mind of England. The national conscience, the national ideals and tests of conduct will be those of the film."

He was eager to become involved. As early as 1914 he appeared, with G. K. Chesterton and William Archer, in a silent-film skit directed by James Barrie. By the 1920s he had appeared in several other brief films, and was fending off requests for his services as film scenarist, and for the use of his already-produced plays, at temptingly rising fees. By 1919 he was being offered up to $30,000 a play, and in 1920 a million dollars for film rights to all his plays. He rejected all offers.

"Filming kills a play stone dead," he objected, "and should therefore be applied to the corpses of plays that have had their run." Besides, he realized, "A play with the words left out is a play spoiled."

Despite flirtations with propositions to make silent movies of his plays, or to create new scenarios, Shaw was the wrong writer for soundless film, even when Hollywood tried to cash in on Gene Tunney's boxing fame and Shaw's old novel *Cashel Byron's Profession.* Talkies immediately attracted Shaw, until he discovered that the producers who approached him thought that sound films were only movies with spoken subtitles. A play for film, Shaw would insist, is not "an exhibition of photography." Bernard F. Dukore's 153 pages of introduction, bolstered by 680 endnotes, is a full-length monograph itself on Shaw's growing attraction to the cinema and his eventual contribution to the soundfilm screenplay. As Dukore observes, this is a contribution not fully apparent in the films as shown, truncated by producer's whims and box-office concerns. Some of the screenplays were never translated into film: Shaw's *Saint Joan* was blocked by the Roman Catholic censorship lobbying group, The Legion of Decency, in the 1930s, and *The Devil's Disciple,* for which Shaw wrote additional scenes, was never made. Shaw's script for *Arms and the Man* (1932) is another rarity, as the film, in the infancy of talkies, had little distribution beyond England, while the even more primitive *How He Lied to Her Husband* (1930), for which Dukore rightly furnishes no screenplay, was only adapted from the stage version via insignificant cuts and variations of a few lines.

The *Saint Joan* screenplay has been published before—separately—in an edition by Dukore. For most readers and scholars the real meat of the volume will be the screenplays of *Major Barbara* and *Pygmalion*. The Penguin "screen version" (1945) of *Major Barbara,* now nearly a rare book, is actually a reading version of the screenplay, and neither the much-cut film of the screenplay nor the screenplay itself, which Dukore has pieced together from shooting scripts and typescripts with holograph alterations by Shaw. All the new filmed sequences are included, whether or not they survived the cutting room. Thus they add to the Shavian canon but emphasize the scrappy nature of the screenplay, produced under wartime conditions and constraints, and updated into the 1930s in some places while left a generation older in others. Thus Mrs. Baines (updated to "General" Baines in a new episode) recalls the Bloody Sunday riots in Trafalgar Square in 1886 almost as if they were yesterday, while motor cars and modern trucks appear, the Japanese incursion into Manchuria is mentioned, and Todger Fairmile in a new scene discusses Welsh heavyweight Tommy Farr, the British ring hope of the immediate prewar years.

Despite the uneven chronology of the script, the new scenes are vintage Shaw, writing at 85 as if producer Gabriel Pascal were Granville Barker of the palmy Court Theatre days. Shaw had long claimed that he wanted someday to write a grand opera—words *and* music—and for the film *Major Barbara* he wrote a scene in which the Utopian industrial town of Perivale St. Andrews utilizes large-screen television to reproduce orchestral performances once heard there live. For his scene Shaw imagined well, writing in a "Wagnerian" symphony orchestra of a hundred instrumentalists led by no less than Arturo Toscanini accompanying a large choir in the quartet and chorus from Rossini's *Moses in Egypt*. As the organ comes in to swell the music, the recitative and chorus are Shaw's own setting to Rossini's score:

BASS SOLO.   In this our hour of darkness
                   We warsmiths of the cannons
                   Where do we stand today?
CHORUS.   We forge our own destruction
                      We shall be slain who slay.
BASS SOLO.   Then from the gods who fail us
                   Ourselves must win the sway.

I

Quartet and Chorus

BASS SOLO.   O thou great soul of all:
                   Say where but here within us
                   The answer to our call
                   Shall we, thy servants, find?
CHORUS.   Say where but here within us
                      Shall we the answer find?
SOLO QUARTET.   Say where?
CHORUS.   In ourselves.

II

TENOR SOLO.   Shall we not then arise
                   And in our hearts the power
                   We sought for in the skies
                   Find ready in our hands?
CHORUS.   In heart and brain discover
                      The godhead in our hands.
SOLO QUARTET.   Where else?
CHORUS.   In our hands.

III

SOPRANO SOLO.   From Women's tortured hearts
                Their slaughtered sons lamenting

	I cry against these arts
	That slay what we create.
CHORUS.	Creation, not destruction,
	Shall henceforth make us great.
SOLO QUARTET.	Dare we hope?
CHORUS.	Yes: we dare.

IV

Soloists and Chorus with Organ ad lib.

ALL.	To thee the god within us
	We trust the world to win us.
	Creation, not destruction,
	Henceforth shall make us great.
SOPRANO SOLO.	Us great.
CHORUS.	Henceforth.

The chorus over, the performers vanish from the screen. Today Shaw's dream is a staple of television, but the concept was too expensive for filming and probably little more anyway than Shaw's fantasy. On paper, at least, he had written for Toscanini's baton. The lyrics, however, epitomize Shaw's mature faith, and deserve to be better known. Now they will be.

Even more vintage Shaw is the more integrated screenplay for *Pygmalion*, first written in 1934 with new scenes, including a phonetics lesson between Higgins and Eliza, added as late as 1938, when filming began. Even there a few discrepancies remain. The *indoor* ambassadorial reception, at which Liza triumphs on screen, is new, composed in 1938, but no one involved with the filming remembered to remove the 1912 reference (Act IV) to Eliza's success occurring at a garden party. Here again Shaw had prepared a hybrid reading edition, combining with the original stage play short scenes from the film and new narrative material to bridge the segments. Dukore does not mention this confusing version, now the "definitive" Bodley Head text, where lines of narrative added as a result of the need for transitions are printed in Roman while Shaw retained italics for stage directions and narrative material from the reading edition of the stage play. Dukore's fuller screenplay is basically the uncut text as prepared in 1938, with a new final scene to satisfy Pascal's claimed box-office need for further ambiguity. As an appendix, Dukore prints Shaw's preferred 1934 ending, which left no doubt that Eliza would marry Freddy, nor that the irascible Higgins was no Prince Charming:

> HIGGINS. Goodbye, mother. [*He is about to kiss her, when he recollects something.*] Oh, by the way, Eliza, order a ham and a Stilton cheese, will

you? And buy me a pair of reindeer gloves, number eights, and a tie to match that new suit of mine. You can choose the color. [*His cheerful, careless, vigorous voice shews that he is incorrigible.*]
LIZA [*Disdainfully.*] Buy them yourself. [*She sweeps out.*]
MRS HIGGINS. I'm afraid youve spoiled that girl, Henry. But never mind, dear: I'll buy you the tie and gloves.
HIGGINS [*Sunnily.*] Oh, dont bother. She'll buy em all right enough. Goodbye.
They kiss. Mrs Higgins runs out. Higgins, left alone, rattles his cash in his pockets; chuckles; and disports himself in a highly self-satisfied manner, and goes out through the window to the balcony.
Higgins on the balcony smiling benevolently down to the party beneath.
Chelsea Embankment. Mrs Higgins's limousine standing opposite her door. Doolittle holds the car door open in a courtly manner for Mrs Higgins, who gets in.
Freddy appears.
LIZA. Here he is, Mrs Higgins. May he come?
MRS HIGGINS. Certainly, dear. Room for four.
Liza kisses Freddy.
The balcony.
Higgins's smile changes to an expression of fury.
He shakes his fist at the kissing couple below.
The Embankment.
Liza cocks a snook prettily at Higgins, and gets into the car.
Freddy takes off his hat to Higgins in the Chaplin manner and follows Liza into the car.
The car drives off. Wedding march.

With Leslie Howard, a leading heartthrob, cast as the curmudgeonly Higgins, the ending would not have worked; however the problem was that Howard was miscast, in the interest of commerce, for the role Shaw had written. As was (is?) usual in the cinema world, what was changed was the play rather than the player.

The scenes not filmed, and the new scenes filmed only to be cut, or cut out, in Shaw's screenplays for these films, *and* for *Caesar and Cleopatra,* produced in Shaw's ninetieth year, add so significantly to the Shavian canon that one puts down the book with regret that it has not been published in a size and format to conform to the Bodley Head *Complete Plays,* and with gratitude to Professor Dukore for making the texts of the screenplays accessible so readably and with so full a scholarly background. Rather than blame anyone for the many typographical errors one can hope instead that the high price of the book will not put off purchasers, and that a second printing will correct the misprints. The work deserves as much—a mine for Shaw scholars and a reading delight for anyone interested in theatre and film. It is tempting to hope that the availability of the scripts will tease producers to film Shaw again, and even that imaginative directors will look for ways to interpolate some of the delicious scenes intended for film into new stage versions of the plays. In the meantime Shaw scholars will count their blessings and read some of the plays anew in the perspective of Shaw's screen treatments.

Stanley Weintraub

Not by Shaw

Lady, Wilt Thou Love Me? Eighteen Love Poems for Ellen Terry Attributed to George Bernard Shaw, ed. by Jack Werner. New York: Stein and Day, 1980. $8.95.

If you believe that the dusty painting in your attic is a Rembrandt, or if you're sure that the chipped old fiddle in your basement is a Stradivarius, then you might even believe that these poems were written by Bernard Shaw for Ellen Terry. The less credulous will note that the poems are written in a suffocatingly sentimental and humorless style that is completely unlike Shaw's. For instance:

> Unrequited tho' it be,
> Tho' I know not whence it came,
> Still, the love I bear to thee,
> Ever must remain the same

or

> Days will pass, and months, and years,
> Love, to me, shall still be Sorrow:
> Hush, fond sighs!—and tarry, tears!
> Joy will never come the morrow

or even

> For sweet Content hath passed this way
> And—smiling at my woes—
> Drawn me her flower'd path along,
> Filling my heart with a glad new song.

The handwriting (the manuscript is reproduced) is quite unlike Shaw's. Werner alleges that Shaw disguised his handwriting, but gives no reason why he would have done so. And it is very difficult to do so consistently.

The Shaw estate (which never should have allowed the reprinting of a genuine poem by Shaw in the introduction) has refused to accept Werner's attribution to Shaw, as has Sotheby's, where these poems were auctioned in 1958. Werner is not able to quote any scholar who thinks that these poems are genuine. There is no mention of them in the Shaw-Terry letters, or in any other books by or about Shaw or Ellen Terry, and there can really be no question that Bernard Shaw had anything whatever to do with these submediocre poems.

All this would hardly make this book worth a review, if it were not for one sad fact. A scholarly study of Shaw, the product of years of work, and published by a university press, can rarely expect to sell more than 2,000 copies. But Stein and Day issued a first printing of this work of 20,000 copies! So the only value this book has is to demonstrate the existence of Gresham's law in literature.

Alexander Seabrook

Tailoring *Heartbreak House* for the Stage

Bernard Shaw. *Heartbreak House. A Facsimile of the Revised Typescript.* Edited by Stanley Weintraub and Anne Wright. (General Editor of the *Early Texts: Play Manuscripts in Facsimile Series:* Dan H. Laurence.) New York and London: Garland Publishing, Inc., 1981. 211pp. Illus. $50.

Garland Publishing has undertaken to issue the draft notebooks of Shaw's plays, the first such volume that of *Heartbreak House.* In the absence of the original shorthand draft of this play, however, the Garland edition is a facsimile of the typescript as amended by Shaw in his spidery but legible hand, augmented by a fine introductory essay detailing the stages through which the play passed on its way to final form. Some pages of supplementary changes and additions to the dialogue are included, as well as a few pages of shorthand notes.

Although the title of this work-in-progress is confidently announced as "Heartbreak House," it is both more and less than the play as finally approved and published by Mr. Shaw—more, because in addition to a surprising amount of the work as it appeared in final form, it includes a good many passages that were subsequently excised or substantially altered, plus the instructive introductory essay; less, because some dialogue that was added at later stages (in proofs) does not appear, and the haunting Shaw preface is not included. Still, this publication makes available an important stage of the final text—fortunately a stage already close enough to the final version to make it doubly fascinating, both for what has been cut out and for what has not yet been included. The sequences of events, the characters, incidents, and most of the passages one remembers are here already, either in type or in holograph emendation. But it is not *Heartbreak House* as Shaw intended it to be read, staged, and studied.

This folio volume ought to interest anyone curious about the process by which plays take shape, are tightened, tailored for the stage, sharpened and pointed by deletion, emendation, addition. The preliminary carpentry has already been done. Characters, settings, lines of development, prevailing tone are already established. Of course the more familiar one is with the play the more engrossing a study of this edition will be; and it will prove especially useful for anybody planning a production of *Heartbreak House*—if there are still a few directors in the theatre who maintain some concern for, and some sense of responsibility towards, the author's intentions—for it proves how little Shaw's intentions wavered, how sequences and fundamentals of character remained constant as the text moved towards the final version, and how in his staging directions he has made movement as much a part of character as dialogue. The importance Shaw gave to stage directions (setting, placement, movement, gesture, attitude) is here made vividly evident: to the typescript he has added by hand his interpretations of character by behavior and gesture; and from these holograph hints to producers, performers, and readers, one can detect the varying emphases he placed on the dialogue at every turn. Mrs. Hushabye "jumping up mischievously, and going to [Mangan] ... slipping her arm under his and pulling him upright" (elaborated from the bland "slipping her arm affectionately through his") or Randall "swinging the poker between his fingers like a well folded umbrella," are clear clues to character and momentary mood. Stage directors who persist in ignoring Shaw's carefully contrived staging will inevitably shift his emphasis and distort his intentions, which are more clearly perceptible in this edition because they are added, for the most part, in the author's own hand and so cannot be passed over as incidental afterthoughts.

Although every character is firmly established by this time, the evident care exercised in the choice of phrase and word does suggest slight adjustments in interpretation. Lady Utterword is described in the typescript as "very comfortably established in the hammock" at the opening of Act III; Shaw has written "lying voluptuously," which is both more vivid for the reader and more suggestive for the actress. (Mr. Weintraub and Ms. Wright point out in their introduction that

Shaw was at some pains to reduce the note of sexuality that sounds in the typescript, particularly relating to Lady Utterword. This fact may cool the ardor of enthusiastic actresses in that role, though there is no doubt that Shaw intended the "demon daughters" to be seductive within strict limits.) The careful shadings of theatricality in the play are suggested by the change Shaw has written in at the conclusion of Ellie's speech to Mrs. Hushabye in which she explains her "understanding" with Mangan. The typescript reads "She breaks down." Shaw has amended this to "[she cannot go on]". A good deal of dialogue is crossed out (less, however, than one would expect in a first draft); but nothing excised seems to alter character in any significant degree, saving perhaps Shotover's early acceptance of Ariadne as his daughter, which Shaw thought better of. The most surprising addition is the announcement in Act III of Ellie's "betrothal" to Shotover, a passage that has been inserted in Shaw's hand. Even here there is no real change of character. The most extraordinary feature of this addition is the unwavering sureness of aim with which Shaw has, in a single page, introduced a stunning surprise and made the dialogue connect effortlessly between two speeches which are sequential in the typescript.

Such technical mastery as this will certainly appeal to working playwrights, at least to those concerned with civilized language and society. The craft of turning mere observation or statement into lively stage dialogue cannot be learned from the finished text, since there is not a flat line in it. But here many handwritten changes transform mundane comments into charged, individualized remarks. Hesione's "We are waiting to hear what it is" has been replaced with "But what is it? Dont be aggravating, Addy." Shotover's "Well, I have helped you to find out that you must help yourself. I can do no more. I am in my dotage" becomes the staccato, bewildered "It confuses me to be answered. It discourages me. I cannot bear men and women. I have to run away. I must run away now." And there is an exchange between Lady Utterword and Mangan in Act III which originally read:

> LADY UTTERWORD. What has the result been, so far, may one ask?
> MANGAN. The result has been that I have put a stop to the games of the other fellows in the other departments.

Shaw has corrected that passage to read

> LADY UTTERWORD. And what have your administrative achievements been, so far?
> MANGAN. Achievements! Well, I dont know what you call achievements; but Ive jolly well put a stop to the games of the other fellows in the other departments.

In each case vigor, individual expression, conversational fluency have been added to bald question-and-answer without the smallest sacrifice of clarity or character.

Shaw's acknowledged intimate familiarity with the requirements and possibilities of the stage has been amply documented; but here are further examples of it. The original opening of the play (page 5 of this edition; renumbered page 4 of the typescript after the new opening was prefixed) read simply "Ellie Dunn sits waiting, gloved and hatted. Nurse Guinness enters and stares at her curiously." This is struck out in ink, and the amended opening is added—the one familiar to readers, in which Guinness crosses the full stage, picks up empty bottles from the pantry, and notices Ellie only on her return: a far more theatrically effective and arresting start. Again: Shotover pours out the "India tea" into a "flower pot" in the typescript, but Shaw has considered the stage manager's problem of that flower pot and substitutes the ship's "leathern" fire bucket. A few pages later a photographic portrait of Ariadne which Shotover brings in to show her ("She was fairer than she looks here. Freckles used to come out black in a photograph in those days") is cut altogether, as is the Captain's description of her as "a gabbling flapper." Shotover's prompt acceptance of her, crossed out in the typescript in order to leave the question of recognition unresolved, also gets rid of an awkward gesture in which he was originally to kiss her and put his hands on her shoulders, "holding her at arms length." The bracketted stage directions are nearly all in Shaw's hand (there are few in the typed script).

What is cut, although nobody will argue that the cuts are better than the final speeches, makes fascinating reading, though it is not easy to slow down sufficiently to pore over the passages scratched out. One usually ends by agreeing that the cut parts are dispensable; for example, Ariadne's command to Randall to "Go to bed instantly ... How dare you? ... How can anyone care for such a creature?" is followed by these (cut) sentences:

> LADY UTTERWORD. ... A costermonger would have more respect.
> Hector: why dont you keep horses?
> HECTOR. Costermongers dont hunt.
> LADY UTTERWORD. They keep donkeys.
> MRS. HUSHABYE. Who would not be proud of so distinguished a grandfather?

All that is cut; and it is unlikely that the most fanatical addict would wish it reinserted.

Unnecessary explanations and specific topical references are eliminated as well. Ellie's account of why she has arrived alone instead of with her father and Mangan is still present in the typescript but will disappear later. Costermongers, Conan Doyle, flappers and photographs, Parsifal and Frederick the Great, "feminist recriminations" and the exact location of Randall's bedroom upstairs, all eventually disappear, letting the play move in a less precise time zone.

Two passages fit so well into the themes of self-reliance and the need to fight for one's own beliefs that they might have been retained except for Shaw's concern for tautness and economy. Shotover's speech "I go on with the dynamite none the less. If I do not go according to my lights I shall be enslaved by men who go according to theirs. And my own lights lead me to seek power for self-defence, for the power to resist evil wills" is cut eventually, though it survives in this version; the three sentences that follow are crossed out in the typescript: "Remember, we are no longer free as we were. They have made hell and cast us into the cauldron. I will fight for my own soul and for yours." (Was that too topical or too personal? The anger and disillusionment that seeps out of such passages brings the dramatist almost as close as his characters.) And in Act III Mazzini observes, "I am only too thankful to have what I wear settled for me, if only I can afford to buy what is settled. But you see, the people who insist on settling my dress insist on settling my religion and my politics and my notions of right and wrong, too." To which Mrs. Hushabye replies (or did until her speech was cut together with Mazzini's), "How kind of them! and how easy for you!" Although these passages eventually disappear, they and others like them are rather like cracks through which one can discern the drift of Shaw's thoughts at successive stages in the composition of the play. Indeed, this edition makes available to us something more than a graphic example of the author's working methods. It is a stage in the process of putting reins to his freer fancy, and a great part of the fascination of this edition is the opportunity it offers for coming a little closer to Shaw's immediate impulses and expressions, and to see just where, and how, he has chosen to adapt, eliminate, or check them.

Whether Shaw himself would have been pleased with the publication of this script is an interesting (and perhaps irrelevant) speculation. Given his scant regard for academic scholarship and his enormous respect for the art of the stage, he is not likely to have been overly pleased at seeing his tentatives exposed to general view. Nor was he keen that younger playwrights should emulate him. If the play (as somebody said) really is the thing, the final version of it is the only text the author would wish to be known and understood by. But even in this Shaw has his oblique revenge upon those who attempt to dissect his work or reduce it to form and technique; for one gets so caught up in the dialogue, even in this unfinished, intermediate version—in the evolution of characters' attitudes, their habits of mind and expression, in the flow of fluent, lucid, literate language, in the keenly felt disappointments, fears and frustrations of author as voiced by character: in a word, in the engrossing company of Shaw—that one often forgets to note the corrections, and reads, as one should do, for the pleasure and excitement and immediacy of the content first of all. Not even this carefully presented facsimile, with its crossings out and interpolated lines and paste-overs, can remain entirely a text for analytical study. Like everything Shaw put on paper, it has a life of its own; and though we may prefer the finished *Heartbreak House*, still, this second step towards its full maturity contains a wealth of fascinating and suggestive material, whether it survived in the final text or was at last deleted.

Robert Chapman

John R. Pfeiffer[1]

A CONTINUING CHECKLIST OF SHAVIANA

I. Works by Shaw

Shaw, Bernard. *Bernard Shaw: Selected Plays.* New York: Dodd, Mead & Company, 1981. Includes a "Preface" by Rex Harrison, "Shaw and His Plays" by David Bearinger (not notable), *Candida, Caesar and Cleopatra, Man and Superman, Major Barbara, Pygmalion, Heartbreak House,* and *Saint Joan,* along with a number of accessory writings GBS supplied for these plays. The purpose of the collection is unclear, as the Collected Plays with their Prefaces text is used, but not the handy small-size format. Perhaps it will become a one-volume text. Price: $19.95. See Bearinger, David, and Harrison, Rex, under "Books and Pamphlets" below.

———. *Bernard Shaw. Plays.* Moscow: Pravda Publishing House, 1981. The paperback volume (2 rubles), edited by N. A. Presnova and introduced by Z. Grazhdanskaya, includes *Mrs Warren's Profession, Caesar and Cleopatra, Pygmalion,* and *Heartbreak House.* The print run may be a record for a Shaw title in an initial printing: 500,000 copies.

———. "Capital Punishment and Imprisonment." In *Prose Models.* Ed. George Levin. Fifth edition. New York: Harcourt, Brace, Jovanovich, 1981. Not seen.

———. *Collected Plays,* vol. 4. Under the general editorship of A.A. Anikst, N. Ya. D'yakonova, Yu. V. Kovalev, A. G. Obraztsova, A. S. Romm, B. A. Stanchits and I. V. Stupnikov. Leningrad: Art Publishing House, 1980. The fourth of six projected volumes, in Russian, containing *The Dark Lady of the Sonnets* (M. Loriye, trans., with preface trans. by N. Rakhmanova), *Fanny's First Play* (A. Krivtsova, trans.), *Androcles and the Lion* (with preface, G. Ostrovskaya, trans.), *Overruled* [Russian title: *Seething with Passion*] (Ye. Lopyryeva, trans.), *Pygmalion* (P. Melkova, trans., with preface and afterword trans. by N. Rakhmanova), *Great Catherine* (with author's defense, G. Ostrovskaya, trans.), *The Music-Cure* (Ye. Lopyryeva, trans.), *O'Flaherty, V.C.* [Russian title: *O'Flaherty, the Cavalier of the Order of Victoria*] (L. Polyakova, trans.), *The Inca of Perusalem* (V. Paperno, trans.), *Augustus Does His Bit* [Russian title: *Augustus Does His Duty*] (I. Zvavich, trans.), *Annajanska, the Wild Grand Duchess* (with preface, V. Paperno, trans.), *Heartbreak House* [Russian title: *The House Where Hearts are Broken*] (S.

---

[1] Professor Pfeiffer, *SHAW* Bibliographer, welcomes information about new or forthcoming Shaviana: books, articles, pamphlets, monographs, dissertations, reprints, etc. His address is Department of English, Central Michigan University, Mount Pleasant, Michigan 48859.

Bobrov and M. Bogoslovskaya, trans., with preface trans. by Ye. Lopyryeva). Translations and transliterations for this note by Roger Freling, Central Michigan University. Professor Freling occasionally makes his service available to parties interested in translations of Russian Shaviana, and welcomes requests.

———. *Collected Plays*, vol. 5. Leningrad: Art Publishing House, 1981. The fifth volume contains, in Russian, *Back to Methuselah* (Yu. Korneev, trans., with preface trans. by S. Sukharev), *Saint Joan* (O. Kholmskaya, trans., with preface trans. by N. Rakhamanova), *The Apple Cart* (E. Kalashnikova, trans., with preface trans. by A. Staviskaya), and *Too True to Be Good—Bitter, but True*, in the Russian rendering (V. Toper, trans.)

———. "The Devil Speaks." In *Reading For Rhetoric*. Ed. Caroline Shrodes, Clifford A. Josephson, and James R. Wilson. Riverside, New Jersey: Macmillan, 1979. Not seen.

———. "George Bernard Shaw." In *Literary Criticism of the English Speaking World*. Out of Print and Used Books & Back Date Periodicals. Catalogue 213. Cleveland: John T. Zubal, Inc., 1980, pp. 54–55; 2969 West 25th St., Cleveland, Ohio 44113. Lists nearly 100 items of Shaviana, including 37 titles presenting GBS correspondence, essays, stories, and plays. Also offers a 1933 sale catalogue of the Archibald Henderson collection, and a 1972 Sotheby, Parke-Bernet sale catalogue of GBS letters, manuscripts, and first editions.

———. *The Intelligent Woman's Guide to Socialism, Capitalism, Sovietism and Fascism*. To be issued in paperback by Penguin Books in May 1981. Price: $3.95.

———. *Lady, Wilt Thou Love Me? Eighteen Love Poems for Ellen Terry*. Ed. Jack Werner. New York: Stein and Day, 1981. Listed here only for bibliographical convenience: This work is not by Shaw. Reviewed in this volume.

———. Letter to a close friend (excerpts), owner of a yeast company, reporting receipt of a yeast shipment and commenting on the fall of Paris, 18 June 1940, advertised for sale in Catalogue 16, James Lowe Autographs Ltd., 667 Madison Ave., Suite 709, New York, New York 10021. Item # 122. Price: $650.00.

———. Letter to Jonathan Cape, 8 November 1924, deliberating whether or not Cape should publish W. H. Davies' confessional work *Young Emma*. Included in an appendix and on dust-jacket of W. H. Davies' *Young Emma*. New York: George Braziller, 1981. Cape issued a British edition of *Young Emma* in 1980.

———. Letter to Kingsley Martin, 1934, in Kingsley Martin's "Shaw and Wells." Reprinted in *H.G. Wells, Interviews and Recollections*. Ed. J. R. Hammond. Totowa, New Jersey: Barnes & Noble, 1980, p. 85. GBS advises against publication of a pamphlet collecting correspondence of a dialogue about socialism made by Wells, Keynes and Shaw, among others.

———. *Major Barbara*. In *The Modern Age*. Ed. Leonard Lief and James F. Light. Fourth edition. New York: Holt, Rinehart and Winston, 1981. Not seen.

———. Musical criticism of Wagner from various publications, in Robert Hartford, ed., *Bayreuth: the early years. An account of the Early Decades of the Wagner Festival as seen by the Celebrated Visitors & Participants* (Cambridge and New York: Cambridge University Press, 1980), 139–148, 160–168, 223–238, 245–247. Shaw's first visit to Bayreuth was in 1889. The account of it, which he wrote for the London journal *The Hawk*, was signed, in Germanic pun, "By Reuter." Other reports of Bayreuth would appear in *The English Illustrated Magazine*, *The World*, *The Star*, and his own *The Perfect Wagnerite*, adding and revising to that through its fourth edition in 1922. Extracts from all of these accounts appear, as well as Shavian reactions to Wagner's music and to Bayreuth in letters to W. T. Stead, Beatrice Webb, his wife Charlotte, and others. Some of Shaw's criticism would hold for any work at any time. "The law of traditional performances," he writes in 1889, "is 'Do what was done last time.'—the law of all living and fruitful performance is, 'Obey the innermost impulse which the music gives, and obey it to the most exhaustive satisfaction.' And as that impulse is never, in a fertile artistic nature, the impulse to do what was done last time, the two laws are incompatible, being laws respectively of death and life in art. Bayreuth has chosen the law of death. Its boast is that it alone knows what was done last time, therefore it alone has the pure and complete tradition, or, as I prefer to put it, that it alone is in a position to strangle Wagner's lyric dramas, note by note, bar by bar, *nuance* by *nuance*. It is in vain for Bayreuth to contend that by faithfully doing what was done last time it arrives at an exact copy of what was done the first time when Wagner was alive, present and approving. The difference consists in just this, that Wagner is dead, absent and indifferent. The powerful, magnetic personality, with all the tension it maintained, is gone; and no manipulation of the dead hand on the keys can ever reproduce the living touch...."

———. *The Screenplays of Bernard Shaw.* Ed. Bernard F. Dukore. Athens: University of Georgia Press, 1980. Reviewed in this issue.

———. *Shaw's Music. The Complete Musical Criticism.* Ed. Dan H. Laurence. London: Max Reinhardt; New York: Dodd, Mead, 1981. Three volumes. Reviewed in the next volume.

———. "So He Took His Hat Round": *A Facsimile of a Manuscript.* St. Louis: Washington University Libraries, 1981. A charity appeal on behalf of the King Edward Memorial Hospital, Ealing, drafted in holograph in pencil by Shaw; with an introduction by Dan H. Laurence limning GBS as "probably ... the most charitable professional man of his generation." Published as "the first in a series of keepsakes to be issued for the Friends of the Libraries." Limited to 600 copies; none for sale. Apply to Friends of the Libraries, Washington University, St. Louis, MO 63130.

II. Books and Pamphlets

Anderson, Robert. "Shaw, (George) Bernard." In *The New Grove Dictionary of Music and Musicians.* Twenty volumes. London: Macmillan, 1981. Entry in vol. 17, pp. 222–23. It is the longest essay on any music critic in the twenty volumes. "Shaw's collected writings on music stand alone in their mastery of English and compulsive readability."

Bearinger, David. "Shaw and His Plays." In *Bernard Shaw: Selected Plays.* New York: Dodd, Mead & Company, 1981. A lightweight "Introductory Essay" to the volume. See "Works by Shaw" above.

Bell, Michael. *The Context of English Literature, 1900–1930.* New York: Holmes and Meier, 1980. Characterizes Shaw's limitations with reference to the process of his "wit" in *Mrs Warren's Profession*, quoting from the play, "No normal woman would be a prostitute if she could afford to marry for love." Bell: "The way this remark appeals to the 'normal' woman involves a reification that if you pause to think about it is surely abstract to the point of untruth." It works because of its rhetorical symmetry. Thus, there is "something untrue" about women not wanting to be prostitutes or to marry for money just as there is something false about the endings of *Mrs Warren* and *Major Barbara*. "Shaw's abstractive simplifications, while leaving him space for satiric points and comic paradox, are in some tangible if ambiguous measure his actual simplifications as well as formally chosen ones, and it is his unwittingness, or ambivalence, in this respect that makes him so irritatingly coy much of the time. Brilliant as they are as ways of criticizing the given, even Shaw's best plays reveal emotional blanknesses when obliged to express a larger sense of life."

Bergman, Ingrid, and Burgess, Alan. *Ingrid Bergman: My Story.* New York: Delacorte

Press, 1980. Bergman met GBS just once in 1948 on the occasion of Pascal's invitation to her to film or stage *Candida*. She used the opportunity to tell Shaw she didn't do *Saint Joan* because she thought it unrealistic. Shaw asked her to visit again. Saying she would like to, Bergman offered to bring her husband. GBS, she reports, indicated he wasn't interested in her husband. Bergman played *Captain Brassbound's Conversion* in 1972. She thought it was a bad play, but this run finished in the black because she was in it.

Berlin, Isaiah. *Personal Impressions*. Ed. Henry Hardy. New York: Viking Press, 1980. Berlin's perception in the 1920s found Shaw, Wells, and Chesterton part of the cultural establishment, recommended by his "solid, sentimental and unimaginative" schoolmasters. The emancipating writers were J.B.S. Haldane, Ezra Pound, and Aldous Huxley. Pointedly, Huxley's exposition was better than Shaw's.

Booth, Michael R. *Prefaces to English Nineteenth-Century Theatre*. Manchester: Manchester University Press, n. d. [1980]. Shaw is excluded from direct treatment here, but his views are enlisted a number of times to comment upon the theatre and playwrights who formed the traditions that Shaw and Wilde drew upon.

Bradbury, Ray. "GBS and the Loin of Pork." In *The Haunted Computer and the Android Pope*. New York: Knopf, 1981. Bradbury, a long-time Shavian, imagines an incident based on Mrs. Campbell's remark, quoted by Shaw himself, that if G.B.S. were to turn to meat-eating, no woman in London would be safe. In Bradbury's verses, the porkchop sits on Shaw's plate while the world trembles at the outcome. ("Will now the atheist of meat turn carnal lover?") His beard quivers; he shuts his eyes in determination. But "The women [remain] unwomened and the pork unporked." He is unable to perform the carnivorous act. "Shaw's fled back to rice and beets." Bradbury concludes, "Safe our daughters, safe our streets." Printed complete in this volume of *Shaw*.

Darracott, Joseph. *The World of Charles Ricketts*. New York and Toronto: Methuen, 1980. The chapter on The Stage has a lot on Shaw, who was a good friend of Ricketts and utilized his stage designs, from *Don Juan in Hell* to *Saint Joan*. Ricketts dedicated to GBS his essay on stage design which appeared in 1913 in *Pages on Art*. The friendship was a cornerstone of Ricketts's career in the theatre. He did designs for *Dark Lady of the Sonnets* in 1910, also making suggestions for incidental music. He also designed costumes for *Fanny's First Play* and *Annajanska*, as well as his most notable Shavian work, the sets and costumes for *Saint Joan*. On seeing them at first, G.B.S. disapproved: "Mr. Shaw came on to the stage and said, 'Scenery and clothes have ruined my play. Why can't you play it in plain clothes, as at rehearsal? Sybil is much more like Joan in her ordinary jumper and skirt than when dressed up like this, with her face all painted.'" But the success of the play soothed Shaw, and he was delighted with the publication of the play in a deluxe edition illustrated with Ricketts's costume designs. At least six photographs of G.B.S., Shavian players and sets are included.

Davies, W. H. *Young Emma*. London: Jonathan Cape, 1980; New York: George Braziller, 1981. Uses a complete Shaw letter as an appendix to Davies' memoir of his wife and again uses the complete letter on the dust-jacket. See "Works by Shaw" above.

Elliot, Vivian. *Images of George Bernard Shaw. An exhibition at the National Theatre 2 March to 25 April 1981*. London: National Theatre, 1981. A large-format, four-page guide to the exhibition mounted in conjunction with performances of the complete *Man and Superman*, including four caricatures of Shaw and one photograph. Ms. Elliot's essay observes that Shaw's success as self-publicist "trapped" him in the image he created, and that since caricature tends toward exaggeration of eccentricity, Shaw's public character diverged more and more, in his fame, from his private self.

Fawkes, Richard. *Dion Boucicault, A Biography.* London, Melbourne, and New York: Quartet Books, 1979. "Shaw, who knew Boucicault's plays well, paid him the compliment of basing the trial scene in *The Devil's Disciple* on Shaun [-the Post's] trail [in Boucicault's *Arrah-na-Pogue*], and there are many parallels between the two, even down to the dialogue. Shaw's character of the languorous British officer, General Burgoyne, has its counterpart in Boucicault's Irish gentleman, Colonel O'Grady; Major Coffin is very similar in attitude and ineptitude to Shaw's Major Swindon; and several other incidents in the Boucicault play found their way into Shaw's."

Fisher, Lois H. *A Literary Gazetteer of England.* New York, London, Toronto, etc.: McGraw-Hill, 1980. Over twenty references to GBS, including connections with Ayot St. Lawrence, Aldbury, Brixham, Buckfastleigh, Great Malvern, Cropthorne, Limpsfield Chart, London, Luton, Manaton, Postling, Sandgate, Sidmouth, and Torquay.

Foley, Martha. *The Story of STORY Magazine.* Edited by Jay Neugeboren. New York and London: W. W. Norton, 1980. Shaw published pieces in *Story*. He is mentioned four times in this account, each time only as a name in a list of distinguished contributors.

Ganz, Arthur, *Realms of the Self. Variations on a Theme in Modern Drama.* New York: Columbia University Press, 1981. A substantial section on Shaw (pp. 57–85) discusses his plays in terms of duality—"that from the beginning they simultaneously embody romantic optimism and romantic disillusion.... Shaw was to be attracted not only by optimism, progress, and social action but by the opposing qualities of passivity, withdrawal, and fulfillment in death." Although there is little fulfillment in death in Shaw's plays, the perspective is persuasive, Ganz seeing the "dramatic tension" in Shaw generated in part "by a conflicting vision of the world—as a place where the self can be perfected; where continuing reform and improvement are possible; or as the abode of vulgarity, greed and brute stupidity in which man retains his distasteful and irredeemable self.... Much of the interest ... lies in tracing the variety and complexity of the balances he contrives between his conflicting impulses. Since the optimistic Shaw is a public personality but the despairing Shaw a private one, his commitments to life and action can be made openly and directly, but his impulse to withdraw must be developed through such extended metaphors as ... the ascent to heaven." Despite the authentic and public despair in a *Heartbreak House, Methusaleh* or *Joan,* the Ganz thesis works for much of Shaw.

Gielgud, Kate Terry. *A Victorian Playgoer.* London: Heinemann, 1980. The author was the niece of Ellen Terry and the mother of John Gielgud. Her account includes her reactions to new plays by Shaw, Wilde, and Pinero, which she saw on opening nights. Information is from publisher's advertisement. Not seen.

Gies, Frances. *Joan of Arc, the Legend and the Reality.* New York: Harper & Row, 1981. Includes a number of references to Shaw's interpretation of Joan. Nothing contentious.

Harrison, Rex. "Preface" to *Bernard Shaw: Selected Plays.* New York: Dodd, Mead & Company, 1981. The celebrity and prestige of Harrison in his own right gives this encomium to GBS importance. Harrison reflects upon the revolutionary subject matter of Shaw's plays, his role in *Pygmalion/My Fair Lady,* Shaw's inspiration to actors and actresses, the key episodes in Shaw's rise to success, and his own awe and unqualified admiration of G.B.S. See "Works by Shaw" above.

Hunt, Hugh. *The Abbey: Ireland's National Theatre, 1904–197[9].* New York: Columbia University Press, 1979. Dotted with about a dozen references to G.B.S., including the trouble with the British and Irish censors over *Blanco Posnet,* and a pro forma mention of *John Bull.*

James, Clive. "A Dinosaur at Sunset." In his *First Reactions, Critical Essays 1968–1979.* New York: Alfred A. Knopf, 1980. Reprint of a 1972 *Listener* review of the second volume of Shaw's correspondence (1898–1910), edited by Dan Laurence. Great admiration for the G.B.S. of these earlier years.

Laurence, Dan H., *The Fifth Gospel of Bernard Shaw*. New Orleans: The Graduate School of Tulane University, 1981. The 17-page Mellon Lecture, given annually at Tulane. A concise look at Shavian religious principles, his views of Christianity and of the Bible, his more poetic than scientific Creative Evolution. Laurence stresses the optimistic side of Shaw's world view, "that the universal movement is towards an irreversible growth and expansion of life."

McGhee, Richard D. *Marriage, Duty & Desire in Victorian Poetry and Drama*. Lawrence, KS: The Regents' Press of Kansas, 1980. Includes predictable discussions of title subjects in *Heartbreak* and *Man and Superman*.

Martin, Kingsley. "Shaw and Wells." In *H.G.Wells, Interviews and Recollections*. Ed., J.R. Hammond. Totowa, New Jersey: Barnes & Noble Books, 1980. A reprint of material from Martin's *A Volume of Autobiography 1931–1945* (London: Hutchinson, 1968) in which Martin reports the powerful influence of Wells and Shaw upon him, detailing the similarities and differences of the two men as he saw them, employing correspondence from G.B.S. and Wells as exhibits, in a piece both scintillating and sometimes simplistic. Martin's sympathy was, finally, with Wells.

Mikhail, E. H. "Bernard Shaw and Sean O'Casey: An Unrecorded Friendship." In *Essays on Sean O'Casey's Autobiographies*. Ed. Robert G. Lowery. Totowa, N.J.: Barnes and Noble, 1981, pp. 123–146. Chronicles the relationship essentially from the *Autobiographies*, the Krause *Letters*, and Eileen O'Casey's memoir. See a somewhat similar essay under Weintraub.

Moody, Richard. *Ned Harrigan. From Corlear's Hook to Herald Square*. Chicago: Nelson-Hall, 1980. Harrigan's theatre, named after him, was renamed the "Garrick" when Richard Mansfield in *Arms and the Man* changed it.

Morley, Frank. *Literary Britain. A Reader's Guide to Its Writers and Landmarks*. New York: Harper & Row, 1980. Notices several of Shaw's addresses and gives a good deal of space to his homes and domestic arrangements.

Morley, Margaret. *Larger than Life. The Biography of Robert Morley*. London: Robson Books, 1979. Morley has been one of the fine and successful Shavian actors. This account mentions his success in *Pygmalion* and the Playhouse 90 production of *Misalliance*. Morley called G.B.S. the only "saint" he ever met, assigning his inspiration to become an actor to Shaw. The volume includes a photo of GBS (side-rear view), Gabriel Pascal, and Morley discussing *Major Barbara*.

Newsome, David. *On the Edge of Paradise, A.C. Benson: The Diarist*. Chicago: University of Chicago Press, 1980. Benson knew G.B.S., but there is little report of their contact here.

Nichols, Mark. *The Importance of Being Oscar, The Wit and Wisdom of Oscar Wilde*. New York: St. Martin's Press, 1980. Lots of references to G.B.S. cover the familiar connections with Wilde.

O'Casey, Sean. *The Letters of Sean O'Casey, 1942–54*. Ed. David Krause. New York: Macmillan, 1980. Includes well over a hundred references to GBS and his works, as well as seven letters to Shaw. Mentions *Blanco Posnet, Art and Socialism, Major Barbara, Methuselah, Saint Joan, John Bull, Intelligent Woman's Guide, Caesar, Disciple, Pygmalion, Hearbreak, Dilemma, Superman, Androcles, Unsocial Socialist, Village Wooing, Arms*, and *Immaturity*.

Quinn, Jim. *American Tongue and Cheek. A Populist Guide to Our Language*. New York: Pantheon Books, 1980. Employs G.B.S. as a usage model a number of times in particular to dispel the pop-grammarians' claim that "there is a connection between clear thinking and good grammar—that bad thinking, and especially bad political thinking, produces bad writing." Witness: "George Bernard Shaw went to the end of his life insisting that the careers of Stalin, Mussolini, and Hitler—whom he defended indiscriminately—demonstrated the failure of democracy as a viable form of government. So whether you are pro-left or pro-right in your personal politics, you have in Shaw a man who never wrote an inexact sentence—and never escaped a reputation for outrageous paradox."

Rix, Walter T. "Shaw und Sudermann: Von der Gemeinsamkeit der Dramatiker und ihrer unerquicklkichen Stücke beim Eintritt ins 20. Jahrhundert." In *Hermann Sudermann. Werk und Wirkung.* Ed. Walter T. Rix. Würzburg: Königshausen & Neumann, 1980, pp. 304–332.

Seelye, John. "New Introduction" to Mark Twain's *Personal Recollections of Joan of arc.* Hartford, Connecticut: The Stowe-Day Foundation, 1980. Seelye's introduction to this facsimile reprint of the 1896 edition remarks on the major literary "Joans," including Shaw's, finding Twain's Joan assuming a singular place, as a Victorian artifact set among Renaissance, Enlightenment and Romantic figures on the one hand, and various versions of Modernism (Shaw's is an example) on the other.

Steel, Ronald. *Walter Lippmann and the American Century.* Boston and Toronto: Little, Brown and Company, 1980. Lippmann acknowledged Shaw as part of his intellectual environment. A number of references here represent this. Lippmann was moved by parts of *Man of Destiny.* "'Ibsen and Shaw have shown us with perfect truth that morality is not respectability, that the Life Force is above marriage laws, that society is against the individual,' he wrote Lucille Elsas, a New York girl with whom he was conducting a shy romance." Lippmann met GBS at least once, through Graham Wallas.

Vidal, Gore. *Views from a Window. Conversations with Gore Vidal.* Selected by Robert J. Stanton. Ed. Gore Vidal and Robert J. Stanton. Secaucus, New Jersey: Lyle Stuart, Inc., 1980. Includes five largely admiring references to GBS, on religion, politics, and Shaw's comic wrapping for his serious messages. Shaw prepared the way for Harold Wilson as Voltaire prepared the way for the French Revolution and Bonaparte. "Echoing Shaw, I'm comfortable only in the presence of the dead goat, which means reading a book. . . ."

Warner, Marina. *Joan of Arc. The Image of Female Heroism.* New York: Alfred A. Knopf, 1981. A number of references to Shaw's utilization of the records in his play about Joan. Her recognition of the Dauphin, Warner observes, is reported only in the testimony of Simon Charles at the Rehabilitation inquiry: "When the King learned that she was approaching, he withdrew behind the others; Joan, however, recognised him perfectly, made him a bow, and spoke to him for some minutes. After hearing her, the King appeared to be joyous." These lines alone, according to Warner, "contain the thread that has been used to embroider with sustained fancy the story that Charles even changes costume with Gilles de Rais and places him on his throne instead." Further, Warner sees some of Joan's "cheeky answers that have made her famous for pluck, defiance, heroic unyieldingness" as revealing "rather more desperation than the lighthearted cussedness so entertainingly rendered by Shaw." And she concludes that Shaw's image of the "young, plainspoken peasant taking on the mighty pillars of the Church . . . has an eloquence that has made it stick in the minds of many as the true Saint Joan. But it is an anachronism: Joan was not . . . [for] modern self-determination. The reason she would not bend to the Inquisition . . . could be that she had pledged herself elsewhere and owed loyalty [to her "voices"]."

Weintraub, Stanley. "Shaw's Other Keegan: O'Casey and G. B. S." In *Sean O'Casey, Centenary Essays.* Ed. David Krause and Robert G. Lowery. Totowa, New Jersey: Barnes & Noble, 1980, pp. 212–27. O'Casey thought of G.B.S. as his "anamchara—

soul-friend—as we say in Ireland." He also thought of himself, perhaps, as a second Shaw. Whatever the case, O'Casey's debts to Shaw appear to be more than O'Casey was conscious of. In O'Casey's *Juno* the figure of Captain Boyle may be a genial parody of *Hearbreak House*'s Captain Shotover. In Boyle's "romanticizing of tawdry reality" can be seen the symptoms identified in Larry Doyle's lament in *John Bull*. In *Plough and the Stars* we are reminded of "the sardonic thrusts of *Major Barbara*." In *Purple Dust* the insipration might have been *John Bull* and/or *Hearbreak*. The article also sketches the principal details of the O'Casey/Shaw friendship. Other essays in the volume that mention Shaw are Bernard Benstock's "Sean O'Casey and/or James Joyce," Mary FitzGerald's "Sean O'Casey and Lady Gregory: The Record of a Friendship," David Krause's "The Druidic affinities of O'Casey and Yeats," and Alan Simpson's "The Unholy Trinity: A Simple Guide to Holy Ireland c.1880–1980." For a somewhat similar essay to Weintraub's see under Mikhail, above.

Werner, Jack, ed. *Lady, Wilt Thou Love Me? Eighteen Love Poems for Ellen Terry* by Bernard Shaw. New York: Stein and Day, 1981. The G.B.S. authorship claim is a fraud. Reviewed in this volume.

Wilson, Colin. *The Quest for Wilhelm Reich*. Garden City, New York: Doubleday, 1981. Wilson's abiding admiration for Shaw is again represented in the largely cosmetic references to him in this biography of a psychoanalyst.

Wilson, Edmund. *The Thirties. From Notebooks and Diaries of the Period*. Ed. Leon Edel. New York: Farrar, Straus and Giroux, 1980. Six references to G.B.S., always in approval or admiration.

III. Periodicals

Adler, Thomas P. Review of Shaw Festival production of *Misalliance*. *Theatre Journal*, XXXII, no. 4 (December 1980), 526–7.

Beerbohm, Max. Letter to Cyril Clemens on cover. *Mark Twain Journal*, XX, no. 2 (Summer 1980). "At a wholly delightful luncheon given by Bernard Shaw in 1907, I was greatly impressed and fascinated by Mark Twain's truly beautiful and graceful hands."

Borkat, Roberta F. S. "Swift, Shaw, and the Idealistic Swain." *English Studies*, LXI, no. 6 (December 1980), 498–506. Shaw's *Arms and the Man* "enacts dramatically the crisis of the romantic idealist, which Jonathan Swift portrays in several of his earthiest poems." Shaw's Major Sergius Saranoff undergoes the same disillusionment as Swift's Cassinus in "Cassinus and Peter: A Tragical Elegy" (1731) experiences. He is also similar to Strephon in "The Lady's Dressing Room" (1730) and "Strephon and Chloe" (1731). Both examined romantic love, the nature of mankind, "the masks and extreme illusions which man employs to deny his mixture of the godlike and the bestial, and the role of the satirical unmasker, the author himself."

Bosworth, Patricia, "He Can't Stop Playing 'Enry 'Iggins." *The New York Times*, Sunday, August 16, 1981, pp. 1, 4. On Rex Harrison's attraction to the Henry Higgins role, his recollections of the creation of *My Fair Lady* from Shaw's play, and his view of the "implied happy ending, which I don't think Shaw would have liked. He was very much a realist." Harrison claims that when the adaptation was broached to him by Lerner and Loewe, "I insisted that Shaw's key scenes be retained."

Bratton, J. S. "Missing the Message." *TLS* (March 20, 1981), p. 321. Review of *Money and Politics in Ibsen, Shaw and Brecht*, by Bernard F. Dukore, and *Ibsen and the Theatre: Essays in Celebration of the 150th Anniversary of Ibsen's Birth*, ed. Errol Durback.

Braun, Eric. Review of Richmond (Surrey) Theatre production of *Heartbreak House*, performed on 2 June 1980. *Plays and Players*, XXVII, no. 9 (June 1980), 27.

Clarke, Peter. "The Music of G.B.S Larking." *TLS* (January 30, 1981), p. 11. Review of National Theatre production of *Man and Superman* at Olivier Theatre. Includes *Don Juan in Hell*.

Cranham, Ronald. Review of Shaw Theatre Company production of *Pygmalion* on 6 May 1980. *Plays and Players*, XXVII, no. 8 (May 1980), 31.

Dinse, John. "From the Left: Distributing our Wealth." *The Buyer's Guide*, Mount Pleasant, Michigan (February 6, 1981), Section A, p. 3. Dinse is a Political Science Professor at Central Michigan University, and regularly makes Shaw's *The Intelligent Woman's Guide* required reading in certain courses. In this installment of his column, aimed at the semi-rural midwestern reader this weekly addresses, he lucidly extracts Shaw's *Guide* to interpret the economic predicament of the early 1980s.

Dukore, Bernard F. Review of *Shaw and Ibsen*, ed. J.L. Wisenthal. *Theatre Journal*, XXXII, no. 4 (December 1980), 542–43.

Francis, R. A. "Romain Rolland and Some British Intellectuals During the First World War." *Journal of European Studies*, X, no. 3 (September 1980), 189–209. Describes a number of Shaw/Rolland contacts: Shaw was on Rolland's 1916 reading lists. Shaw was a voice for freedom and a citizen of the world. During the war the two men clashed on at least three occasions: 1) On Shaw's refusal to sign Rolland's "petition" on Rheims and Louvain, 2) on Shaw's defense of Roger Casement, and 3) on Shaw's refusal to sign the *Declaration de l'independence de l'esprit*. He hoped G.B.S. and Wells would rise to their pre-war reputations as internationalists. They disappointed him mostly. To Rolland Shaw belonged to an honorable tradition of Anglo-Saxon writers against hypocrisy who sound cynical to avoid seeming hypocritical. Shaw and Rolland never lost respect for each other.

Ganz, Arthur. Review of *Shaw and Ibsen* ed. J.L. Wisenthal. *Comparative Drama*, XIV, no. 3 (Fall 1980), 286–8.

Harrison, James. "Destiny or Descent?: Responses to Darwin." *Mosaic*, XIV, no. 1 (Winter 1981), 109–24. "Shaw's case is both clearer and more complex. His much more vehement dislike of natural selection, with all its stupid, blundering, non-vegetarian' cruelty, its ghastly and damnable reduction of beauty and intelligence, of strength and purpose, . . .' is largely, one feels, a fastidious mistrust by Shaw the rationalist of life's irreducible physicalness, its messy, unpredictable, irrational ugliness and beauties. But there is a romantic side to him as well: so strongly was he influenced, through Wagner and Nietzsche, by a Continental line of thought which virtually bypasses Darwin, that his 'Life Force' turns out to be a kind of simplistic, painting-by-numbers version of Bergson's *élan vital*, with even a common emphasis on mind as the ultimate outcomes of the whole process."

Holroyd, Michael, "Devotions of a Dramatist," *Times Literary Supplement*, May 1, 1981, pp. 481–82. An essay-review based upon Margot Peters' *Bernard Shaw and the Actresses*, which discusses the "mother-figure" which attracted him in literature and the possibility that "scholars may have been too ready to write off Shaw's sexual drive."

Kakutani, Michiko, "G. B. Shaw and the Women in His Life and Art." *The New York Times*, Sunday, September 27, 1981, Section 2, pp. 1, 14–15. On the occasion of three major Shavian productions onstage in Manhattan at the same time (*Misalliance*, *Candida* and *Pygmalion* via *My Fair Lady*), Kakutani discusses Shaw's presentation of women on the stage and what the author sees as his attitude toward women: "intense and contradictory . . . , part flirtation, part defensiveness and quite thorough fascination."

Klein, Alfons. Review of *Bernard Shaw. Du reformateur Victorien au prophète édouardien*, by Jean-Claude Amalric (in German). *Anglia, Zeitschrift für Englische Philologie*. Band 98, Heft 3/4 (1980), 534–36.

Lassam, Robert. "George Bernard Shaw as Photographer." *National Trust* (Spring 1981), p. 12. The article, illustrated with a G.B.S. self-portrait as a crippled beggar and a photo of his first car, a 1920 AC Cobra, sketches Shaw's keen interest in photography and the latest equipment. Of particular interest to Lassam are the whereabouts of Shaw's Leica and the photos he must have taken with it. Information may be conveyed to him, Curator of the Fox Talbot Museum, Lacock, Wiltshire (Telephone Lacock 459).

MacKay, Patricia. "Broadway, Las Vegas, and the Road." *Theatre Crafts*, XV, no. 2 (February 1981), 12–19. Sub-titled "Ken Billington—Lighting Designer," the piece includes photos of Billington-lighted sets of *My Fair Lady*, a production on tour through Los Angeles, Chicago, Detroit, Miami Beach, Boston, and New York until August 1981.

Review of "Die heilige Johanna [*Saint Joan*]" at the International Theater in Zurich. *Die Bühne*, N. 267 (December 1980), p. 23.

Symons, Julian. "Value for Money." *Ellery Queen's Mystery Magazine*, LXXVI, no. 6 (December 1, 1980), 140–55. Symons' protagonist is named George Bernard Shaw because his parents (surnamed Shaw) conceived him on the night of a visit to *Arms and the Man*. He grows up to epitomize an oversimplified stereotype of the real Shaw's character—"a ruthless realist in his business, in his nonpersonal relationships, in his marriage. A man accustomed to success, to having his own way, he was 'the ruler of his world.' " Naturally, it would be unkind to reveal here the fate devised for the fictional G.B.S. namesake in this mildly amusing tale.

Szirtes, George. "Sheep Shearing at Ayot St. Lawrence." *TLS* (December 12, 1980), p. 1403. A poem, a pastoral vignette; no reference to G.B.S.

Taylor, Thomas J. "Cumberland, Kotzebue, Scribe, Simon: Are We Teaching the Wrong Playwrights?" *College English*, XLIII, no.1 (January 1981), 45–50. In the process of proposing that "bad plays" not be taught, Taylor makes several positive references to Shaw, who is among the "big five" with Ibsen, Chekhov, Strindberg, and Pirandello. Notices Ibsen and Shaw as the brilliant transformers of the play design and melodramatic content of second rate plays. In graduate school, "we read *all* of Jonson, *all* of Ibsen, *all* of Racine, or (the bravest among us) *all* of Shaw."

Taylor, John Russell. Review of Shaw Theatre production of *Pygmalion*. *Drama* (July 1980), p. 49.

Wallis, Claudia. "People." *Time* (November 10, 1980), p. 77. Reports Diana Rigg is making an anthology of hostile "brickbat" critics' reviews of actors, to be titled "No Turn Unstoned," after G.B.S's definition of what a critic leaves behind him.

Weintraub, Stanley. Review of *Shaw and Ibsen*, by J. M. Wisenthal. *Nineteenth-Century Theatre Research*, VIII (Autumn, 1980), 123–26.

GBS, no. 8 (June 1980). Newsletter of the Shaw Society of Japan. Includes Genji Takahashi's "Reminiscences of Bernard Shaw," "Obituaries," "*Candida*—Mask and Self" by Hisashi Morikawa, "Shaw and British Society in 19th Century" by Fumiko Takahashi, "Shaw's Image of Artist in *The Doctor's Dilemma*" by Yoshikazu Shimizu, "Shaw's View of Man" by Masafumi Ogiso, "Malvern Festival and Shaw" by Junko Matoba, "News from Abroad," "Recent Shaw Studies in Japan," "News about Our Members," "Past Activities of the Society," and "Editor's Note." *GBS* inquiries to Masahiko Masumoto, The Language Centre, Nagoya University, Furocho, Chikuaku, Nagoya, 464 *Japan*.

The Independent Shavian, XVIII, no. 3 (1980). Journal of the Bernard Shaw Society. Includes "Vivisection: The Real Thing" by G.B.S, "Good out of Vivisection?" by

G.B.S., "Honor Among Fellow creatures" by G.B.S., "The Prime Minister [Thatcher] is not Amused," "The Royal Academy Versus art" by G.B.S., "Bernard Shaw for President," "Memories of George Bernard Shaw" by Arthur Lynnford Smith, "O'Casey and G.B.S." by Joseph Ricciardi, "Shaw Cornered," "Hurry Hurry Hurry," "News About Our Members," and "Shaw's Finest Hour."

IV. Dissertations

Bandler, David B. *Theatricality: A Theory of the Role of Theatre Implicit in Drama with Special Reference to Hamlet, Man and Superman, and Waiting for Godot* (Carnegie-Mellon University, 1980). *DAI*, 41 (November 1980), 1840-A. Makes an effort to "resolve the 'literary-theatrical' dispute among critics by arguing for greater emphasis on the experience of performance, rather than on traditional literary values, in developing full understanding of a play's meaning." Treats the plays of the title to "illuminate the neglected significance of implicit theatricality" in them.

Chancellor, Gary Lynn. *Stage Directions in Western Drama: Studies in Form and Function* (University of Wisconsin—Madison, 1980). *DAI*, 41 (November 1980), 2096-A. Abstract does *not* mention Shaw or his work.

Clemon-Karp, Sheila. *The Female Androgyne in Tragic Drama* (Brandeis University, 1980). *DAI*, 41 (November 1980), 2096-7-A. "Great dramatists, the classical Greek tragedians, Shakespeare, Ibsen, and Shaw among them, have often used drama as a means of demonstrating the artificiality of sex-role limitations and their inherent potential for harm. . . . through these master playwrights, the ideal of wholeness that is androgyny has made an appearance in the theatre." Examples are Antigone, Cleopatra, Hedda Gabler, and St. Joan.

Lucas, James Lavard. *The Religious Dimension of Twentieth-Century British and American Literature: A Textbook in the Analysis of Types* (Northern Illinois University, 1980). *DAI*, 41 (November 1980), 2103-A. G.B.S. is treated in the taxonomy of the major body of the study as among the "heretical," in particular among the "social humanists," along with Archibald MacLeish, Faulkner, Hemingway, and Bellow.

Rackard, Benny Gene. *A Directorial Analysis and Production Guide to Three Musical Theatre Forms for High School Production: La Vida Breve, The Sound of Music, and The Chocolate Soldier* (University of Southern Mississippi, 1980). *DAI*, 41 (November 1980), 1820-A. Thesis title is sufficient here.

Turner, Dennis Geoffrey. *A Demonstration of Changing a Theatrical Genre to Communicate an Intensification of the Original Theme* (United States International University). *DAI*, 41 (January 1981), 2835-A. Attempts to "demonstrate the feasibility of altering a mode of theatrical presentation with the purpose of communicating a timeless theme entertainingly expressed, in a currently popular thetrical genre." The theme chosen: "The inevitability of youth, however much disparaged by their elders, coming at last to power and responsibility. Concommittant to that theme was the probability of age reluctant to accept it and clinging to youth. . . ." Both themes are in G.B.S.'s *Caesar and Cleopatra*. Purposes transforming *Caesar* to a musical comedy with lyrics and dance. Presumably, a script of some degree of finish is a working part of this study, though the abstract does not say so explicitly. The author asserts his conviction that adapting an existing work to a new genre is far harder than original composition.

CONTRIBUTORS

Thomas P. Adler teaches English at Purdue University.

Charles A. Berst teaches English at the University of California, Los Angeles. He is the author of *Bernard Shaw and the Art of Drama*.

Ray Bradbury is the author of *Martian Chronicles, Fahrenheit 451* and other novels.

Robert Chapman, Professor of English at Harvard University, was formerly Director of the Loeb Drama Center at Harvard.

Robert Coskren teaches English and Humanities at Oklahoma State University, Stillwater.

Thomas F. Hale teaches History at Idaho State University, Pocatello.

Joseph M. Hassett, who recently returned from a sabbatical year in Irish studies in Ireland, is a member of the Washington law firm of Hogan and Hartson.

The late Christopher Hollis was an author, journalist, and Member of Parliament.

Philip Klass writes science fiction as *William Tenn*.

Daniel Leary teaches English at the City College of the City University of New York. He is editor of the next volume of *Shaw*, "Shaws's Plays in Performance."

Cecil Lewis, an R.A.F. flier in the Great War, got to know Shaw when Lewis became involved in theatre, films and broadcasting in the 1920s.

Margot Peters teaches English at the University of Wisconsin, Whitewater. She is the author of *Bernard Shaw and the Actresses*.

Edgar Rosenberg is Professor of English and Comparative Literature at Cornell University.

Susan Rusinko teaches English at Bloomsburg (Pennsylvania) State College. Her book on Terence Rattigan is about to appear.

The Rev. Alexander Seabrook is rector of St. Mark's Episcopal Church in Pittsburgh and a long-time Shavian amateur.

Tony Jason Stafford teaches English at the University of Texas at El Paso.

Robert Wexelblatt teaches Philosophy at Boston University.